The Complete Vocal Workout
A Step-By-Step Guide To Tough Vocals

Cover and CD image courtesy of Getty Images

ISBN 978-1-84492-003-7

© Copyright 2003, Roger Kain,
published under exclusive licence by SMT, an imprint and
registered trade mark of Bobcat Books Limited.

Visit Hal Leonard Online at
www.halleonard.com

World headquarters, contact:
Hal Leonard
7777 West Bluemound Road
Milwaukee, WI 53213
Email: info@halleonard.com

In Europe, contact:
Hal Leonard Europe Limited
1 Red Place
London, W1K 6PL
Email: info@halleonardeurope.com

In Australia, contact:
Hal Leonard Australia Pty. Ltd.
4 Lentara Court
Cheltenham, Victoria, 3192 Australia
Email: info@halleonard.com.au

The Complete Vocal Workout

A Step-By-Step Guide To Tough Vocals

Roger Kain

CD recorded and compiled by Roger Kain, 2003. Produced and edited by Jim Dickinson and Phil Hilborne at WM Studios. Web: www.philhilborne.com.

Vocals: Skye, Stephen Taylor, Roger Kain. Speech and keyboards: Roger Kain.

CONTENTS

INTRODUCTION

This book and the accompanying CD are aimed at singers working on their own, but also at singing teachers, to provide a scheme of exercises designed to produce modern rock and pop sounds and ranges. At the time of writing, there is no other such scheme available. In this book I have notated the exercises in the conventional way to make them accessible for singing lessons and to enable teachers to expand on them.

Modern commercial singing is a highly professional and skilled occupation. It covers a wide variety of styles, including rock, metal, grunge, pop, etc, each with an enormous range of sounds and pitches. Between these classifications are the subdivisions: hard rock, soft rock, melodic rock, heavy metal, death metal, grunge metal – does anyone remember thrash? Indie? Garage? The name of each genre varies with changing times and fashions, so for the purposes of this book I shall use the generic terms, *rock* and *pop* to mean all of these styles, as these names do not seem to change.

The one obvious thing these different styles have in common is that they are totally different from opera or any other 'classical' style of singing. The sound is different, the technique is different, the range is different, the pronunciation is different. Indeed, the thinking is different, so the training has to be different. Opera isn't a good preparation for rock singing – the operatic range isn't big enough. Neither can rock singers be divided into the classical divisions of soprano, mezzo-soprano, contralto, tenor, baritone and bass – each female singer has to cover the entire female range and each male singer has to cover the entire male range.

One of the problems of teaching rock singers is that rock and pop have given rise to a new breed of feeble singing teachers who do not know enough. Many of them will tell you that you will never get up to a G or an A 'because you're a baritone or a mezzo. Only tenors or sopranos can go that high.' As if being a tenor or a soprano were somehow especially virtuous! As a matter of fact,

the tenor and baritone ranges are the same, and most mezzos can sing soprano perfectly well. Similarly, any decent baritone should be able to hit a top C, which annoys the tenors who can't! I was trained as a baritone, I am well over 50, and I can still sing a perfectly good top C, while I can also sing a good bottom C, three octaves below. The difference is in the *sound*, not in the range. Many of my students can encompass an even bigger range than I can, but they were stretched earlier than I was. This process usually takes about four years, although some of my luckier students have managed it more quickly.

The worrying thing is that most singing teachers have learned nothing from the heavy-metal boom of the '70s, '80s and '90s. That phenomenal development in singing was led by singers, not teachers. They achieved their spectacular results largely by disobeying their teachers, who no doubt continued to wag their fingers, uttering dire warnings of the ruin that their charges were inflicting on their voices. The vast ranges of singers like Skye, Skin, Sebastian Bach, Michael Bolton, David Coverdale, Stephen Tyler, Jeff Tate *et al* (the list is enormous!) has meant nothing to most teachers. Throughout the whole of the last 20 years, teachers have been saying things like 'His voice is going' about each of the great heavy-metal singers – and they're still saying it. Yet these singers are still going strong, a fact which many teachers fail to notice.

Then there's the other great finger-wagging phrase, usually uttered in deep, slow lugubrious tones: '(S)he's had a few problems with his/her voice.' So what? Every singer in the world has had trouble with 'the voice' at one time or another. It's called being human.

One of the purposes of this book and CD is to dispel some of the myths and fears of rock singing. If you hear a rock singer doing something wonderful, the chances are that you too are capable of it. Great rock singers have nothing that you don't have, physically. Perhaps they have more will power, a better 'ear', or more of the actors' instinct than you. That is dependent on your mind. A good teacher should be able to help you sort out the mental approach.

You go to a teacher mainly for three reasons:

- To find out what is available to you. A lot of songs you'll want to sing are very difficult, particularly those with very high notes, and you might start to wonder if it will ever be possible for you to sing them. Unfortunately, there are always a lot of teachers ready to tell you, 'It's out of your range.' They will usually follow this up with two insidious statements: 'If you try to force the voice up, you'll do permanent damage' and 'Anyone who tells you that you can get up to these notes is a liar.' This is nothing less than moral blackmail designed to hide the teacher's lack of knowledge. If a teacher says, 'You can't go that high because you're [or you're not] this, that or the other, it probably means, 'I don't know how to teach you to sing up there.' There are perfectly safe ways of opening up recalcitrant high notes, and this book contains exercises for several different approaches (I'm not bigoted). Even most true basses – the rarest voice of all – can eventually reach a top C and high sopranos can build up a chest voice capable of sustaining a gutsy bottom E (below middle C).

- To tap into the accumulated knowledge of centuries. This is often the giveaway that great singers have had singing lessons: they know too much to have been self-taught. There are techniques available for solving every single problem in singing, including the development of a good chest voice for singers who think they can't get deep notes and the opening up of a glorious head voice for singers who keep hitting that 'ceiling'. These are common problems. What makes them serious is that they tend to induce a mental block. If you can't hit the notes your heroes are singing, it's probably because you haven't found the right technique – and maybe your singing teacher hasn't, either!

- To deal with the psychological problems of singing. Or, to put it in modern terms, to sort out the mind-set, the mental blocks, the fear of auditions, the fear of meeting the band for the first time, the fear of high notes, the fear of looking a prat, the fear of letting go so that you always hold back on notes that you should really just go for. You want that wonderful high note, and you know you can do it, but every time you come to it, you hold back on it

– you clench your throat immediately before you try to sing it, strangling it. But the damage is done before you utter a sound.

To make matters worse, somebody will tell you that it's out of your range. The real problem here is that high notes are terrifying, but you *know* that fear is something to be dealt with; you *know* that you shouldn't give in to it.

Singing involves the emotions more than any other form of music-making. You are your own instrument. You must make all your notes. You are totally responsible for the quality of all your sounds, in a way that instrumentalists are not, and that is a terrifying responsibility. It makes you vulnerable. As you approach difficult notes, they can almost seem to be lying in wait for you, like time bombs ticking away. All sorts of questions run through your mind:

- Am I going to hit that note?

- Is it going to go wrong?

- Can the neighbours hear me?

- Is it going to hurt my throat?

- Could I sing it quietly, so that nobody will hear me missing it?

You feel you can be blamed for every sound that isn't perfect. That's pressure! It's not like pressing a switch or depressing a key on a keyboard. You can press down the highest key on a keyboard and the highest note will come out, easily, perfectly. If it doesn't, you can blame the sound engineer. It's no hardship for the keyboard player. But for you to sing your highest possible note is traumatic. It's frightening. It can also be incredibly exciting.

You'll have problems with sore throats, certainly at the beginning – the early-day sore throat – and also with colds in the early stages. All singers do. I won't be dealing with those ailments here, although there is an extended section about sore throats in Chapter 11, 'Solving Problems'.

The real message of this introduction is this: Don't concern yourself with what you *can* do; concentrate on what you *want* to do.

How To Use The CD With This Book

Although the accompanying CD is self-explanatory, singers who can't read music should still follow it in the book. In the process, you might pick up some music-reading skills.

Have the book open at the exercise on which you are planning to work. Listen to it on the CD while following it in the book. Read the guidance notes. Then, using the CD as a backing track, sing the exercise. If you get into difficulties, re-read the guidance notes. Don't worry if a lot of these exercises are difficult – they're supposed to be. You have to start somewhere. Do as much of each exercise as you can and, next time, try to do a bit more or a bit better. (See Chapter 11, 'Solving Problems'.) Above all, always bear in mind that, if you don't get it right first time, you have a choice: you can either give up or have another go. That's always the choice.

Written Music

To be able to sing at sight (that means first sight!) is the most lucrative skill in music. A studio will pay a huge recording fee for a singer who can pick up a sheet of new music (which might be thick with harmonies) and sing it accurately, in the right sounds, straight away – that's professionalism – so it's worthwhile building up your skills.

Reading music frightens many singers, but it's really not very difficult. All you need to know is your alphabet from A to G and how to count up to 13. Even if you can't be precise about it at first, you can see when the dots (noteheads) go up and down, so your voice should go up or down correspondingly, and you can estimate at a glance from the spacing how long to hold each note. I'm not exaggerating – that really covers all that music involves. If in doubt, you can always make an intelligent

guess! Written music is entirely logical, unlike learning languages, all of which are illogical (some more so than others) and require you to learn far more information than reading music does. The best way to learn to read music is to learn to play keyboards. This will very quickly give you an understanding of the complete structure of music.

Now, although it's not strictly necessary for a singer to be able to read music or to play keyboards, most successful singers can do both. A lot of them paid for their first bands and demos out of the proceeds of session singing and playing. In general, the more you know, the better equipped you are to succeed and to remain successful.

This is where I appear to contradict myself. Earlier, I said that written music is entirely logical, and this is true, but the *conventions* of written music for voices are a bit confused. Usually, the female voice is written in the treble clef at the actual pitch (ie the pitch that is sung), but not always. Sometimes, for convenience, it's written an octave higher or lower. Don't worry about that.

In contrast, conventions of notation for the male voice are in a right old historical muddle. Sometimes it's written in the bass clef and should be sung at the written pitch, while at other times it's written in the treble clef, usually (but not always) to be sung an octave lower than written. None of these strange conventions makes music-reading any more difficult. You get used to them.

In order to avoid confusion, all of the exercises in this book are written at their actual pitches, whether in the bass or treble clef, except where the guidance notes specifically state otherwise.

1 THE RANGE

The first thing to notice about the vocal range is that it is very wide. The notation on pages 11–12 isn't a misprint; many modern rock singers really can cover that range. This wouldn't be possible for anyone trained only in the classical tradition, and it was certainly not thought possible before about 1970. Singing teachers at that time were extremely wary of men who wanted to extend their range upwards and women who wanted to extend their chest voices downward, and indeed many still are – they usually described it as 'forcing the voice'. However, as you go through the exercises contained in this book, you'll find that there's no need to force the voice. You will find it extremely hard work, but *hard work* is not the same as *forcing*.

It was the emergence of heavy metal that brought about the extension of the vocal range. The sound of the bands became so hard and piercing that singers made a terrible discovery: microphones do not turn a woolly sound into a well-focused sound; they only transmit what the singer puts into them. Singers were being drowned out. They had to find a way of cutting through the backing or riding over it. Men mostly rode over it by going higher and louder, and singing above A♭ (the start of the second register of the natural head voice), where most men can produce a voice that is indestructible. It's very difficult for most men to get into that register, but all men can, even true basses.

Women's voices don't work in quite the same way. The strategy employed by most women was to open up the deep resonance of the chest voice, producing a massive sound, and then to extend it upwards as far as possible. For most women, that means up to E♭ in the top space of the treble clef. A lot of women also wanted the highest possible notes of the head voice, where outrageousness is very exciting. In the process, both men and women discovered that their voices doubled in power right down through the range to the very lowest notes, which became known as *death-metal notes*. With this, another interesting fact emerged: singers who can go highest are often the same singers who can go lowest. Don't believe anyone who says that you can't sing both high and low – you can. It might take a few years, but the techniques for it are in this book and on the CD.

Some singing teachers and voice experts predicted that these heavy-metal singers would ruin their voices in five minutes, when in fact the reverse happened: the more they extended their ranges, the better their voices became. The empirical evidence is now overwhelming: singers who extend their ranges improve as they get older, while singers who don't…don't. They either hang on or they deteriorate. Most of the great heavy-metal singers of the '70s are still big names, and their voices are still improving. The interesting fact that emerges is this: the massive improvements in singing were made by performers who disobeyed their teachers.

The second thing to notice is that the voice changes on A♭ and E♭. It's the same for everybody, and it never varies. This is a useful fact to know when you're trying to work out why your voice seems to be refusing to do what (or sound the way) you want it to.

The Range Of The Rock Voice

Showing what becomes possible when you can mix the voices. These are all notated at *actual pitch.*

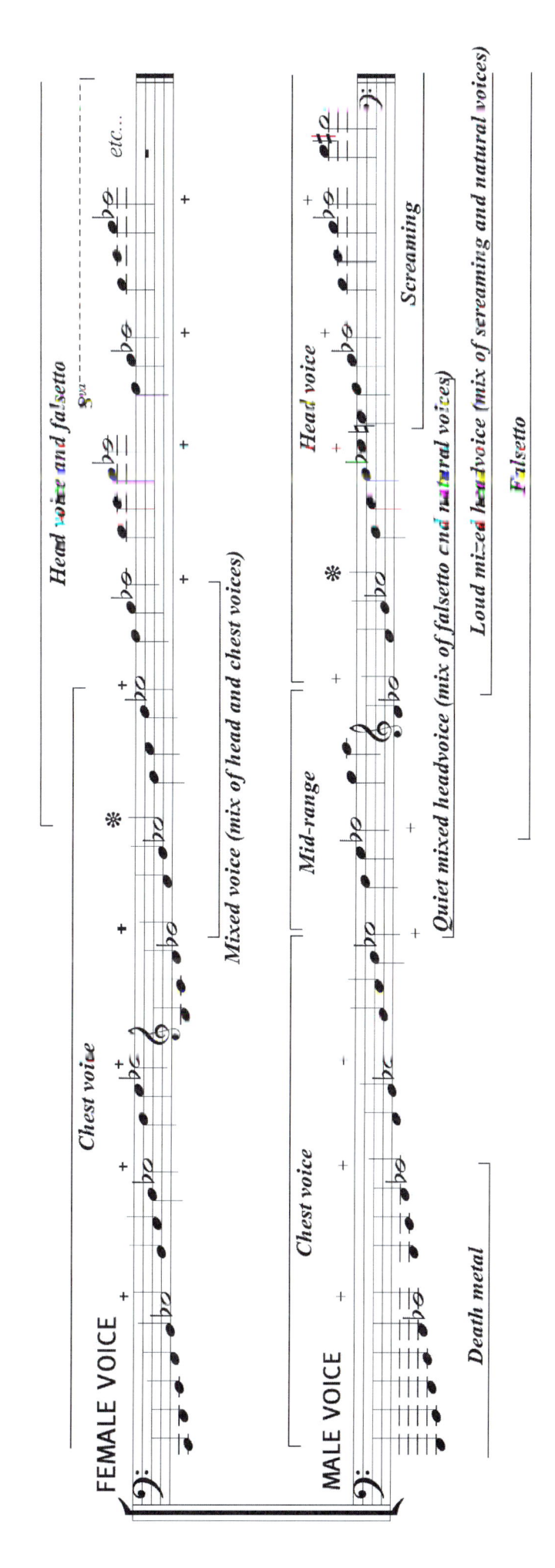

※ Ab, the note on which all voices change dramatically. In a woman's voice it is the dividing line between the head and chest voices. It is called the *passaggio*. By extending the chest voice upwards and the head voice downwards, it is possible to achieve a wide overlap and choose the note on which to change voices and, eventually, to develop a smooth mixed voice. Some men have difficulty in singing above this note, but every man can, including a true bass, the rarest male voice of all.

+ The changes in the voice are invariably on Ab and Eb. These are usually small changes, but they can become serious divisions if the technique is not right for that pitch.

By Contrast, The Well-Developed Classical Ranges

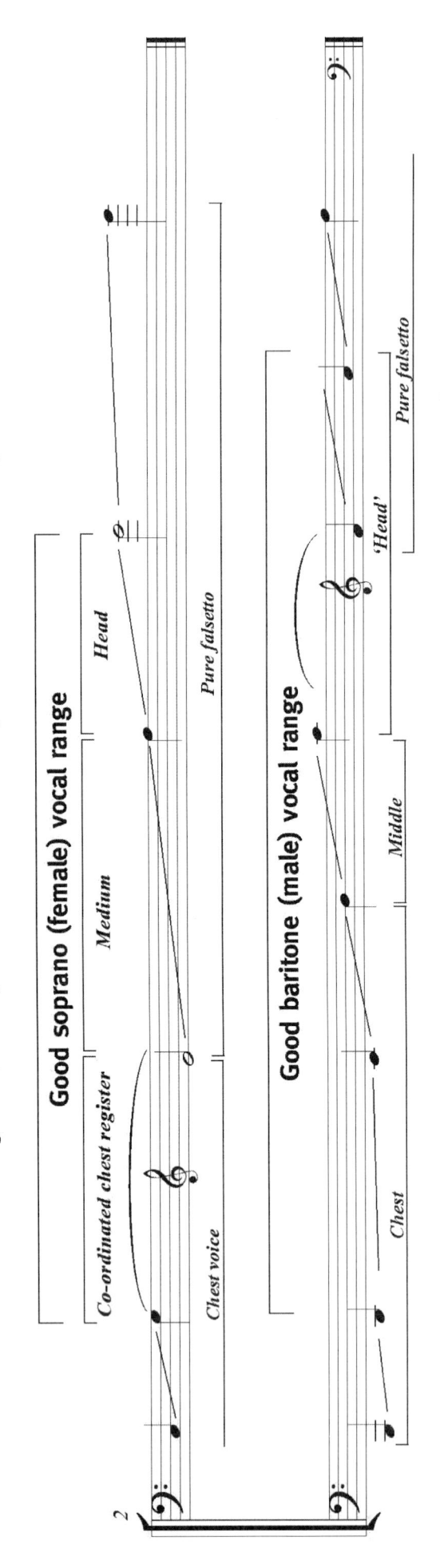

Good soprano (female) vocal range

Co-ordinated chest register — Medium — Head — Pure falsetto

Chest voice

Good baritone (male) vocal range

Chest — Middle — 'Head' — Pure falsetto

Given in *Bel Canto: Principles And Practices* by Cornelius L Reid (New York, 1950, pp 89-91). This has been largely ignored by teachers who thought it was hopelessly ambitious, that you couldn't sing both high and low, but Professor Reid was right. If anything, he *underestimated* what was possible. I exercise nearly all male singers to the extremities of this range from the first lesson. They are usually surprised that they can do it, and without ill effects.

Examples Of Poor Ranges

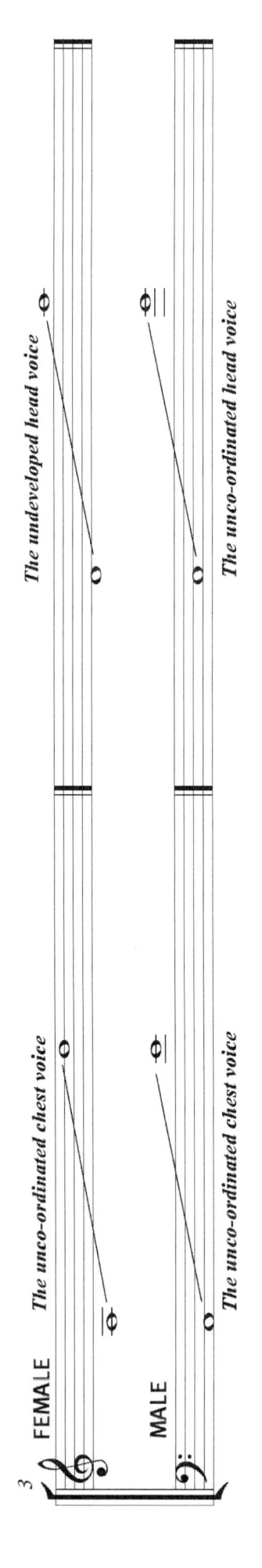

The undeveloped head voice

The unco-ordinated head voice

FEMALE — The unco-ordinated chest voice

MALE — The unco-ordinated chest voice

2 OPENING UP THE VOICE

Basic Exercises For Power And Range

Why Do Exercises At All? Why Not Just Sing Songs?

Exercises are targeted at problem solving in a way that songs are not. A lot of songs are very good exercises in their own right, but that isn't their main purpose. Exercises should do two things. Firstly, they should stretch you, which will help you to get at the notes and sounds that excite you. Secondly, they should build up good habits so that your technique becomes automatic. In other words, exercises help you to cope with your voice under any circumstance. Whatever your problem, there's an exercise to solve it.

Getting Started

The first and, indeed, one of the most difficult things to do is to try to get some high notes. You'll find that, after singing high notes, your whole voice will be much brighter than it was before, all the way down (unless you try to do it from the throat – that would be disastrous). High notes stretch the soft palate (see the 'Glossary' at the back of this book), and they are also exhilarating. You also need some notes in reserve, and so, however high you go in your songs, to make them secure you need to try to go even higher in exercises. Don't be put off by people who say, 'Stick to your natural range,' whatever that may be! If you give up on high notes just because they're more difficult than low notes, you'll never achieve anything. As long as you follow the step-by-step guidance notes listed here, you'll be all right.

You don't have to get everything right straight away. You should be able to get up to A♭ (bar 6), but don't worry if you can't. Do as much as you can. Tomorrow's another day.

Exercise 1: Making A Start On The High Notes

This is the perfect exercise to start your warm-up.

CD 1, Tracks 1–3

This exercise is *loud*. if you try to do it quietly, you won't get up to the top notes – at least, not in the right voice. Top notes are louder than bottom notes. This is particularly important for men – women can sometimes get away with quiet top notes as long as they can get hold of them. But the general rule is to go a little bit louder (sometimes a *lot* louder) when you go up; you can usually let the notes look after themselves when you come down.

Keep the tip of the tongue against the bottom teeth. This is very important indeed, as it will stop you putting pressure on the throat and will focus your voice, making singing a lot easier. When the tongue goes back or is left flapping in mid-air, it's usually because you're clenching the base of the tongue. The antidote is to place the tip against something at the front of the mouth, preferably the bottom teeth or the bottom gum. (See the note on the *tongue* in the 'Glossary').

Take in as big a breath as you can manage with the diaphragm (in practice, that really means your stomach) before you sing. As you hit the highest note in each phrase (accented ^), pull the diaphragm in hard and take the strain with the stomach. (See Exercise 2, 'Breath Control' and the entry for the *diaphragm* in the 'Glossary'.)

There must be no pressure on the neck, no veins or arteries standing out like drainpipes. They will stop you getting up to your highest notes, I guarantee it. High notes take a lot of effort, a lot of struggle. You must take the strain with the diaphragm. If your neck hurts but your diaphragm doesn't, you're not doing enough with the diaphragm. (See *carotid arteries* in the 'Glossary'.)

If this doesn't work, there's another technique: constipate the note. This is an instruction my first singing teacher gave me. It has rescued my students (and me) from a lot of difficulties over the years. As you go for the top note, pull in the diaphragm – and try to push it out through your bottom. To put it another way, for top notes, go for a fart! It's better than straining the neck.

Women shouldn't try to sing it all in the big, gutsy chest voice; let it go into the head voice, or falsetto voice. You need these notes. Don't worry about it sounding girly or classical or squeaky or silly – that doesn't matter. You must exercise the head voice if you want the chest voice to work really well for you.

Men, however, should keep it all in the natural voice. Don't let it go into falsetto at all. That means *keep it loud*. There's no way of getting a Top B or a Top C quietly, at least not until you're very experienced. (See *constipate the note* in the 'Glossary'.)

CD 1, Tracks 1-3

Steady 4, strong, driving rhythm.

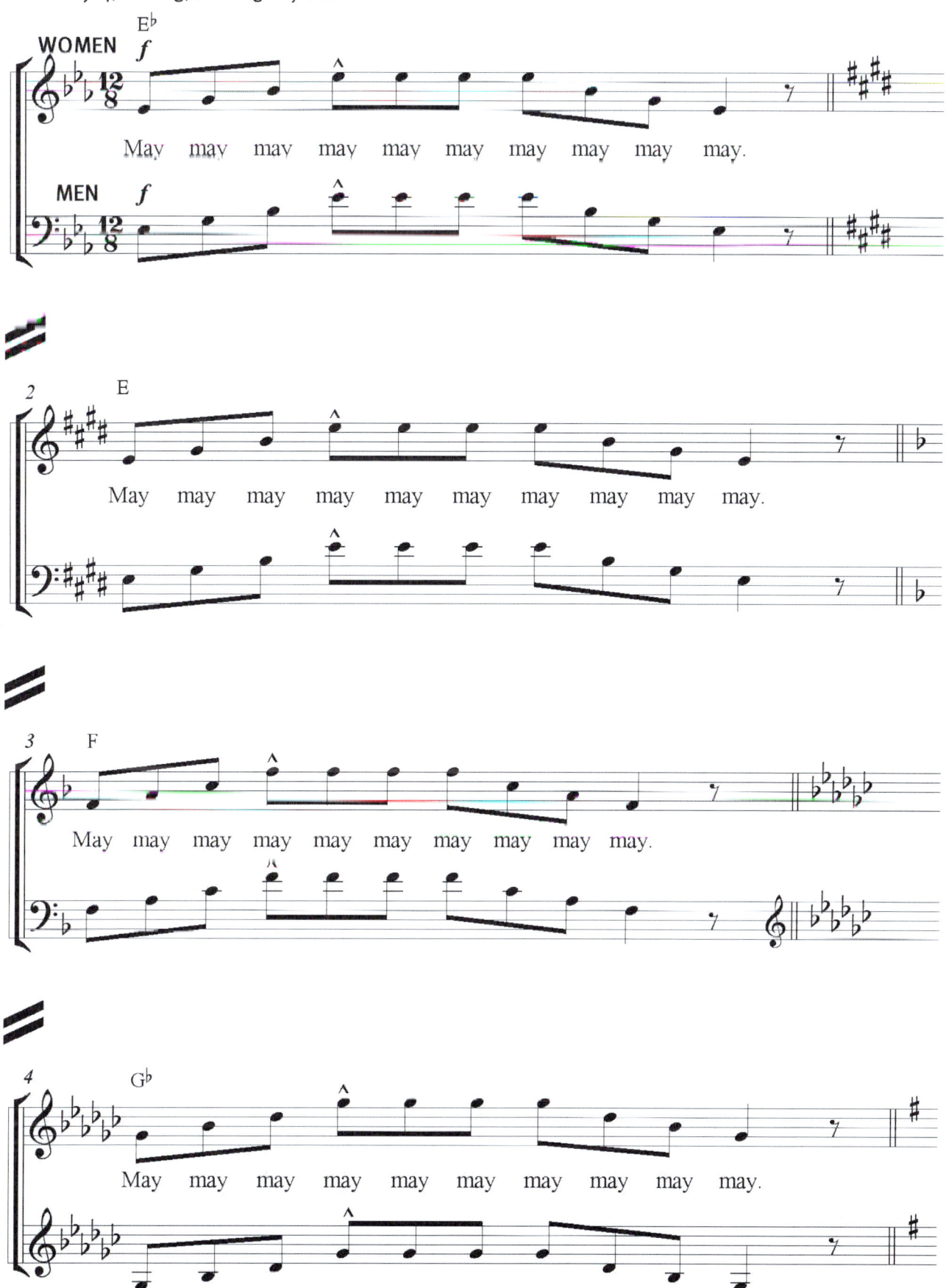

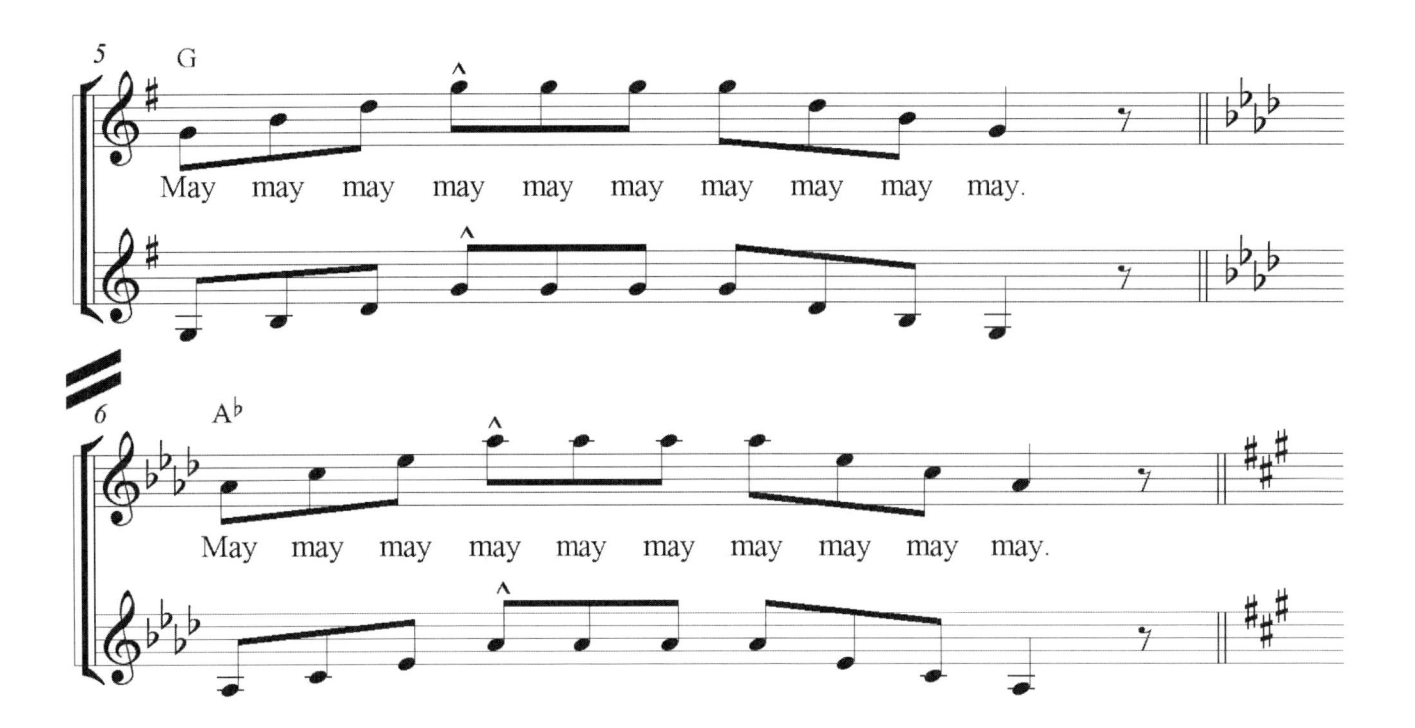

Don't worry if you can't go as high as this; it's very difficult for some singers. Do as much as you can today. There's another day tomorrow.

Women, let it go into head voice (falsetto)

Men, do NOT let it go into falsetto

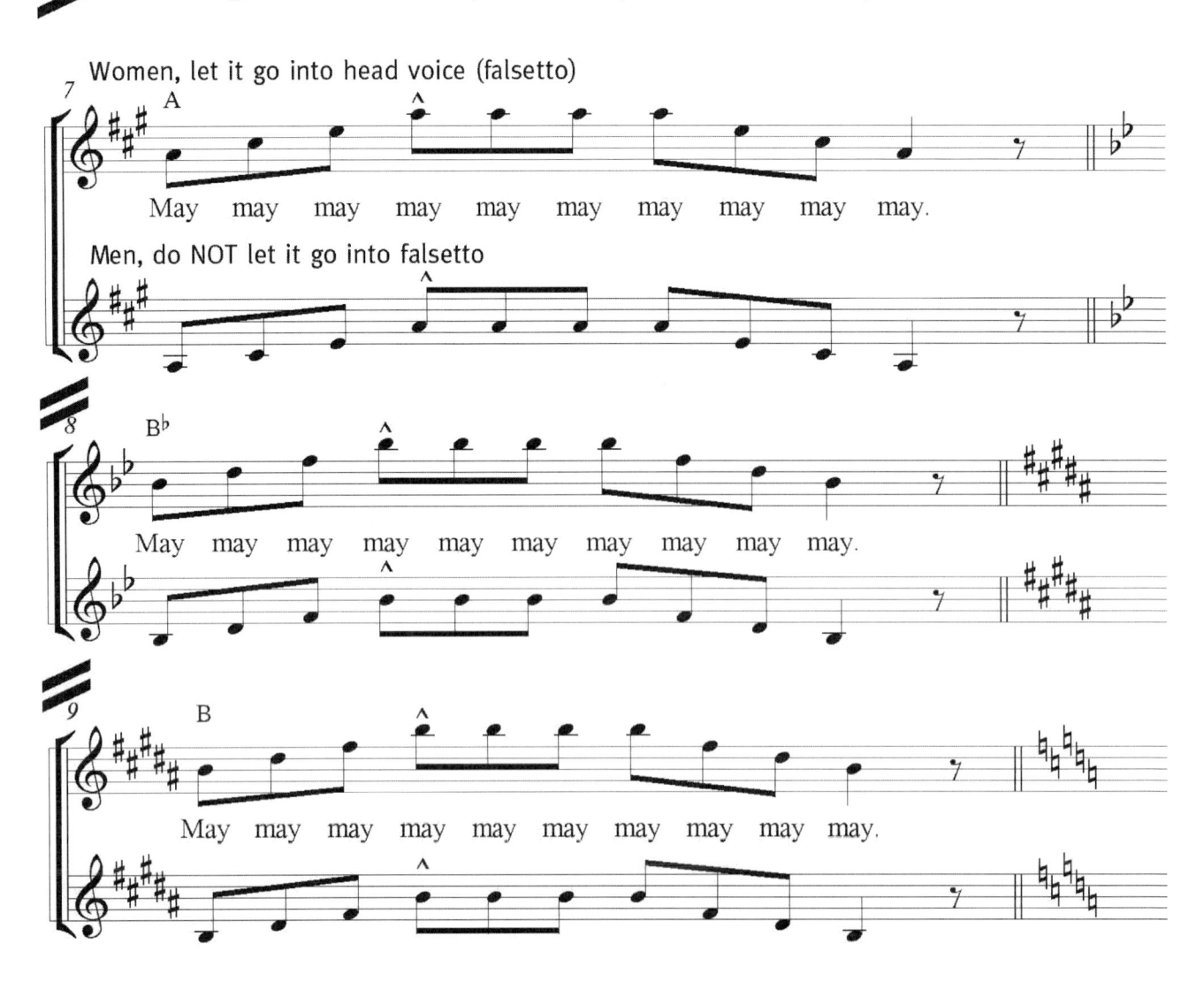

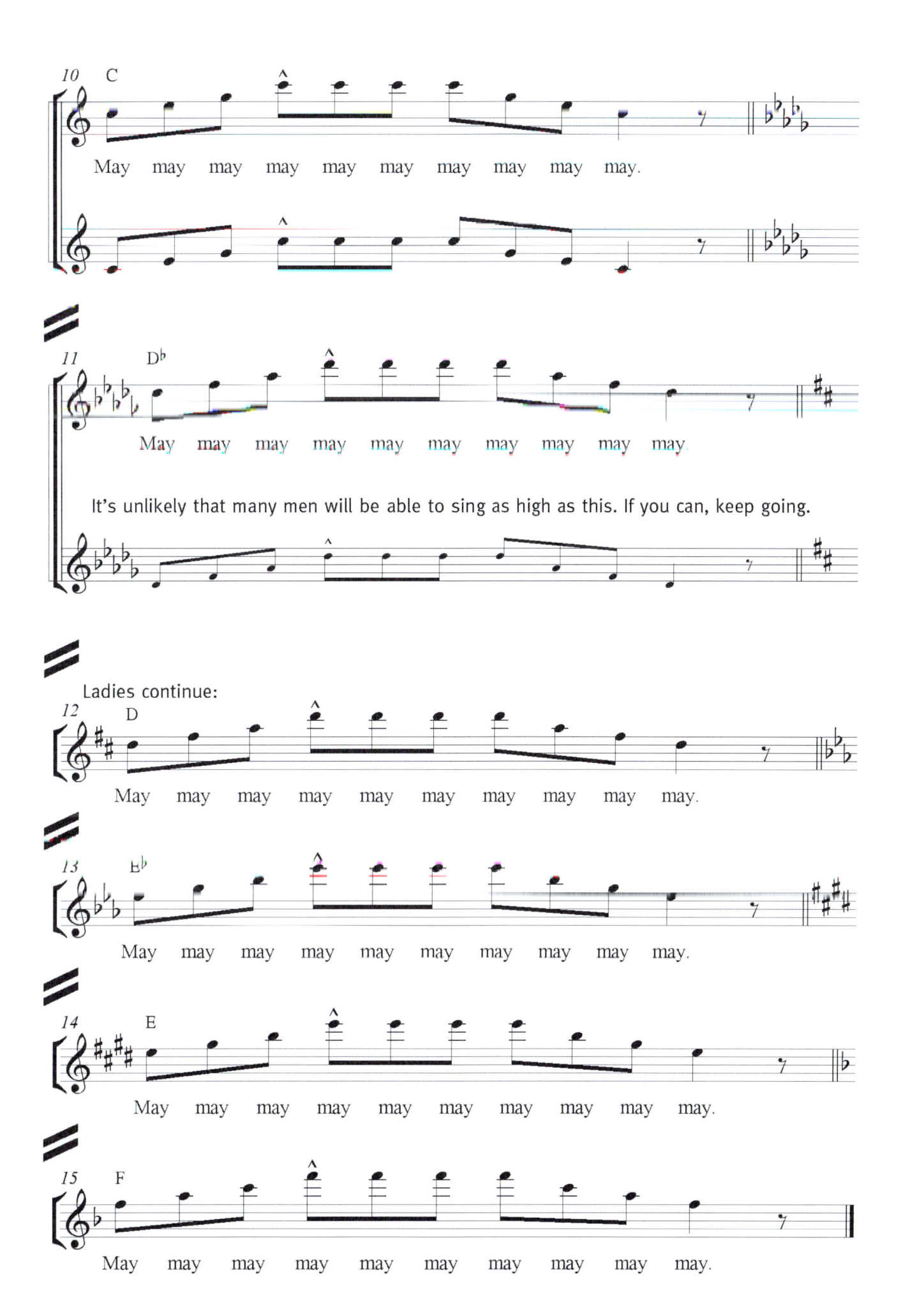

It's unlikely that many men will be able to sing as high as this. If you can, keep going.

Ladies continue:

Exercise 2: Learning To Control The Breath

You don't need to be a genius to realise that this subject is very important to any singer. You don't want to be approaching your big note only to find that you've run out of breath at the crucial moment. But what you might not realise is that you need extra breath in reserve to *support* your top notes. If your high notes are going flat, it might mean that you need a bigger breath than you thought you did.

Most people misunderstand the phrases 'breathe in' and 'breathe out'; they get them the wrong way around. When you breathe in deeply, the base of your lungs gets bigger – like a balloon. When you breathe out, it gets smaller – flat, like an empty balloon.

The basic technique is this: you breathe with the diaphragm. Think of it as breathing with your stomach. You do *not* breathe with your neck – there should be no movement there at all. This enables you to store air in the base of the lungs. When you use it to support high notes or power singing, this air becomes compressed and very strong, like the air in the inner tube of a car tyre – the whole car is supported on compressed air, and this is the type of power-house you need to build in order to support your voice. What you'll now have worked out (and I'm sure you're there before me) is that not only does the diaphragm control the breathing, but also that the diaphragm has no power to do *anything* unless you take in a big enough breath in the first place. What happy logic!

GUIDANCE NOTES

Sit in an upright chair (office or dining type) and lean back without lifting its front legs off the floor. Place one hand *lightly* around the front of your neck and the other hand on your stomach – that is, the base of your lungs, your diaphragm. This is where you're going to do most of the work.

Now breathe out. That means, expel all the air by pulling the diaphragm in as far as you can. Use your hand to help it. Now breathe in, puffing up the lower part of your stomach like a balloon, so that it pushes your hand out.

All this must be done *without moving your neck at all*. You should be able to detect unwanted movement with the hand placed lightly on your neck. Do this for a few minutes each day. Get used to breathing as deeply as possible, moving the stomach as much as possible with each breath (it should move about five inches) with no movement in the neck or throat at all.

You may well experience dizziness. This is quite normal, it probably means that you're breathing more deeply than you've ever done before. This is a good

sign. Pause until it passes. You will adjust very quickly. What makes you dizzy today won't do so in a few weeks' time. (See also *dizziness* in the 'Glossary'.)

Exercise 3: An Easy Way To Start Opening Up The Low Notes

The object of this exercise is to get the lowest possible notes by relaxing. Low notes are easy – as long as you don't force them and you're patient. Nevertheless, they might take a while. Every singer has both a head voice and a chest voice; this means that everybody can eventually sing both high notes and low notes. You need to exercise both of them because they both have a lot to contribute to the sound of the whole voice. You need the low notes, even if you never intend to sing any low numbers, as they improve the tone of the whole voice and stop your high notes from sounding shrill or strident.

Specifically, women need the low notes so that they can extend the chest voice upwards and build up the power in the middle of the voice. This, of course, is essential if you want to compete with the big stars.

Men need the low notes to give the middle register a bit of 'bite'. Most men have a problem in the middle of the voice, which is often weak. If you force these notes, you'll lose all of your high notes. The weakness is due to half of the voice being under-developed, usually the chest voice. What you need to do is work patiently on extending your lowest notes. But – and I cannot repeat it often enough – don't force them; open up your throat and let them start developing in the following way:

GUIDANCE NOTES

Keep the notes very short and make sure all the Hs are crisp, short and clear, or you'll find your throat taking an active part in the proceedings, and you don't want that. You should bypass the throat by keeping it wide open and focusing the sound in the nose. Let the sound sail through your mouth without touching the sides, so to speak.

The pronunciation should be very open, ie 'Ha!' as in *hat*, not 'Haw' as in *law* – these sounds are too closed and operatic. They'll probably knock you out of tune before you're halfway down.

Push the jaw right down, keeping the mouth open wide, like a yawn. The tip of the tongue should be against the bottom teeth – this is always a good way of keeping the voice off the throat and of focusing it in the nose.

Start loudly. Keep your head down. Ease off the volume when you get really low, or when the tuning becomes difficult.

CD1, Tracks 4–5

CD1, Track 5

GUIDANCE NOTES (CONTINUED)

At this pitch, you might be finding it difficult to relax. Perhaps your jaw is becoming stiff, or the notes are less easy to control. If so, you can now change the technique. Start easing your head right back, and feel your whole throat opening up. Push your jaw right down with the tip of your tongue, and feel the notes focusing, gently and effortlessly, in the bridge of your nose.

Make sure you're not pulling your head back into your neck — that will cause a lot of tightness. The lower you sing, the more open and relaxed you should feel.

Ease your head back (see Guidance Notes above). Keep the notes short and crisp.

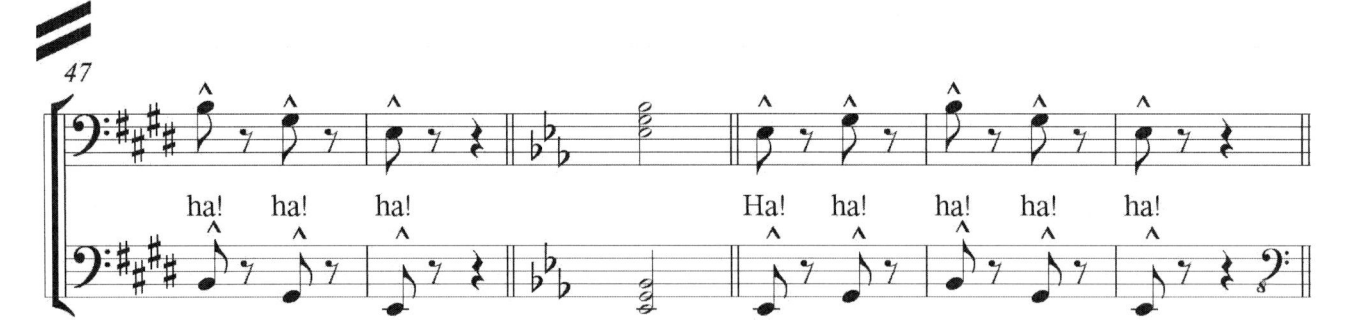

Continue very gently down to here, if you can. Nearly all singers can get down to these pitches, if they take the head back far enough, relax enough and feel the entire throat open enough.

Don't force these notes.

To be sung an octave lower than written (note the figure eight below the clef).

Now you might encounter a problem in switching from very low notes to very high notes. The secret is this: If you were using the throat to produce the sounds in Exercise 3, you might experience difficulty in getting up to the high notes in Exercise 4, but if you follow the Guidance Notes, keeping the pressure off the throat, you should have no difficulty at all in switching directly to the high notes. (See *the throat* in the 'Glossary'.)

Exercise 4: A Second Go At The High Notes – Improving The Tone

GUIDANCE NOTES

Because this consists mostly of downward scales, with an introductory note leading up to the top note, you need to concentrate on only the first two notes. Let the downward notes look after themselves; just keep them in tune.

This is a loud exercise; do not try to do it quietly. Take in a big breath with the diaphragm (that means puff out the stomach) and pull it in for the highest note in each phrase (the note with the ^ symbol over it).

Pronunciation

- **Too-wee** – These two sounds (which are very easy) both have closed vowels, and this seems to cause people a lot of psychological problems. They don't trust them, so they tend to sing 'toe-way'. Stick your lips out for 'too' – this forms a tunnel going both forward and backward down the throat, and is very good for resonance. For 'wee', pull the corners of your lips back into a forced smile. This focuses the voice onto the hard palate, making the sound very bright, particularly on the high notes. (See *resonance* in the 'Glossary'.)

- **No Hs** – The temptation to use Hs to separate the notes in the downward scales seems irresistible to a lot of my students, probably because they can't quite shake the habit of doing things, or defining things, with the throat. In this exercise, Hs very quickly turn themselves into glottal stops, and singers find themselves coughing their way down the scales. (See *glottal stops* in the 'Glossary'.)

- **Don't avoid the W** – People tend to think this is intrusive. In fact, it is essential for smoothness.

- Men should not go into falsetto at all in this exercise.

CD1, Track 7

Pull in the diaphragm on notes accented ^

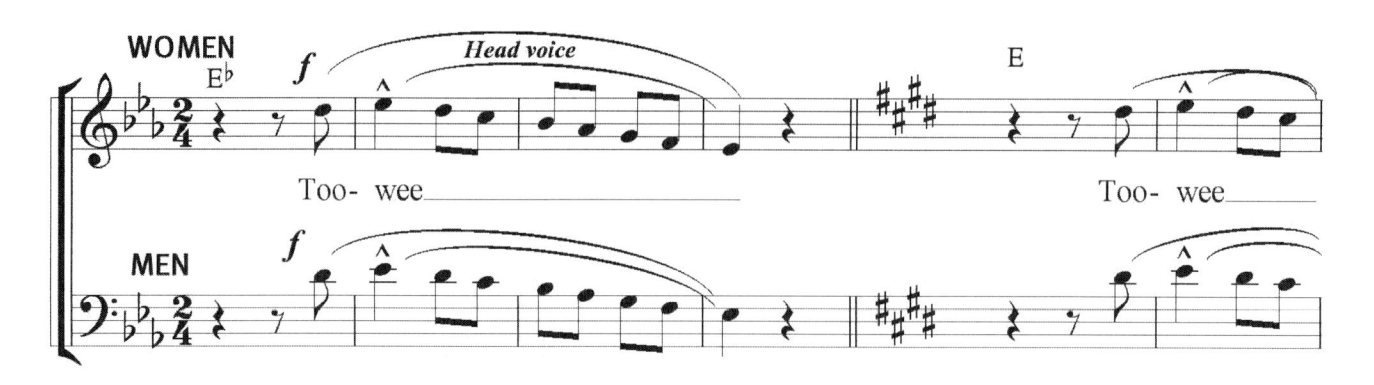

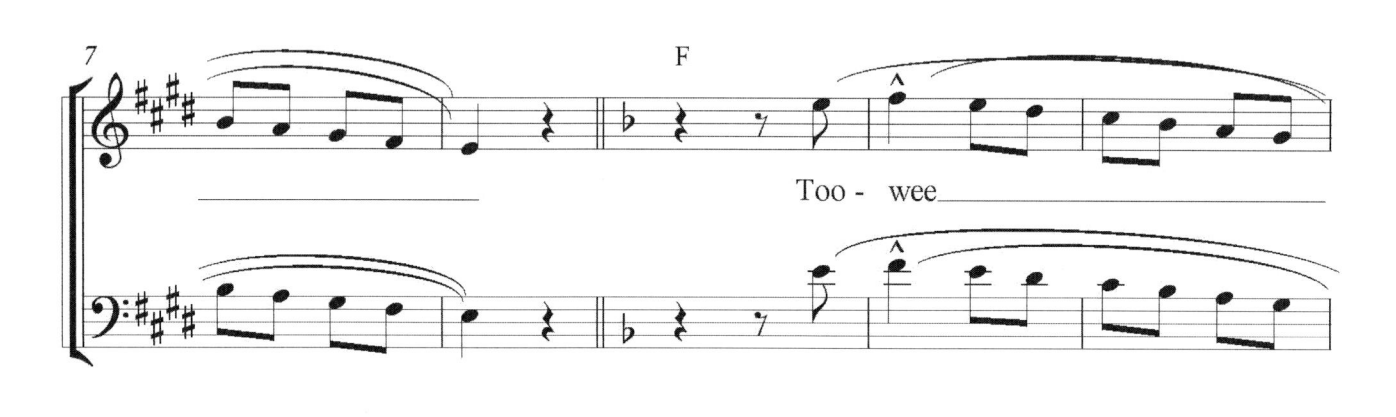

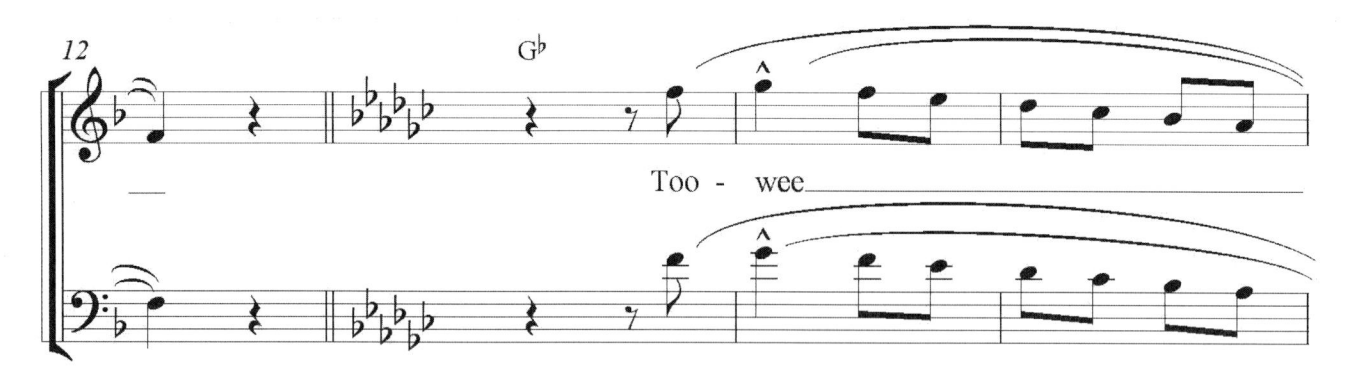

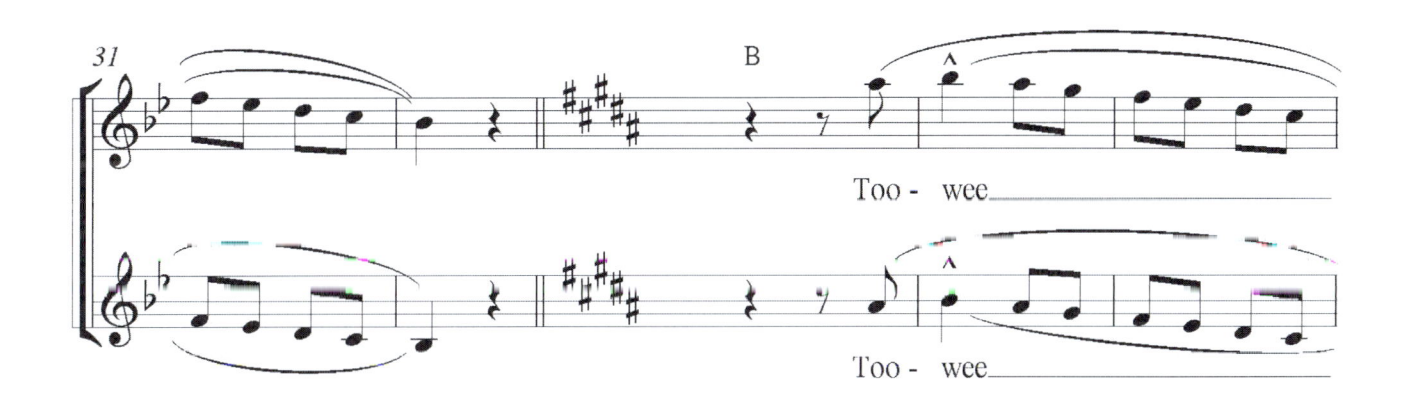

Exercise 5: Crying And Screaming

Not all modern commercial singers want to scream. If you *do* want to, this is the place to start. If you don't want to scream, move on to Exercise 6.

GUIDANCE NOTES

Screaming is the loudest sound a human being can make. If you try to do it quietly, you'll hurt your throat. This is mostly acting. Go flat out for it and it won't hurt, as long as you take the strain with the power muscles.

First, you're going to start crying like a child in the natural voice – chest voice, more or less – and go as high as you can in that. Then, very soon, the women will go into head voice, still sounding like a crying child, but the men will go on for another four or five phrases and then go into a whimpering voice (which doesn't need to be too loud). Then, at bar 28, we go ballistic!

Here's a step-by-step reminder of the techniques. Take a big breath with the diaphragm before you start each phrase, and really *use* it to take the strain.

Get your jaw right down, keeping your tongue firmly against your bottom teeth, even when you're taking the preliminary breath. Give the inside of your throat plenty of space; in fact, push your jaw down with your tongue.

Don't worry if you go over the top, but make sure you're not *under* the note. That's a hiding to nowhere!

When you come to the screaming pitch, go flat-out for it. Take the strain where the human body is supposed to take strain: with the stomach, legs and buttocks. Constipate!

If the throat hurts, but neither your stomach nor your bum do, you're not supporting your sound properly.

This exercise is just the start of a long sequence. It leads on to joining up the screaming with the rest of the voice so that you become versatile with your sounds. You want to be able to choose when to make it smooth, clean and innocent, and when to dirty it up by mixing screaming in with the natural voice. Apart from that, just act! (See *screaming* in the 'Glossary'.)

CD1, Track 9: Crying And Screaming

You must use all your technique for this: jaw, tongue, diaphragm and constipating.

Start in the chest voice if you can, then go into head voice as soon as you like.

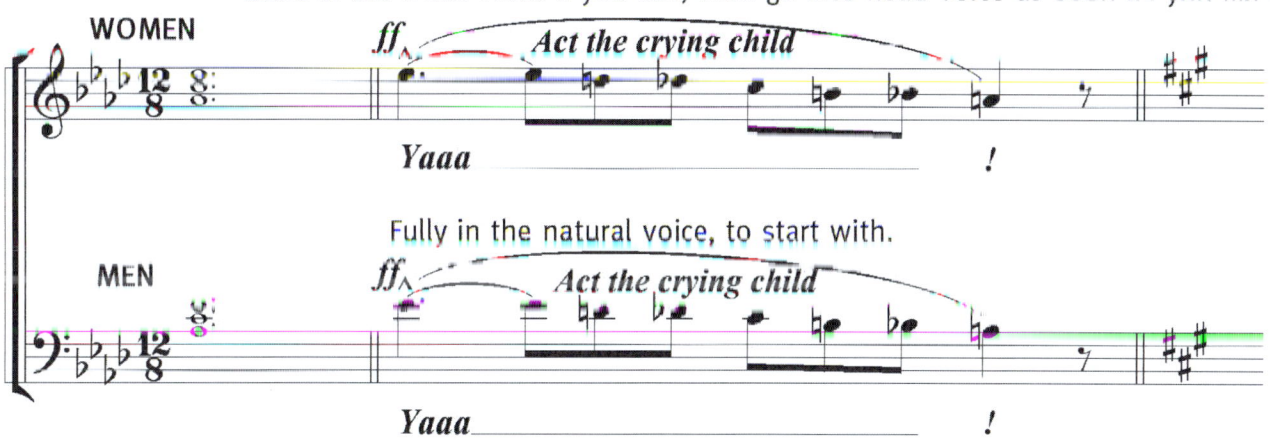

In order to go higher, each phrase must start louder than the previous phrase.

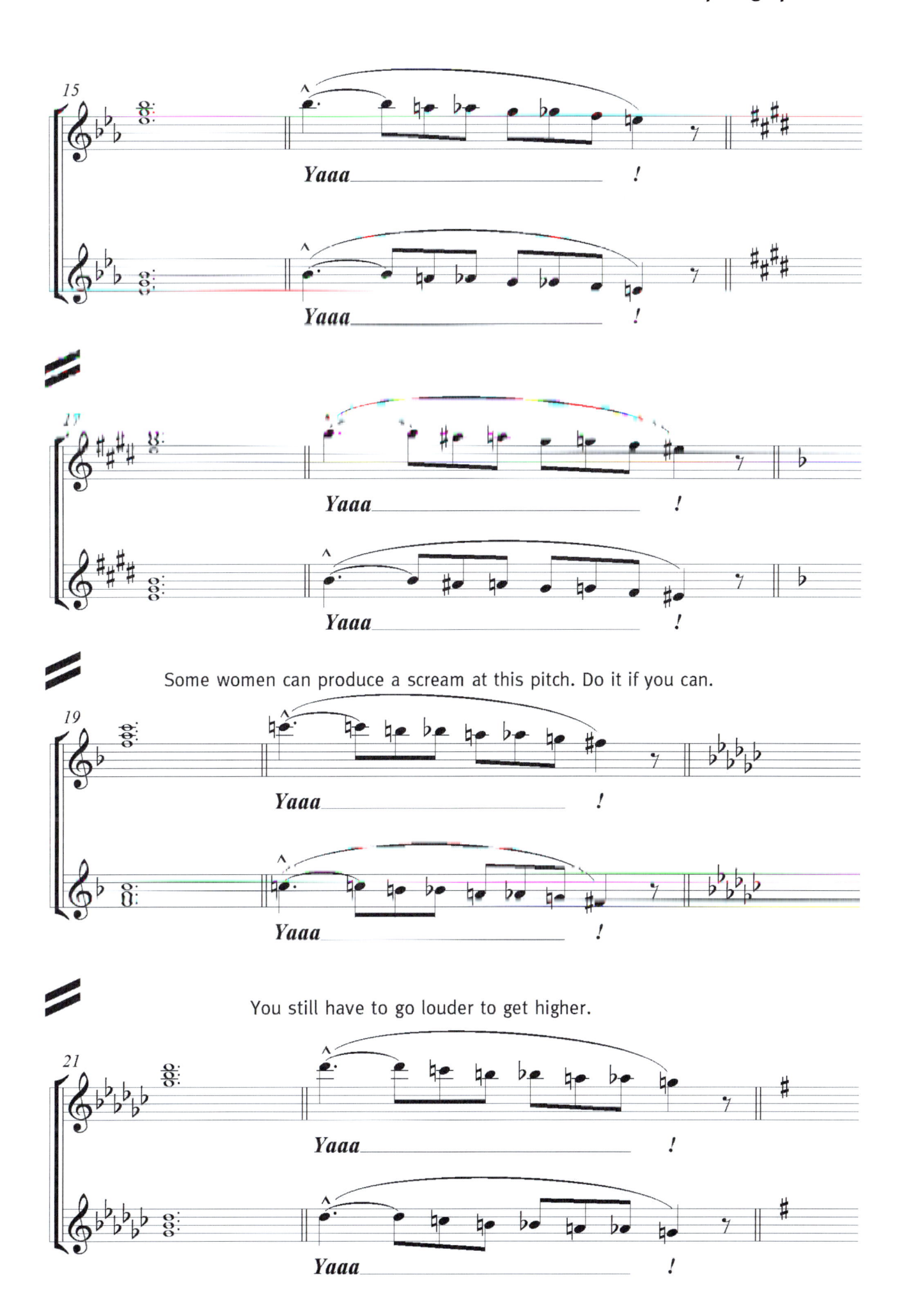

Some women can produce a scream at this pitch. Do it if you can.

You still have to go louder to get higher.

Now scream — constipate!

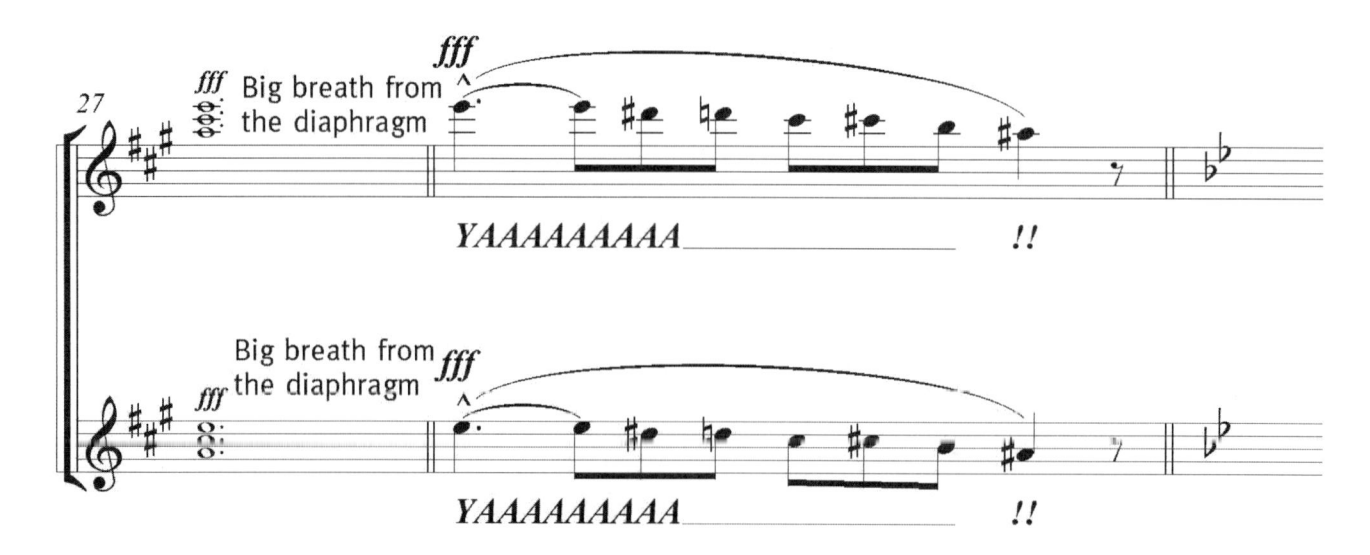

You may need to slow it down in order to get full value out of the screams.

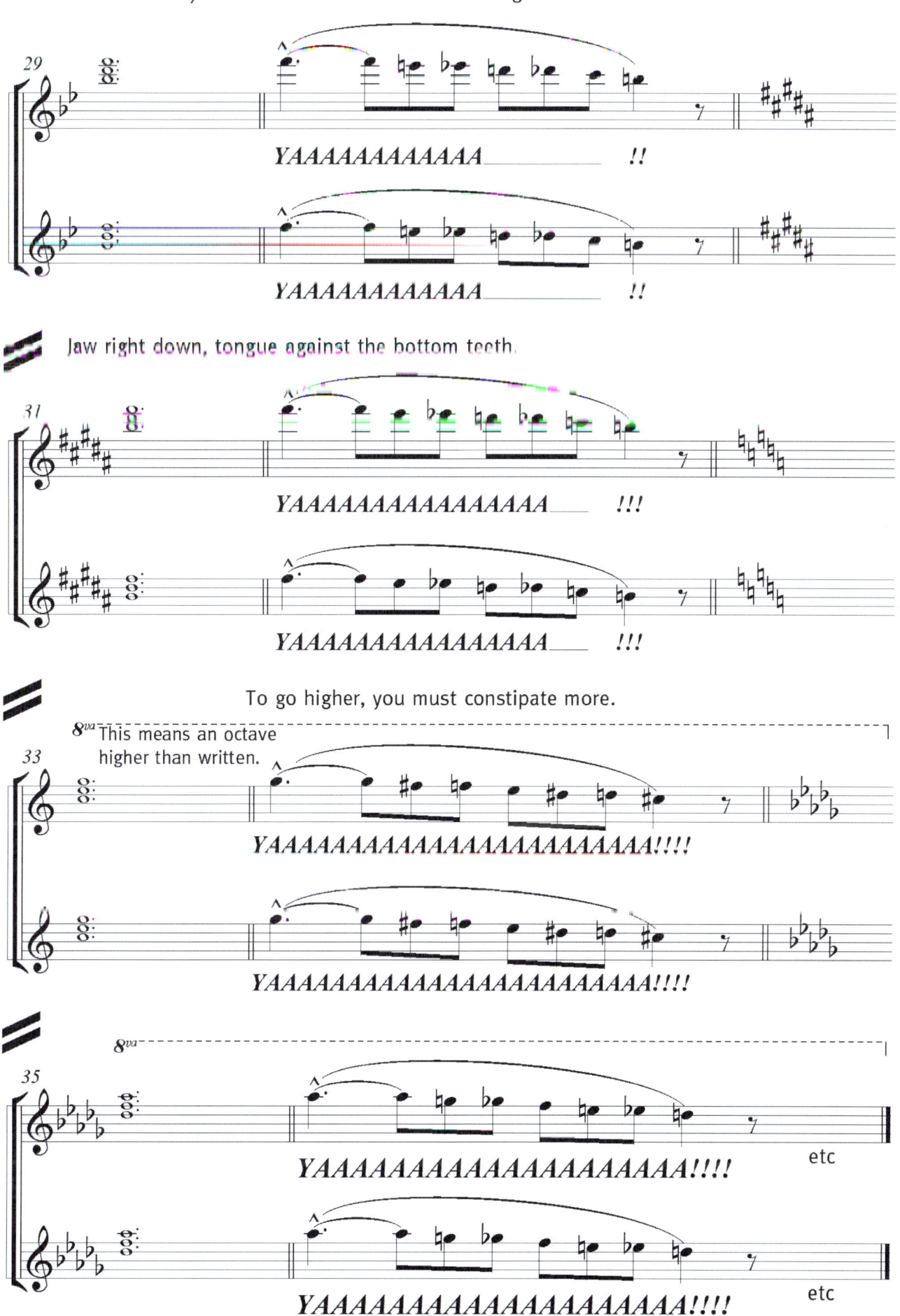

Obviously your jaw should have gone right down to give you plenty of space. If it didn't, you weren't really going flat-out for it. I rarely need to tell my students to drop the jaw on that exercise; if they're really acting, it happens automatically.

Exercise 6: Smoothing Over The Joins In The Female Voice

This isn't a big, belting exercise, unlike most of my exercises; this is for fine-tuning and smoothing over the *passaggio*. The male version of this exercise is on Tracks 18–21.

GUIDANCE NOTES

This exercise is in two parts: (a) the staccato version and (b) the legato version. Although it appears to be lightweight and trivial, you'll find that this is the most important exercise of all. It solves most of the problems of tuning and smoothes over all the 'breaks'. This exercise is, in fact, at least 300 years old. It is very simple and effective.

Watch the tuning. Be precise about every note, especially the second note of each scale, which, you will find, is particularly liable to go flat, which in this context means that the pitch is slightly too low. If your tuning is suspect, help the first note (marked ^) by gently squeezing the diaphragm to support it.

Keep it all quiet, but don't let it become inaudible. Keep the notes well-focused right to the end.

In the staccato version, keep it all very crisp. Let the voice change where it wants to; don't try to do it all in one voice or the other.

In the legato version, keep it very smooth indeed, with no jolts. Smoothness is everything.

If you find yourself running out of breath, take a bigger breath with the diaphragm and squeeze *all the air out* on the last two or three notes of each phrase. That will force you to take a big breath for the next phrase.

You need both halves of the voice to work, and you need to be able to join them up. The higher you can start this exercise, the better. Surprisingly, most of the problems in the middle of the voice can be solved by working downward from your highest possible notes.

CD1, Tracks 13: (a) The Staccato Version

CD1, Track 15: (b) The Legato Version

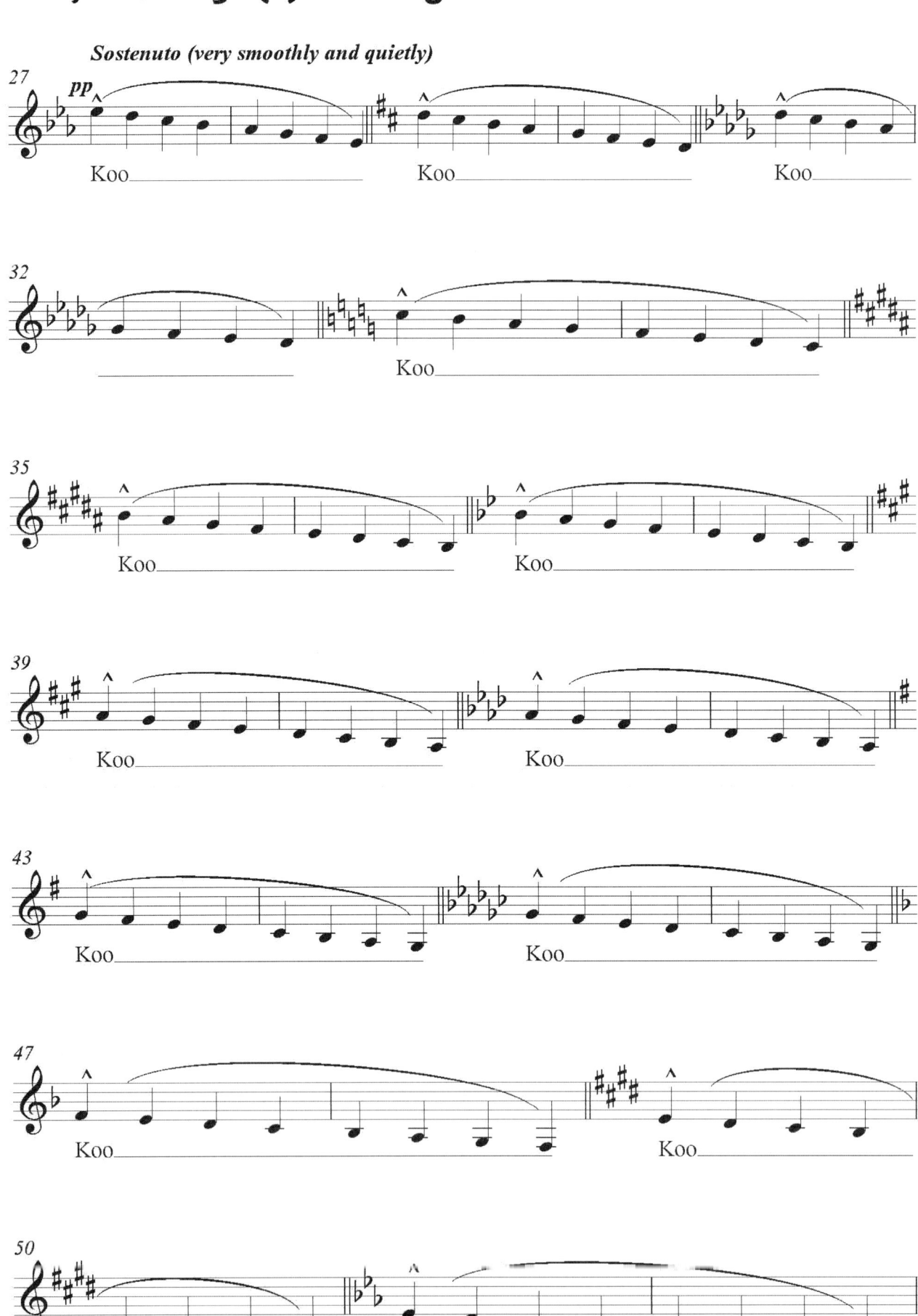

A common error: scooping up to the notes. This causes jolts to occur, thus defeating the object of the exercise.

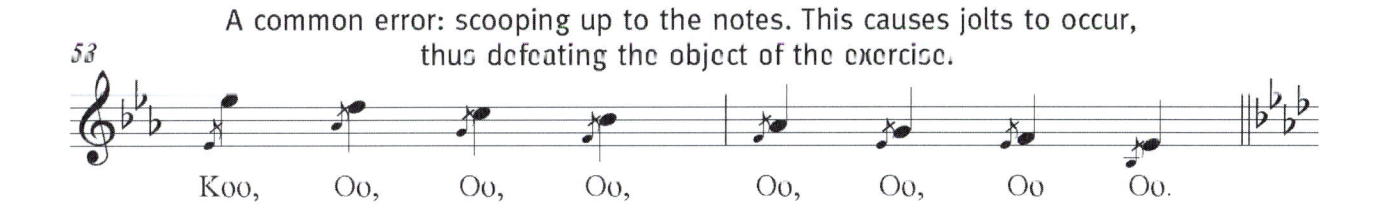

Koo,   Oo,   Oo,   Oo,   Oo,   Oo,   Oo   Oo.

CD1, Tracks 12 And 16

At the second or third lesson, if the first scale (E♭) has been succesful, try starting from here:

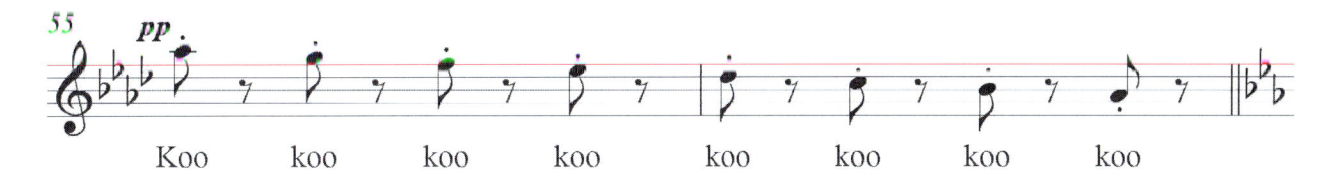

Koo   koo   koo   koo   koo   koo   koo   koo

CD1, Tracks 11 And 15

And, at a later lesson, from here...

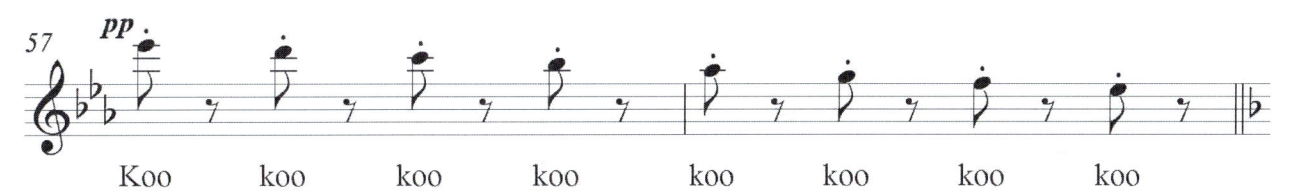

Koo   koo   koo   koo   koo   koo   koo   koo

...and eventually from here.

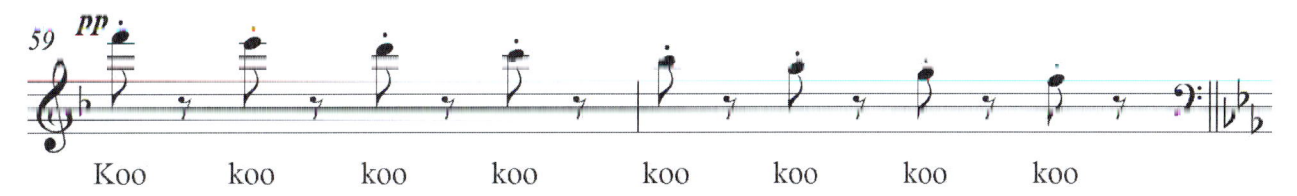

Koo   koo   koo   koo   koo   koo   koo   koo

It is important to exercise these high notes so that the soft palate is stretched. This gives you control over the tone throughout the voice and also smoothes over the *passaggios*, or 'breaks'.

Always finish the entire sequence here:

Koo_____

Exercise 7: Joining Up The Male Voices

Although at first glance you might think this exercise is very similar to the girls' version (Exercise 6), it varies in two ways: it is loud, and the change from falsetto into the natural head voice is specific. You can try to smoothe over it, but it is very difficult; you'll have a much better chance of disguising the join (the *passaggio*) later, when we come to look at the *quiet mixed voice*. Nonetheless, the objects are to smoothe the voice down after the excesses of previous exercises, to begin the process of blending the different head voices and, most importantly, to start working the falsetto voice as early as possible.

GUIDANCE NOTES

The music for this exercise is printed at the actual pitch. It is not a misprint.

First, sing the staccato version. Starting with the A♭ major scale, bar (or measure) 1, sing the first five scales entirely in falsetto (the childish voice). You'll need to do this loudly or you won't get up to the first note. You'll also need a lot of help from the diaphragm, so pull the stomach in hard to get hold of the first note. If you can't reach the A♭, try it from the F major scale (bar 4) to get yourself started, then try the A♭ again.

When you get down to the E♭ scale (bar 6), let it change into the natural voice midway down the scale, somewhere around A♭ (the fifth note of the scale) or G (the sixth note). You may need to squeeze the diaphragm to make a smooth change. Everyone has a natural voice-change on that particular A♭, but it's often difficult to control, but this exercise is designed to help you to control it. (So always try to effect the change on A♭ or G. All scales contain one or the other, but sometimes

the A♭ is called G♯.) Change higher if you can, lower if you can't.

Watch the tuning. Be precise about every note, especially the second note of each scale, which, you'll find, is particularly liable to go flat. Don't try to change voices on the second note of any scale; it will be almost impossible to keep it in tune.

From the A♭ scale (bar 13) onwards, try to do it all in the natural voice. If you can't, change on the third note, not the second.

When you've done the staccato version, have a go at the legato version.

The Trap
The Unwanted Extra Note

This is very common. Indeed, we've all done it. We have this psychological need to 'try out' difficult notes at easier pitches before we commit ourselves to the proper pitch. Obviously, it defeats the object of the exercise, which is to smoothe over the join between the falsetto and 'natural' voices, or to try to. To avoid such a trap, start by taking a bigger breath than you think you need and, just before you arrive at the change, squeeze the diaphragm, gently but firmly, and *concentrate*. You'll understand this exercise better when you work on the quiet mixed head voice, but you need to do this loud version first.

After you've worked on the quiet mixed head voice for a while, you'll no longer need to do the legato version (version [b]) of this exercise – the former exercise will take care of the smoothness – but you'll still need the staccato version (version [a]) to exercise your highest possible falsetto notes as, apart from the screaming exercises, this is the only exercise that enables you to get at them.

CD1, Track 19: (a) The Staccato Version
Read the Guidance Notes on page 34 carefully.

Do the first five scales entirely in falsetto. If you can't manage the first scale straight away, start with the fourth scale.

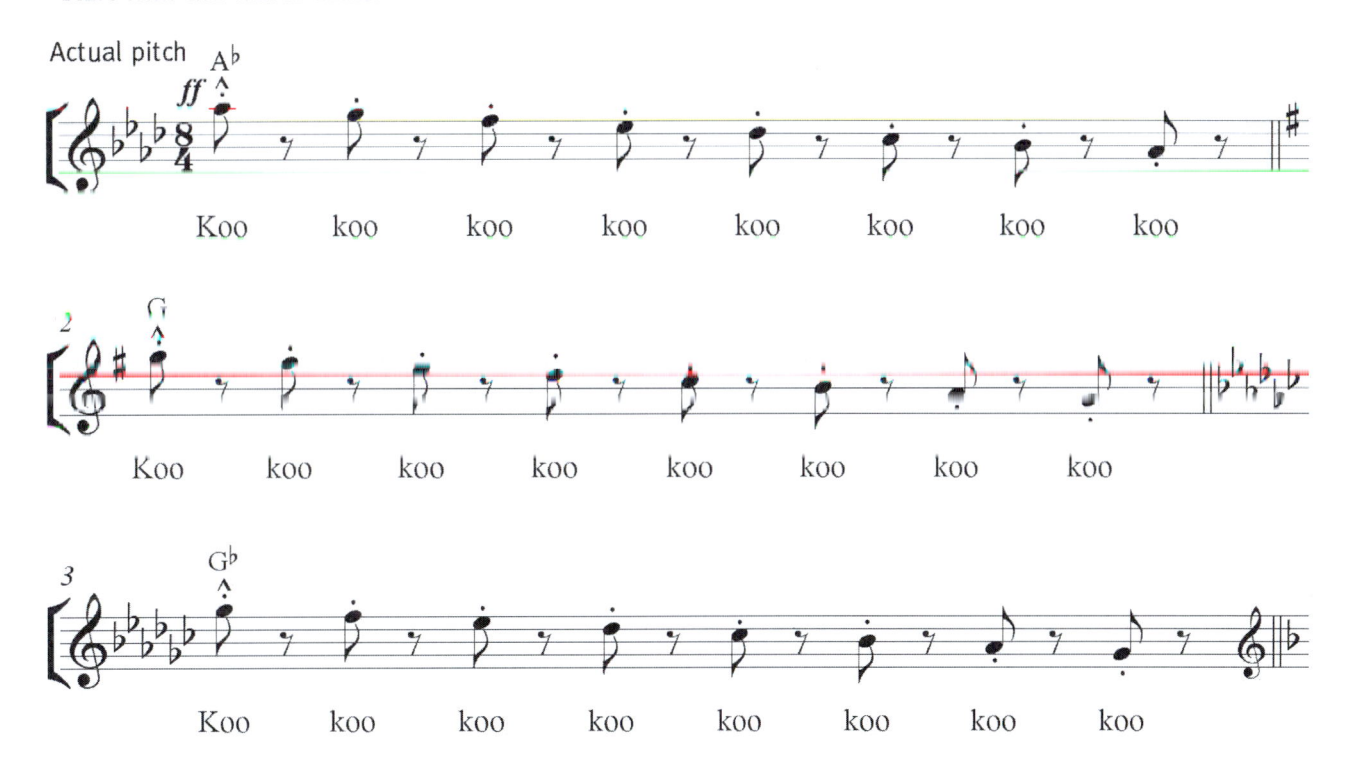

If you can't manage the higher scales, start here and then try the higher scales:

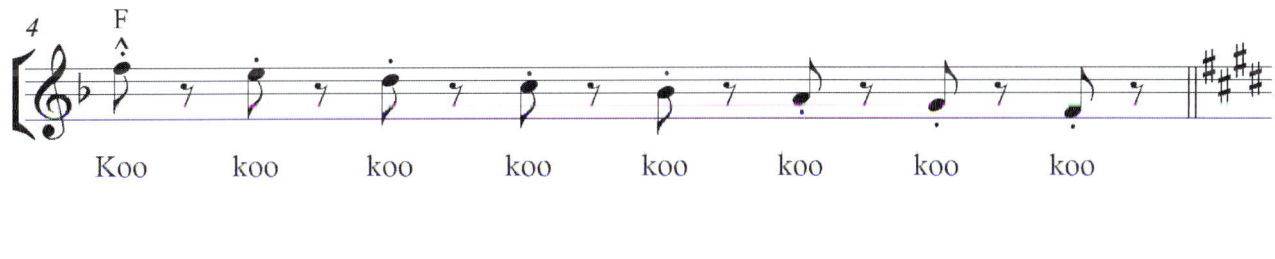

Now change from the falsetto voice into the natural voice on the note marked ✳

Do the remaining scales entirely in the natural voice, if you can.

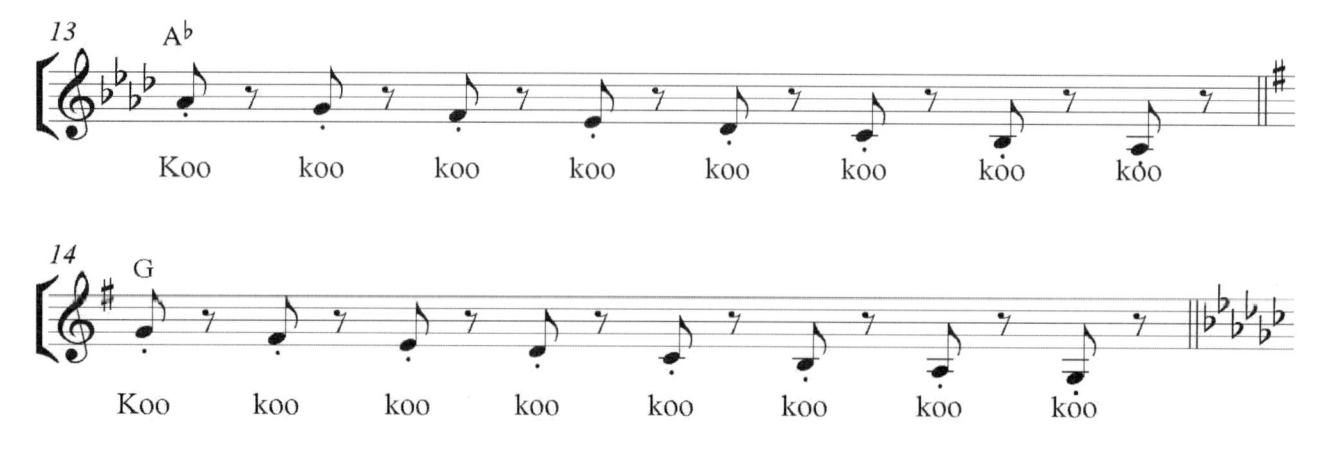

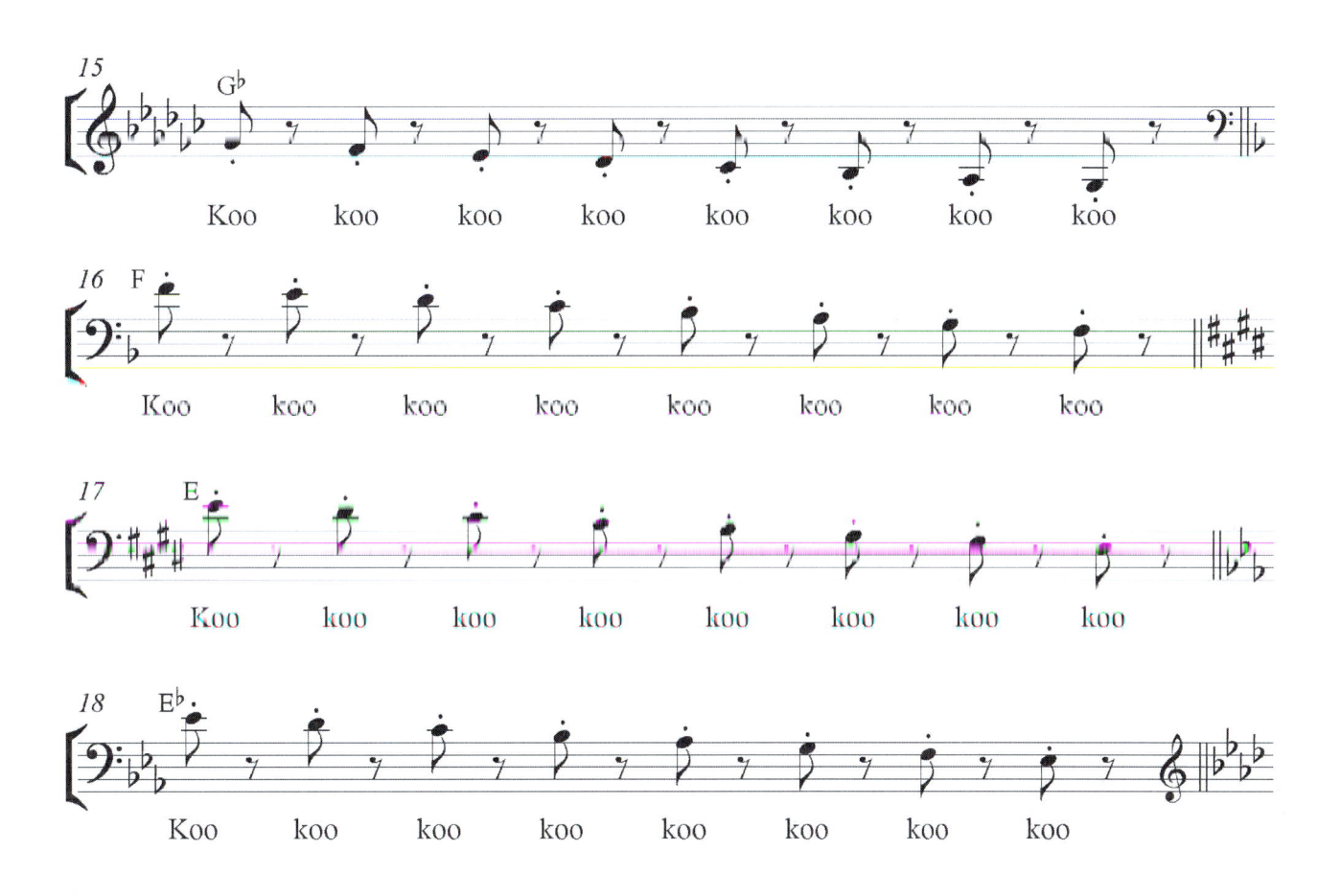

CD1, Track 21: (b) The Legato Version
Read the Guidance Notes on 34 carefully

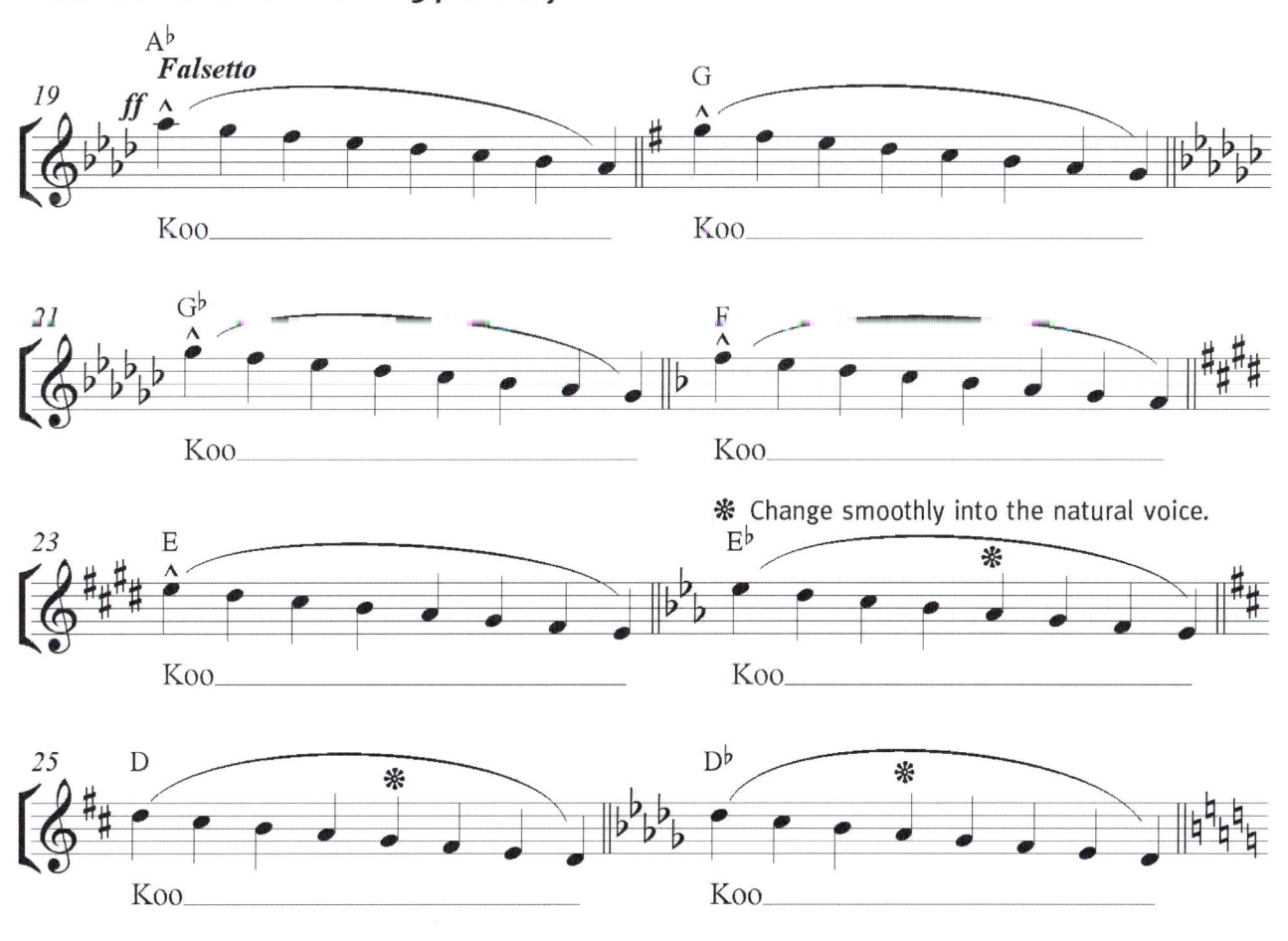

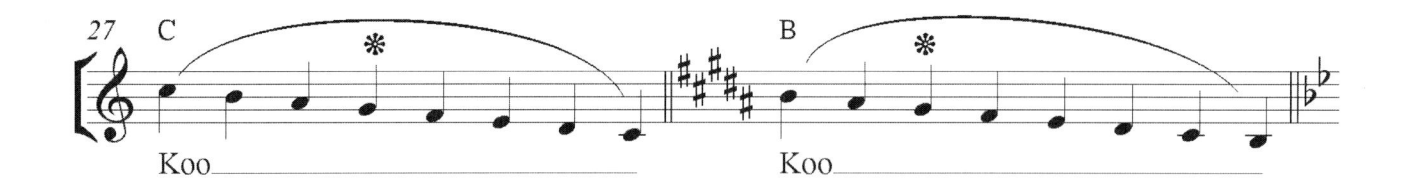

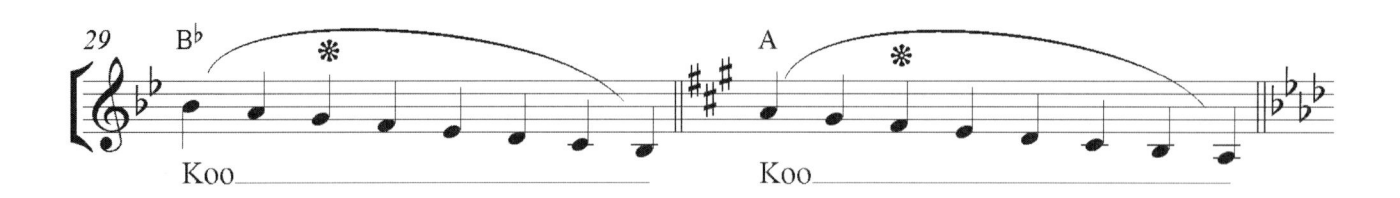

Entirely in the natural voice from here on.

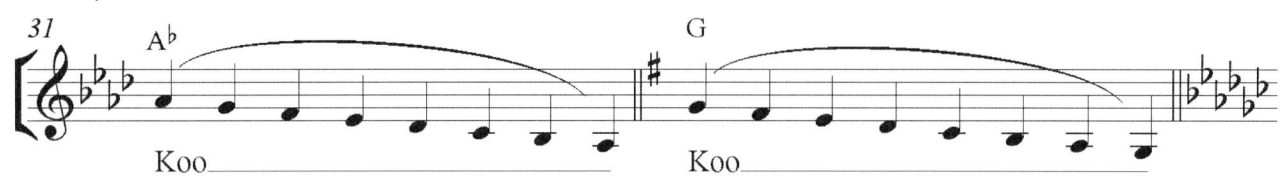

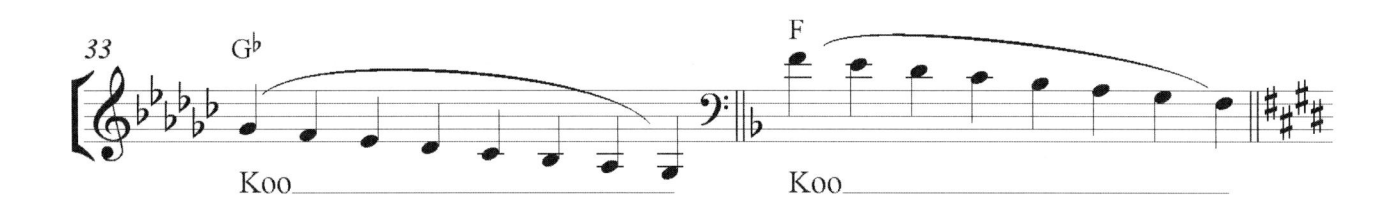

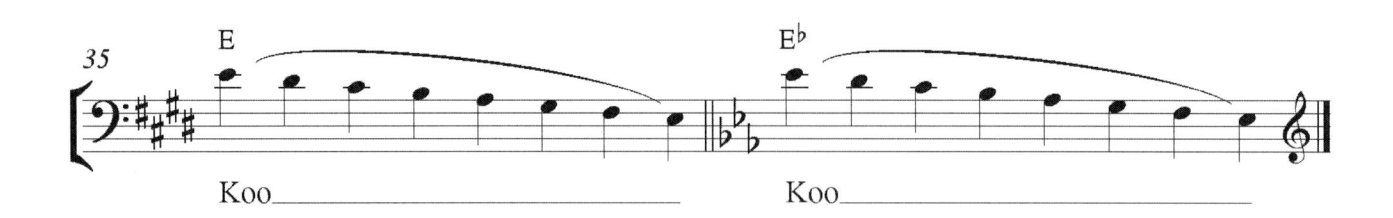

THE TRAP

The Unwanted Extra Note

(Read the Guidance Notes on page 34)

CD1, Tracks 22–23

Exercise 8: Pistol Shots

This is a superb way of waking up the power in the middle of the voice, but don't *start* your warm-up with this exercise; do some high-and-low exercises first.

GUIDANCE NOTES

These are short, sharp notes, as loud as you can make them. The title says it all: they should sound like pistol shots, motivated sharply from the diaphragm and focused in the nose, bypassing the throat altogether. If you use the throat, they won't sound like pistol shots at all but like growls – very unappealing. Also, they will hurt.

Take a good breath with the diaphragm, push the jaw right down, giving you plenty of space, and put the tongue firmly against the bottom teeth.

The Hs must come from the diaphragm and the voice must focus in the nose. You must do nothing with the throat but keep it open. Both Hs and vowels should be produced in one action: slam the diaphragm in sharply for the H.

Pronunciation

Ha! as in 'hat', but don't end it with a glottal stop; instead, keep the throat open. Make the sound as bright as you can. Brightness is crucial in this exercise. Make the sound brash, even brassy.

First, try it slowly without a specific pitch: '[breath] Ha! [breath] Ha! [breath] Ha!', etc.

CD1, Track 22: Pistol Shots

First try it without a note.

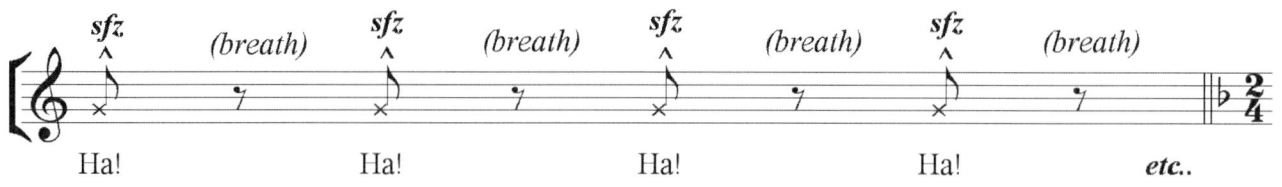

Now sing it in strict time and tune.

CD1, Track 23: Ladies First

Short and sharp. Nasal, not throaty.

Now The Men...

Short and sharp. Nasal, not throaty.

The Story So Far.

So, you've made a start on building up the voice. Maybe you've got everything right pretty much first time and without any real difficulty – some people do. If so, you've done very well indeed. It's much more likely, however, that you found it very difficult, that the notes you wanted remained obstinately out of reach and that the strain on your throat may make you think that all of these exercises are out of your range. You might even be wondering if you will ever be able to sing like a great rock singer. Don't be discouraged – I never promised that it would be easy. Self-doubt is almost the natural state for a singer.

Next, let's tackle the problem of excessive pressure on the throat. Ideally, there should be no veins, arteries or lumpiness showing on the outside of the neck when you sing (although at this stage, that's too much to hope for!). Instead, all of that pressure must be transferred to the power muscles, particularly the diaphragm.

Exercise 9: Co-ordinating The Power Muscles On The High Notes

GUIDANCE NOTES

This exercise is loud and mechanical – diaphragm *in* for the high notes, *out* for the low notes. In order for this to work, you *must* take a very big breath with the diaphragm: puff up your stomach like a balloon so that you have plenty to pull in for the high notes.

Keep the lips almost closed for 'mee' (try pulling the corners of the lips back into a forced smile), and the jaw should be right down for 'yaa'. The tongue should be firmly against the bottom teeth *all the time*.

Keep your head down. Sing the whole of the exercise loudly or you won't be able to control the top notes. This is true for both sexes, but particularly important for men. Women should allow the top notes to go into the head voice, but men must keep it all in the natural voice with no falsetto at all.

If you can't get down to the bottom notes, it means that you're getting stuck in the top register. You're probably locking the jaw in the halfway position, neither closed enough for 'mee' nor open enough for 'yaa'. The solution is to push the jaw right down on 'yaa' – that will usually release the lock.

Make a meal of the Y in 'yaa'. Overdo it. Wallow in it. Y is always a godsend to singers; it focuses the voice wonderfully by exercising the tongue and jaw in the perfect way.

When you reach the highest phrase, come back down, singing the phrases in the reverse order.

CD1, Tracks 24–25

41

CD1, Track 25: Octave Leaps

Pull the diaphragm in for the high notes (marked ^). Let it out for the low notes.

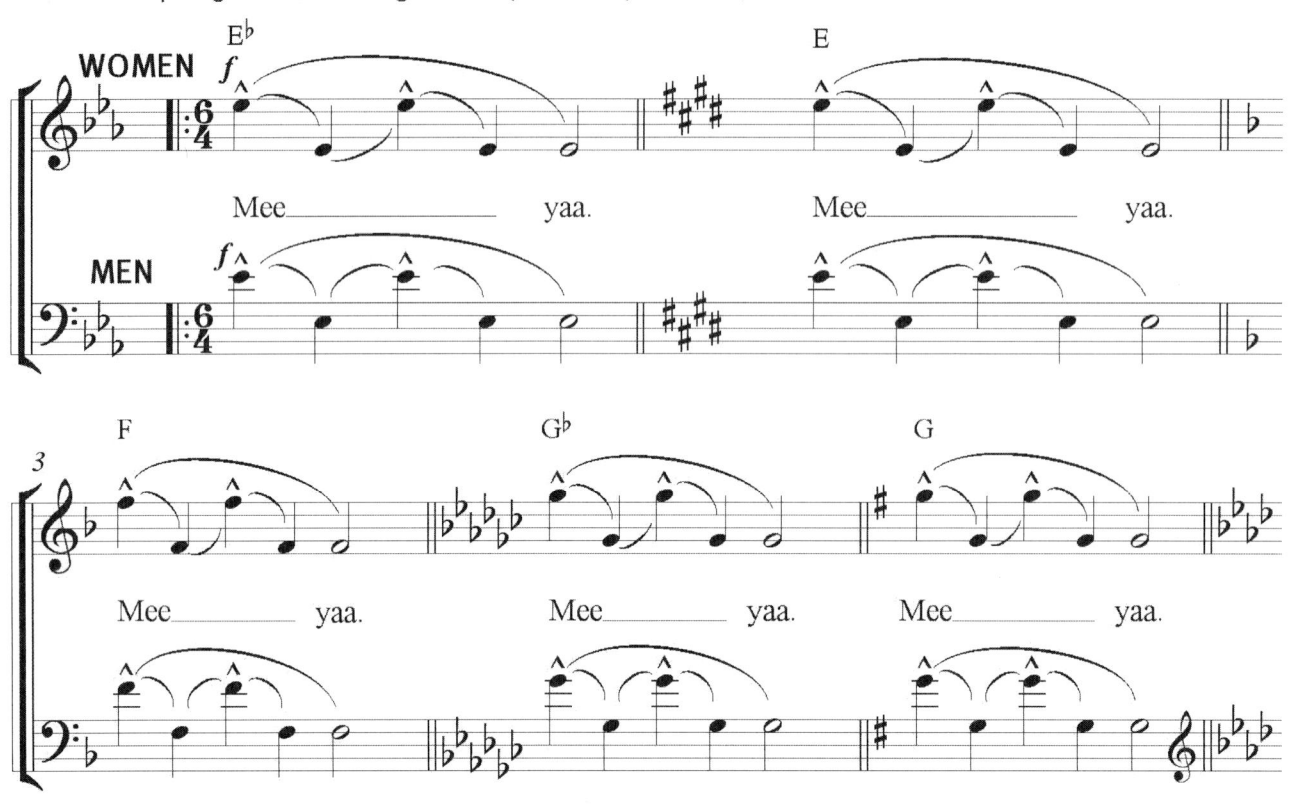

To sing higher you need to sing louder. High notes are louder than low notes, generally.

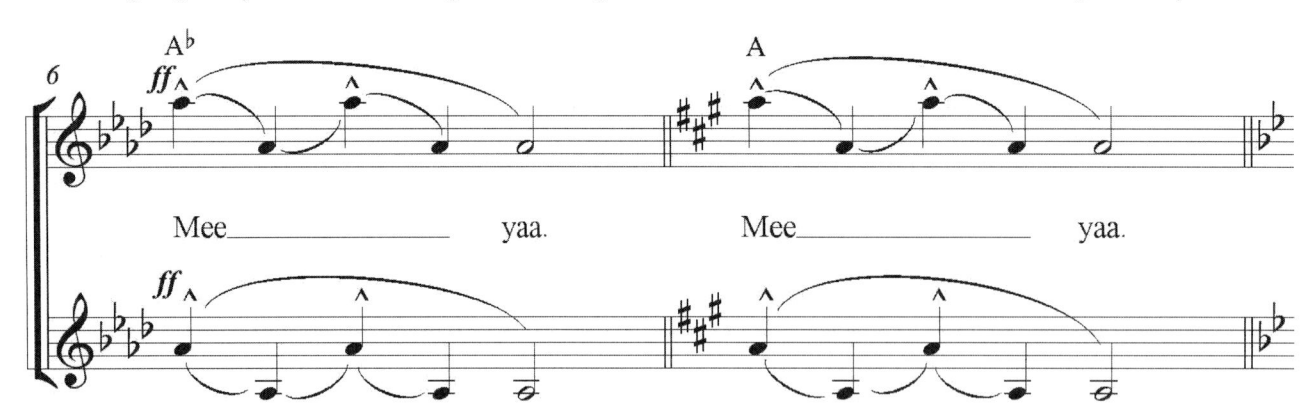

Now go back down, singing the phrases in the reverse order.

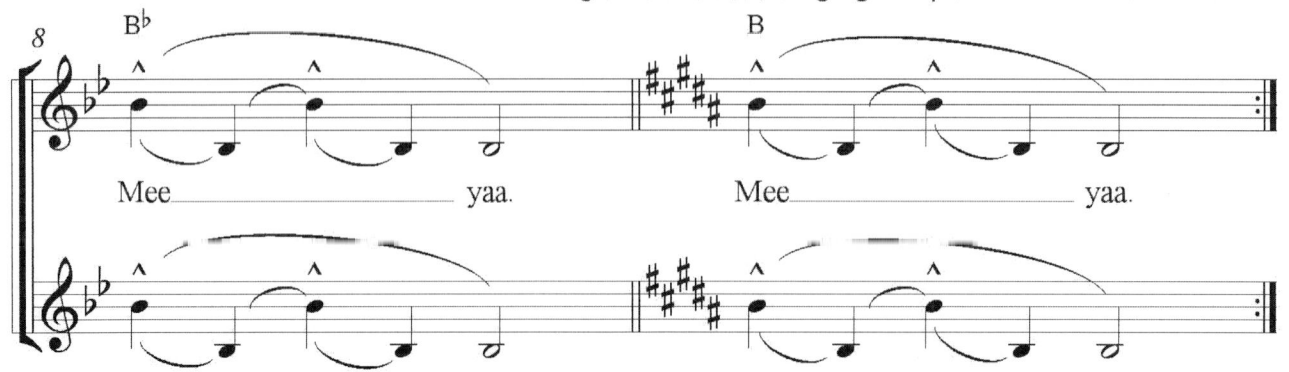

3 THE CHEST VOICE

Exercises For The Middle And Lower Notes

A good, rich, powerful and deep chest voice is very saleable – probably because it is comparatively rare among male pop or rock singers and is the most distinguishing characteristic of female rock and pop singers.

This is where the main difference lies in the female voice, between opera singing and rock. For women, opera singing takes place mostly in the head voice, even in the contralto roles, and they will put a great deal of work into bringing the sound of the sweetest head notes down into the middle register. But, for a woman, rock and pop singing is mostly in the chest voice, which needs to be powerful and should be extended as high as possible for the power, and as low as possible for the tone, so that it is rich rather than strident.

Most men are better at the head voice than the chest voice. So, if you're a man and the deep sounds come easily and powerfully, you are very lucky.

However, whether you're a man or a woman, don't be fooled into thinking that you have a naturally deep voice, or that you're a contralto or a bass just because you find low notes easier than high notes – we all do. You might be mistaking the need for hard work on the high notes for impossibility. There is an easy test: If you have a naturally resonant chest voice, it will be apparent in your speaking voice – it will be the first thing that people notice about you the first time they hear you speak. It will surprise them.

We all have a chest voice, with very deep notes available to us, but it may take a lot of patient work to open it up. Even when you're able to sing all the really low notes well, with a good, hard edge, the sound might still be thin and unresonant. You can't force low notes or they go out of tune and may even hurt; they must be exercised gently and persistently over a long period – months, or even years. If they are not exercised frequently, they will dry up and become unavailable to you temporarily, although you can get them back with a few days' work.

Even if you have a wide top register with wonderful high notes, you can still develop very good deep notes without losing anything at the top end of your voice. Contrariwise, your top notes are likely to become warmer and richer the more you develop your chest voice. Don't believe people who say that you can't sing both high and low: you can – and the CDs accompanying this book are proof of this – as long as you don't use your throat to produce any of the sounds.

Most of my chest-voice exercises include a lot of work either for the diaphragm or for breath control. This is very useful for the teacher, as it provides a distraction from one of the chief objectives of all these exercises: building up some resonance with prolonged use. So, while the students are struggling with endless repetitions of exercises for diaphragm agility, for instance, they are unwittingly exercising the chest voice without pressure on the throat. Also, they tend to stop worrying about their ability to sing in tune (a constant problem with many students in the early stages) and the instinct for accurate tuning takes over, usually – but not always, alas.

Exercise 10: Long Notes To Build Up Deep Sounds

Resonance and vocal technique are best developed with long notes and sustained phrases, not to mention breath control.

GUIDANCE NOTES

The object is to hold the third note – 'yaa' – loudly for at least 20 seconds.

Take a big breath, puffing up the diaphragm, and begin to sing, keeping the tongue against the bottom teeth throughout. Be very grudging, at first, about using up the breath – don't use it up all at once but, when you feel it running out, squeeze the diaphragm so that you use up all of the air. This tends to induce you to take a huge breath for the next go. By the end of the note, you may need to pull in the diaphragm so far that you feel yourself bending over. Breath control doesn't improve with age, unlike most things to do with singing, so make it as good as you can right now.

Push the jaw right down with the tip of the tongue at the *beginning* of 'yaa', not as an afterthought. This is very important, as it will focus the sound on the hard palate, but if you're doing it right it will feel as if you're focusing in the nose.

The breath will last much longer if you sing it with a good hard edge on the voice – not harsh but focused. If the sound is woolly, the breath will not last. If this happens, try singing louder.

Start with the head down. As you go lower, you'll need to ease off the volume. The printed music will tell you when to do this, but you'll probably feel when to ease off.

CD1, Track 27

Get a good, hard edge on the sound. Focus in the nose.

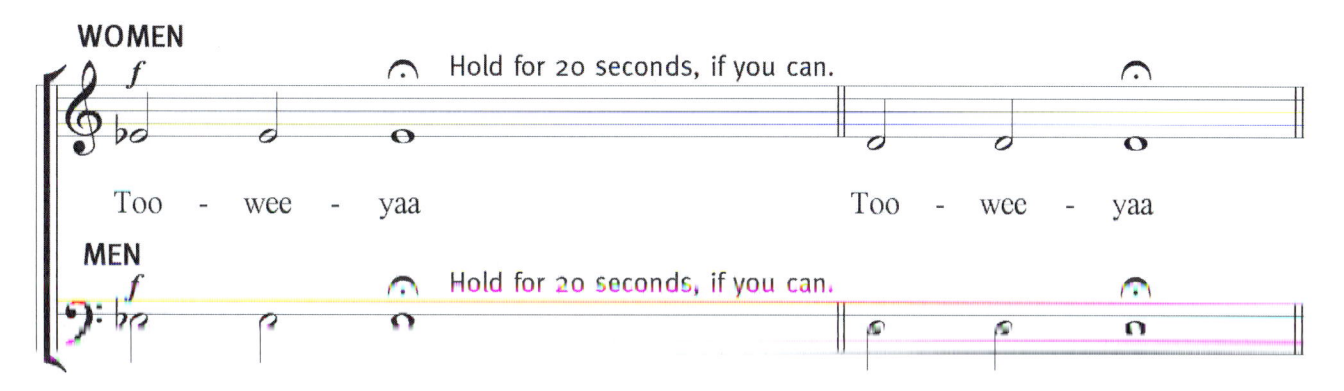

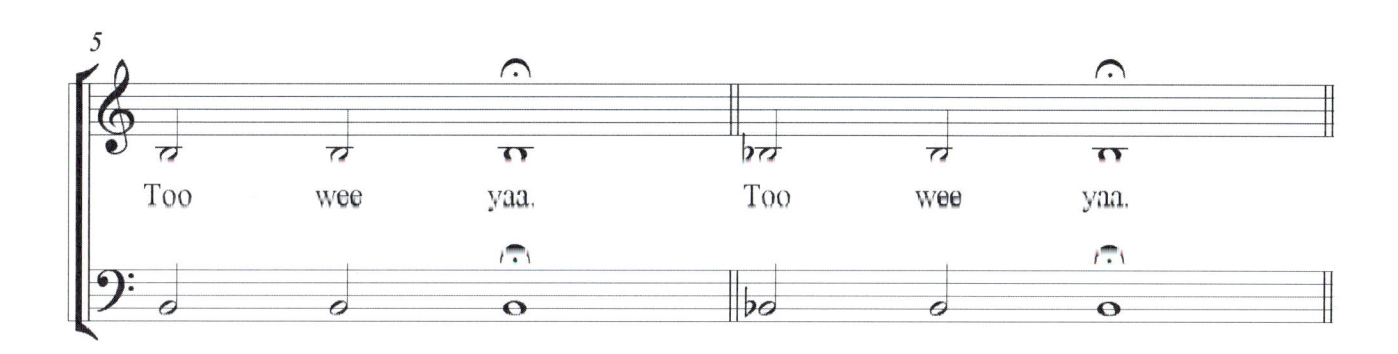

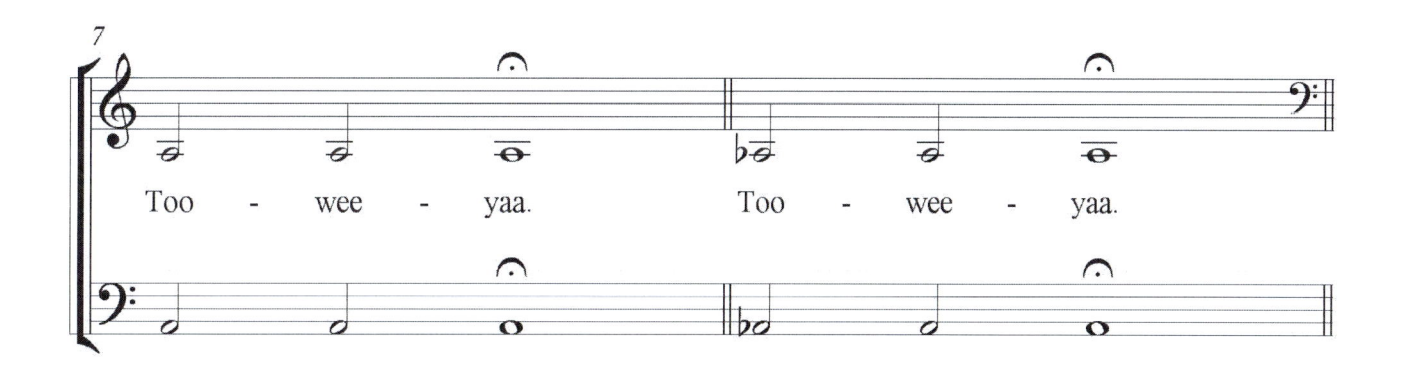

GUIDANCE NOTES (CONTINUED)

From here on, you may have difficulty in producing a convincing sound. The tuning may become awkward, you might not be able to get down to the required note, or perhaps you find yourself cramping the jaw or the root of the tongue in order to produce a hard-edged sound. If any of those happens, change the technique.

Ease your head right back. Relax. Allow your whole throat to open, as if you're a patient receiving mouth-to-mouth respiration. Sing gently. Don't try to 'make' the sound; let it grow. Still keep the tongue against the bottom teeth. Still focus in the nose.

In this, the lower half of the exercise, it can feel as if you are meditating. Sometimes it feels as if the sound is not really being made by you, but by someone else — a very pleasant feeling. If you can't get to the lowest notes (not even by doing them very quietly indeed) or can't get a good focus in the nose, don't worry; there's another day tomorrow.

Low notes should be focused, not forced.

CD1, Tracks 28–29

Exercise 11: Chest Voice Crying Sound

Crying and screaming, as we have established in previous exercises, are the loudest and most natural sounds that human voices can make. This particular exercise is the quickest and easiest way of opening up deep, resonant sounds in the chest voice.

GUIDANCE NOTES

First, sing Exercise 1 – 'May, may, may' – in order to stretch the soft palate. This will wake up your voice and give it a good focus, which is always a helpful preparation for the low sounds because it stretches the soft palate.

The object of this exercise is to make the loudest possible sound with the least possible effort. Imitate a baby crying loudly for attention. Ignore the fact that it's about an octave lower than the sounds a baby could manage – it's the same basic technique. And remember, you've been practising it since the day you were born, so you should be good at it by now!

The sound you produce should be nasal and loud, at least at the start. Just push the jaw down as far as it will go with the tip of the tongue – and wallow in a disgraceful sound. Don't sing it; act it!

Don't go up high by mistake. This may seem a strange thing to warn you against, but many people switch to higher notes in an unintentional yodel, which defeats the object of the exercise. The precise notes are important, but they don't need to be sung precisely. This fine distinction needs a bit of explanation: you need to sing these particular notes, but they don't have to be totally in tune, just totally acted.

You might find the lowest notes a bit difficult. This could be because there is a natural change in the voice on A♭ (marked *), although the problem doesn't always show up until one or two notes after that. So, in bar 111, show it down and, on the sixth or seventh note, push the jaw down with the tip of the tongue as far as it will go and let the voice change *in your nose* – there must be absolutely no pressure on the throat. Wrinkle up your nose to help you focus there. This is a psychological help rather than a technical one: it also focuses your concentration in your nose. Let the same change happen round about the same note (A♭ or G) in the subsequent scales.

Don't try to force it. Keep the sharp nasal focus all the way; let the loud, easy crying sound do all the work.

CD1, Track 29: Wallow In Disgraceful Noises

Don't rush this. Give yourself time to make a good crying sound on every note.

Make sure you get a good crying sound on the first note. That will set up the lower sounds.

✤ There is a natural change in the voice here which you can delay slightly.

Yaa - haa - haa - haa - haa haa haa - haa.

Slower. Make the change in the nose.

Yaa - haa - haa - haa - haa - haa - haa - haa.

Push the jaw down with the tongue, as far as it will go, to get a good focus in the nose.

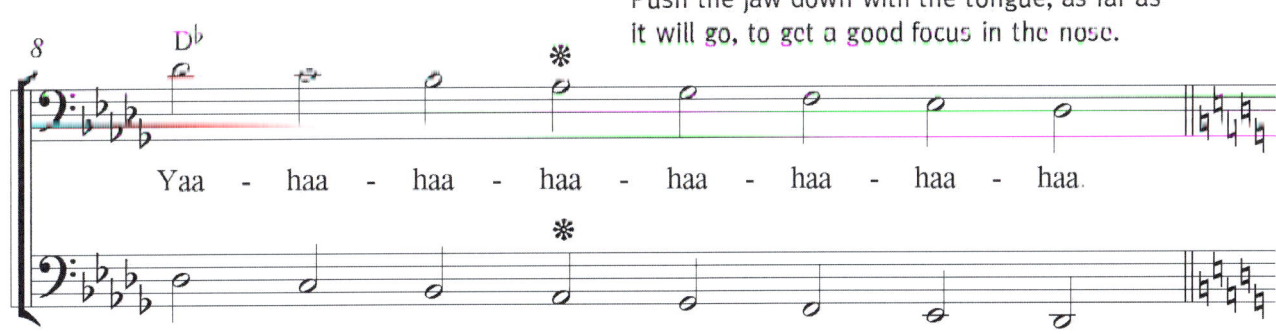

Yaa - haa - haa - haa - haa - haa - haa - haa.

Don't force this. Make the sound in the nose.

Yaa - haa - haa - haa - haa - haa - haa - haa.

Don't rush. Give yourself enough time to control it.

The first note is still crucial.

Now do the whole exercise again.

4 THE POWER MUSCLES AND THE CHEST VOICE

All diaphragm exercises are difficult and require a lot of hard work. It's easier to learn to manipulate the diaphragm in the chest voice than in any other part of the voice, because low notes are generally easier than high notes.

These exercises are much easier to learn when you're young – in your middle teens, for instance. At that age, many students can learn these techniques in a matter of weeks. After that, it takes far more perseverance. Students in their 30s and 40s generally take a few years to learn them, but it's worth it. Once mastered, you never lose them.

There are three principle objectives here. Firstly, you need to take all the activity away from the throat, which has little stamina, and replace it with activity performed by the diaphragm, which has enormous stamina and can be trained to perform almost endlessly. Sometimes – on tour, in rehearsal, in the studio – you may have to sing for 10 or 12 hours in a day, maybe for a couple of weeks at a stretch. If you're using the throat for everything, it will be sore for a lot of that time, but if you're using the diaphragm, although you will still be tired, your singing isn't likely to let you down. Even if you go down with a cold (quite probable when you're exhausted), you may well find that your technique enables you to keep singing well – for a while.

Secondly, you need to develop the habit of working from the diaphragm so that controlling the tone and power becomes automatic.

Thirdly, you need to develop well-controlled vibrato from the diaphragm. Once you've learned how to do this, you'll never lose it, and you'll rarely have throat problems again – at least, not from singing. Make sure that you don't rely on the throat for vibrato (that will develop naturally and gently, unless you force it); instead, rely on the diaphragm – it will never let you down. (See also the notes on the *diaphragm* and *vibrato* in the 'Glossary'.)

Exercises 12–13
GUIDANCE NOTES
Pronunciation
'**Mee-yaa**' – Use the tongue to push the jaw right down on 'yaa' and focus the sound in the nose. This is essential.

The object is to achieve as much power from the diaphragm as possible by pulling it in sharply on every note, so it must be *loud*. Most people find these exercises very difficult, and you may need to practise them for a long time, but even if you don't get it right, making a serious attempt at it will give your voice tremendous support throughout your range, taking pressure away from the throat. Most singers who have mastered these exercises say they never suffer from sore throats now. I presume that they mean not from singing, anyway!

For the fast versions, move the diaphragm violently in order to motivate the notes. One movement on every single note: that's the objective. Make sure that it really is your diaphragm that you're moving (from inside) and not just your chest and shoulders that are bouncing up and down. At first, you may need to use your hands to manipulate your diaphragm at the speed required. Place your hands on your stomach (clenching your fists can be helpful here) and really use them to shake your front abdominal muscles. Don't just bat the outside.

For the slow version, slam the diaphragm in hard at the start of every note (gentleness will get you nowhere in these two exercises) and then relax it. Do the same for every note, trying to work up a rhythm. Make sure that you make a loud sound when you pull the diaphragm in – let the voice thunder. You may need to *act* the connection between the voice and the diaphragm at first; don't expect it to work like magic.

Keep your head down throughout, or the throat will start to take the pressure off the diaphragm, which is like the tail wagging the dog.

Also, don't let the jaw creep up on 'yaa'; push it down with the tip of the tongue, or the throat will take over, you will lose the focus and the sound will be woolly.

There must be no Hs or silences, as these allow the throat to play too active a part. Instead, all of the articulation must be achieved by the diaphragm.

Don't fall into the trap of controlling the articulation by clicking in the throat as if you were singing Handel's *Messiah*. You're not supposed to be practising delicate coloratura (which *can* be done by clicking in the throat, although I wouldn't advise it); instead, you're preparing for spectacular rock singing by exercising the voice with the power muscles.

Exercise 12
CD1, Tracks 31-32: Power And Speed From The Diaphragm
Read the Guidance Notes on page 51-52.

Do this three times: First time fast
       Second time slow
       Third time fast

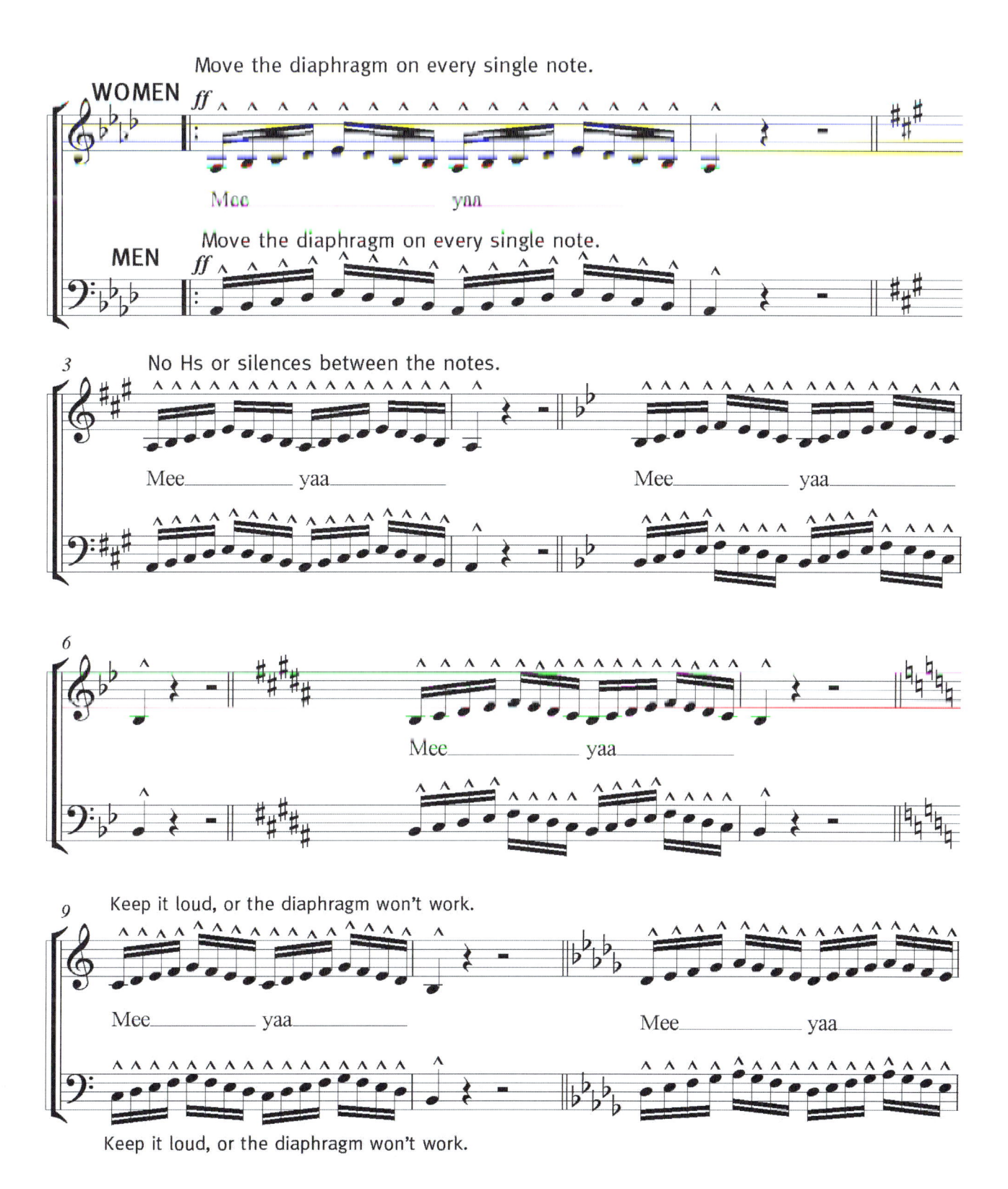

Exercise 13
CD1, Track 34: Vibrato From The Power Muscles
Read the Guidance Notes on page 51–52.

This is not the only way of achieving vibrato, but it is the most reliable. This exercise need not be done very fast; go fast enough to give it a strong rhythmic drive. However, it must be *loud*.

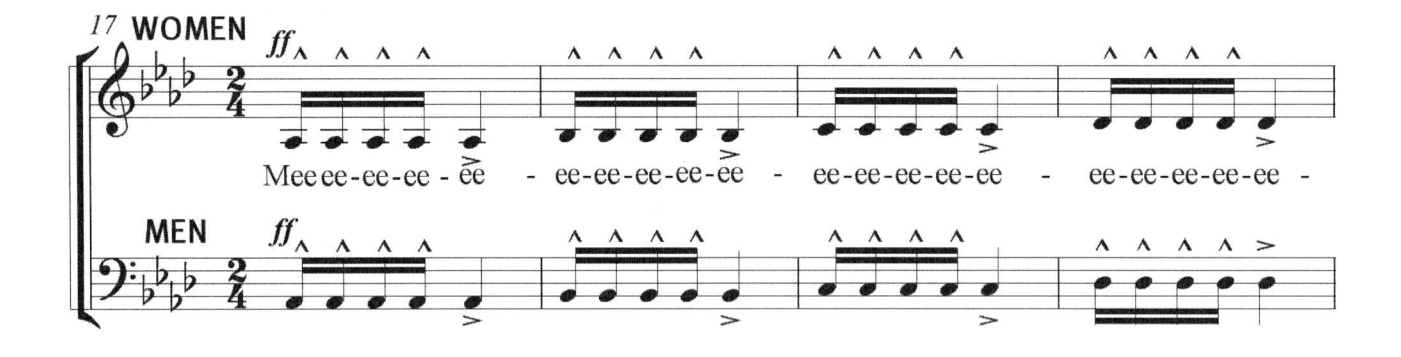

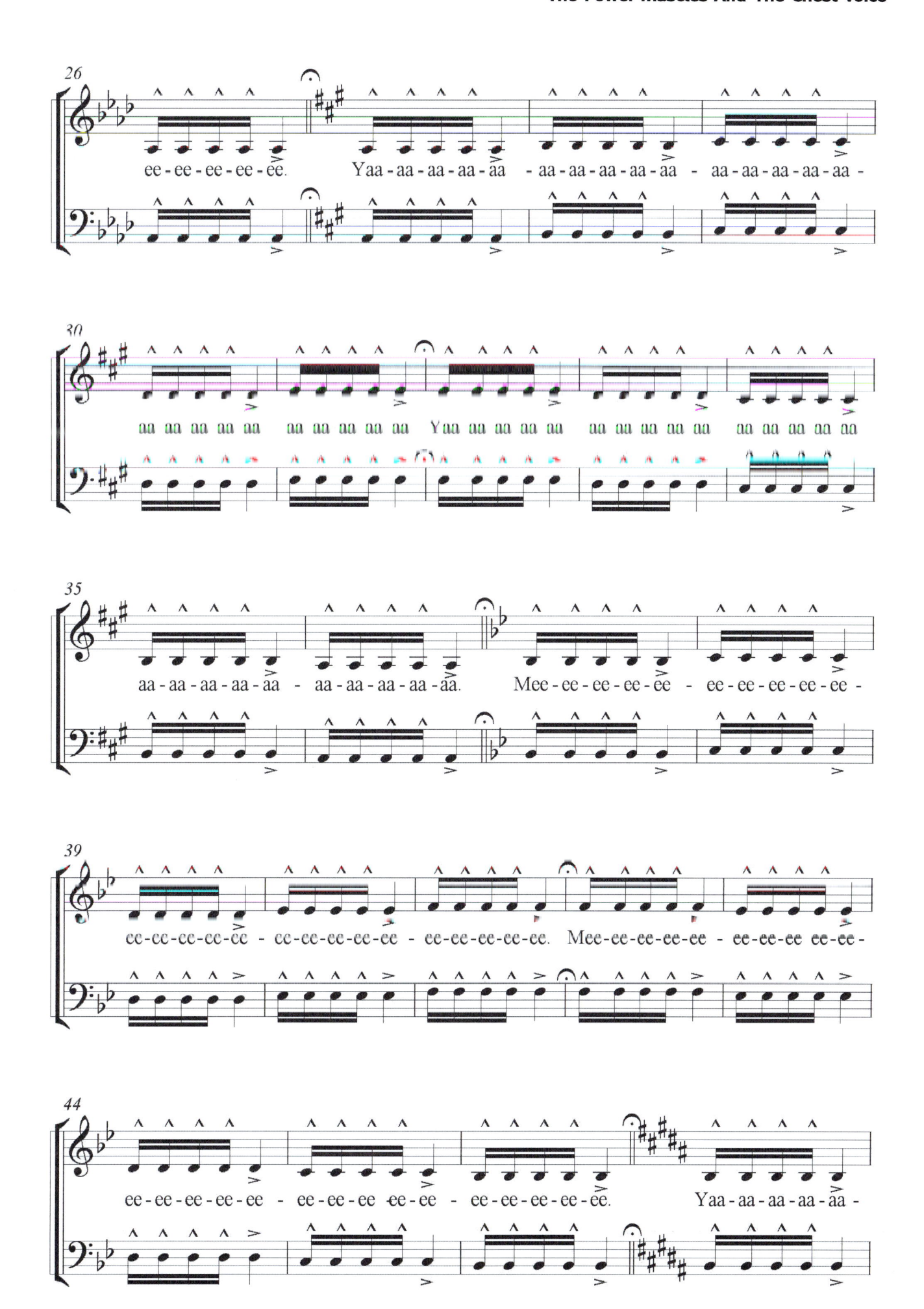

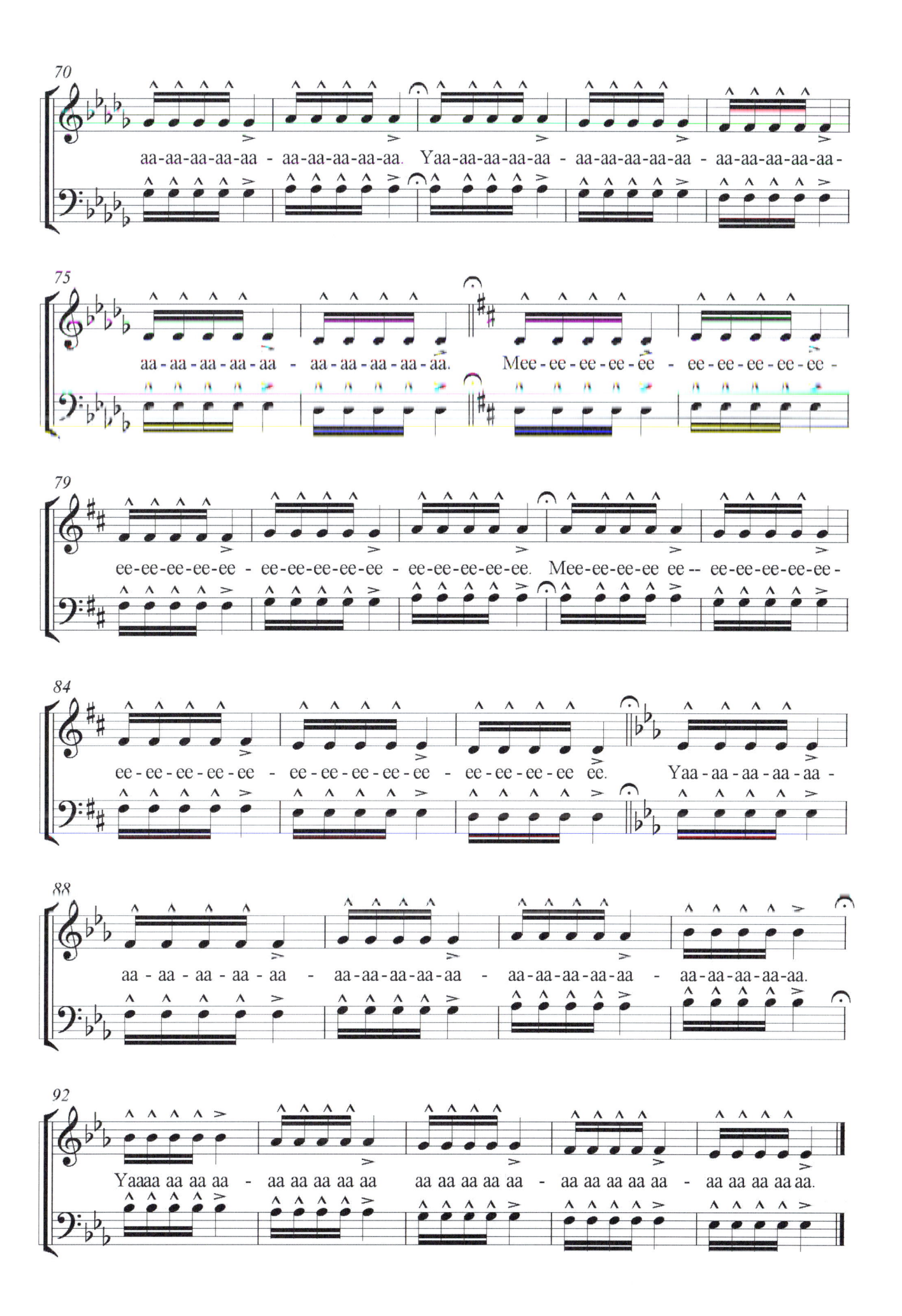

Exercise 14: Even More Power From The Diaphragm

GUIDANCE NOTES

This is a longer and more demanding version of Exercise 12, so it might be a good idea to re-read the Guidance Notes for Exercise 12 on pages 51–52. One big difference between this one and the previous diaphragm exercises is that most of this one can't really be done slowly; you need to take a run at it, as you will discover.

This exercise is loud – fortissimo. If you try to sing it quietly, it will fall apart. As with all loud singing, you must keep your head down, or it will all go onto the throat: disaster!

The top note of each group or phrase must be the loudest note, and very obviously so. Pull the diaphragm in extra hard on this note. You'll find that the top note will hold this very difficult exercise together.

Pay particular attention to the accents. ^ means 'pull the diaphragm in'; when a note has two accents, ^ and >, give the diaphragm an extra kick to get the mechanism started. (You'll notice that the lowest notes in each phrase aren't accented at all. This is to allow you to relax on the first note of each rising scale, ready to give the second note an extra wallop.)

On these fast-articulated scales, it's easier to control everything when you're going up than when you're coming down. This is because rising pitches require increasing tension, which helps you to hold it all together, but the falling pitches require you to slacken the tension, which can allow it all to fall apart. Your brain sorts out the tension for you subconsciously – you don't have to do anything apart from operate the diaphragm while singing the notes. That's quite enough to occupy anyone's consciousness.

One big advantage of the lack of tension in the lower scales is that you can slow them down (from bar 40 onward). Here, co-ordination becomes easier. You can go slow enough to move the diaphragm on every single note. At this pitch (having stretched the soft palate and worked up the tension on the highest scales – you must do the high ones first), you can now work up the technique in slow motion and make it perfect, ready to do the higher scales again. The rubric in the notation is quite clear about this.

Don't worry if you can't get this exercise together quickly. Just keep trying.

CD1, Track 36: Octave Scales

This is very difficult and will test your technique to the limit. Read the Guidance Notes on page 58.

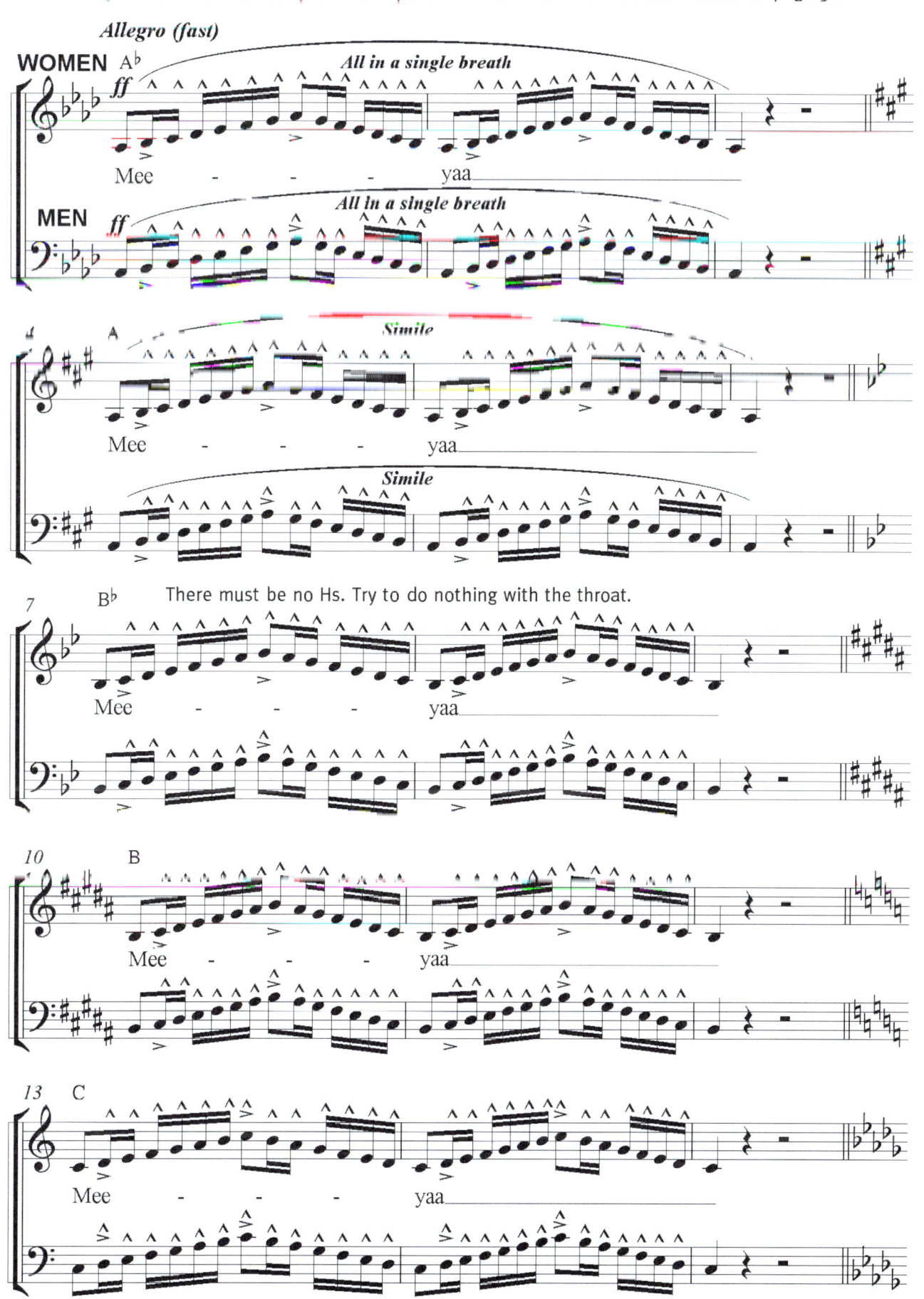

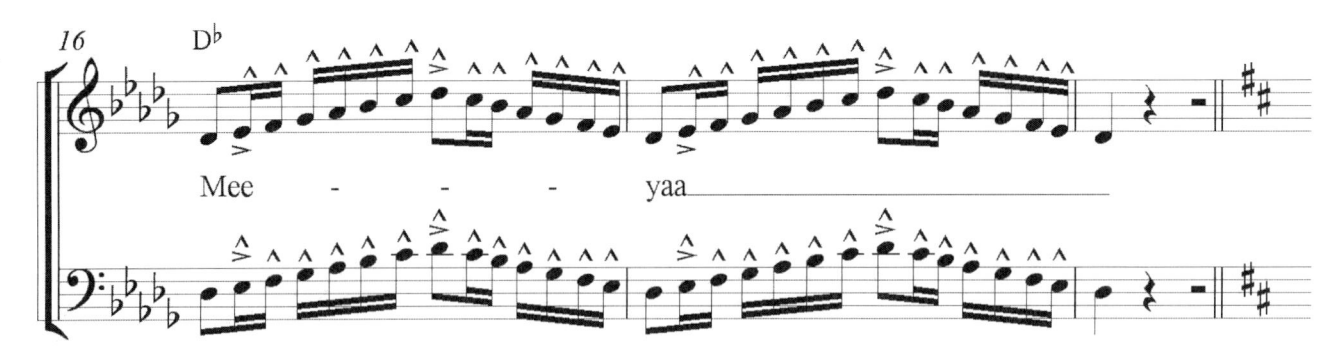

Push the jaw down on 'yaa' or the throat will start helping out the diaphragm, which is the tail wagging the dog.

Few ladies will be able to continue in the chest voice further than this.
Do so if you can, otherwise cut to bar 40.

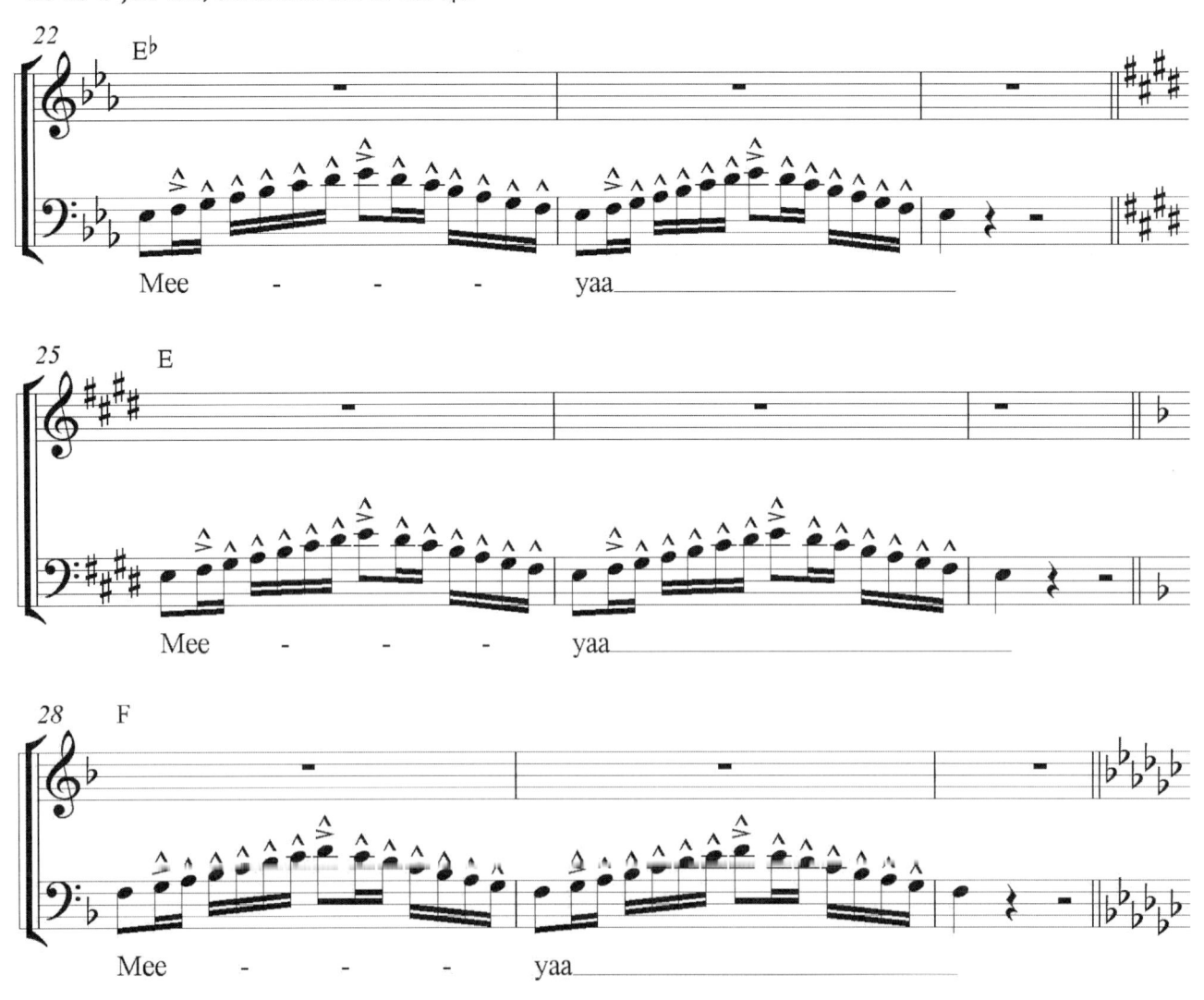

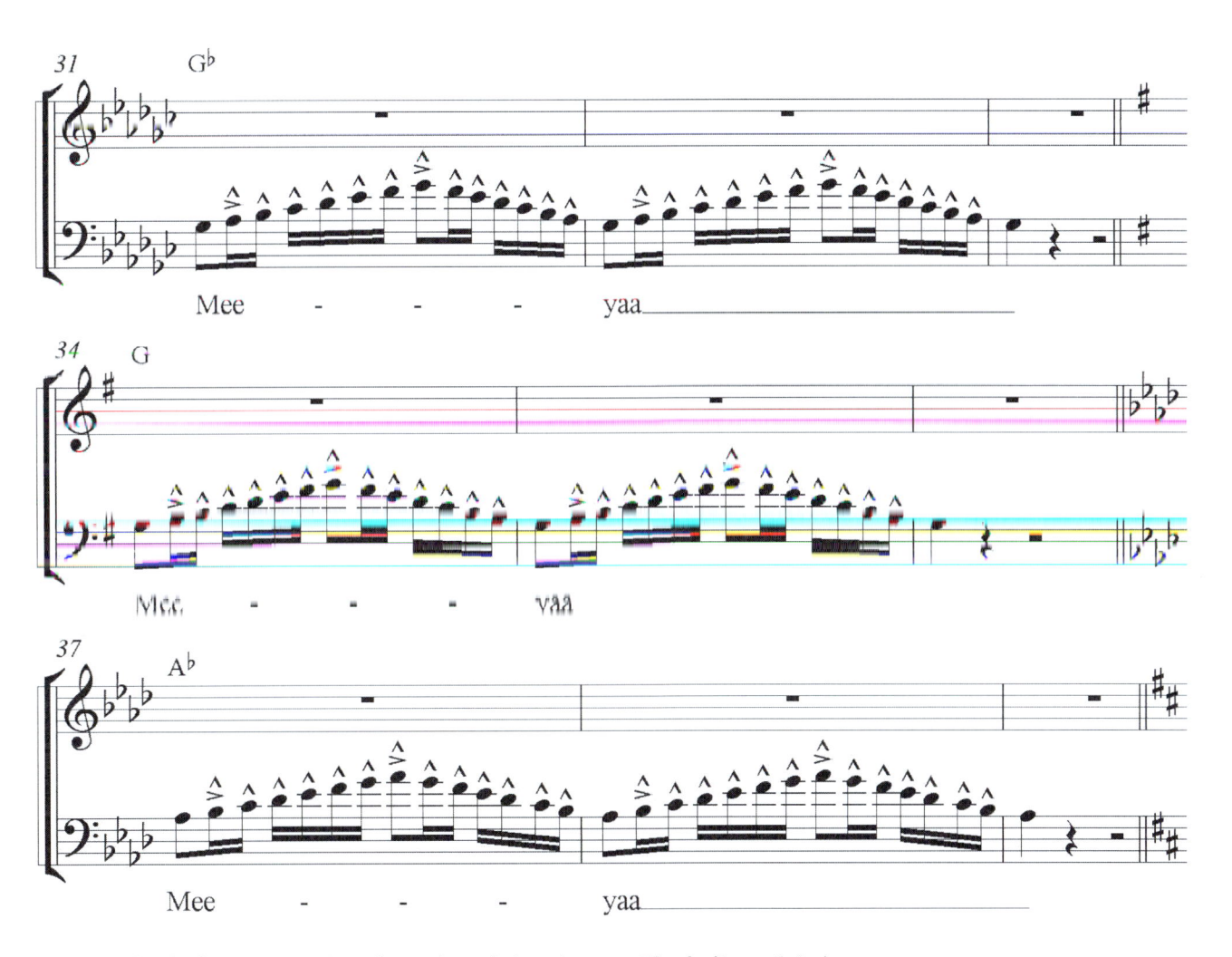

Now go back down, reversing the order of the phrases. The ladies rejoin here:

Continue downward through the scales until you get to here. Now slow it right down.
At this pitch, you can really move the diaphragm on every single note.

Much slower. Look at the change in the notation.

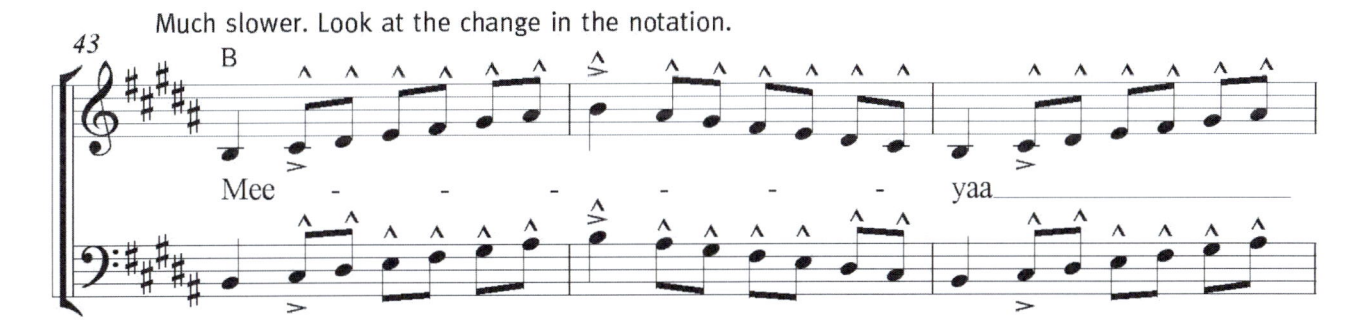

Relax on the lowest note. Do an extra-hard pull on the diaphragm on the second note of each rising scale marked ›.

Now start to come up.

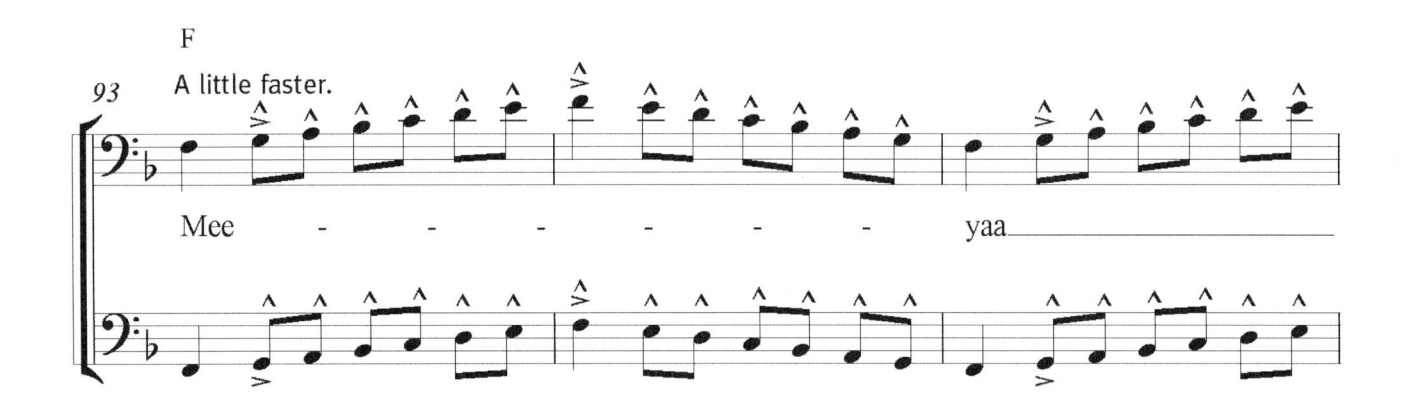

Faster. Watch your technique with the diaphragm.

Back up to speed.

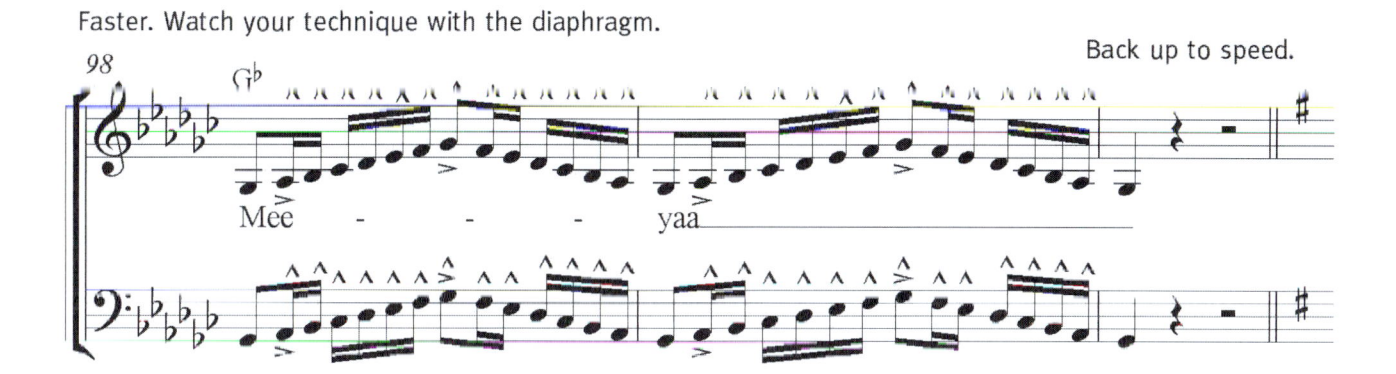

5 BRINGING THE CHEST VOICE UP TO THE HIGH NOTES

This is part of the process of joining up the voices, and very hard work it is, too, but all my students seem to enjoy it. You can really feel the power. (That sounds like a quote from *MTV*!) Broadly speaking, women have two voices, head voice and chest voice, while men have three: natural head voice, falsetto head voice and chest voice.

Bringing the chest voice up to meet and blend with the head voice gives warmth and richness to the entire voice, as well as a general increase in power. It means that, however quietly and gently you sing, however 'throwaway' your style, your voice will never sound trivial.

You should make sure that the chest voice is well exercised before you try this. Always do some of the earlier chest voice and diaphragm exercises first so that you start with a good deep chest sound and, therefore, have something to take up to the high notes. Exercise 14 is also good for this, which is why I have put the two exercises close together.

Men may find that Exercises 14 and 15 will work better after they've learned to do some of the quiet mixed head voice exercises. Everyone should certainly work the chest voice alongside the head voice, but don't try to alternate them. When men are going to be working on both voices on the same day, it's important that they do the chest-voice exercises first, before they move on to the mixed head voice. Women, on the other hand, should do the head-voice exercises first.

Contrary to popular belief, singers should usually do the big, heavy exercises before they move on to the lighter, more delicate stuff. This is where the big mistakes are made in warm-ups: too many teachers start with gentle exercises, so no real stretching is done. With Exercises 14 and 15, start with 'may, may, may' (Exercise 1). The women should then do the highest 'koos' (the downward scales) that they can manage and then go on to the chest-voice exercises. The men, meanwhile, should go from 'may, may, may' straight to the chest-voice exercises. Everybody is then ready for Exercises 14 and/or

15. After all that, the delicate exercises (most of which are for *blending* your different voices) can be used to smoothe down the whole voice so that you can build on the tone quality you've gained from all that stretching and thundering. (See *warming up* in the 'Glossary'.)

Exercise 15: Vocal Thunder From The Diaphragm

CD1, Tracks 37–38

All the notes in this exercise are important. Do not regard any of them as being of less importance than any of the others. And they should all be *loud*.

GUIDANCE NOTES

This is a great voice builder. Keep your head fairly well down throughout – this is a loud and demanding exercise, so you don't want any pressure to go onto the throat. Keep your tongue against your bottom teeth throughout as an added precaution, *even when you're taking a breath*.

Pronunciation

- **Mee** – keep the lips fairly closed. You might find it helpful to pull the corners of the lips back slightly, which will focus the sound in the nose and (hopefully) stop you using the throat.

- **Yaa** – this should be as open as possible. Push the jaw down with the tongue, again focusing the sound in the nose. This applies to *all* of the 'yaas', not just the one on the top note. Remember, *every* note is important in this exercise. Make good use of the Y of 'yaa'. Wallow in it. This will help you to position everything correctly. This exercise is difficult enough when you're using all of your technique; don't make it more difficult by forgetfulness or laziness.

Pull in the diaphragm hard on both of the top notes (marked ^), then slide down to the next note (marked with a *trill* – a squiggly line over the note). Don't drop suddenly, or the voice will change in the throat. Then release the diaphragm and shake it, thus making the sound of the trill. (You should be able to work up a nice vibrato from the diaphragm in this exercise.) Then take a breath, ready for the last part.

Start the last part of the phrase at the same volume at which you finished the trill – don't start it quieter. Pull in the diaphragm on the first note (marked ^), which has now become the highest note in that phrase, and

finish the exercise with a good resonant sound.

As this exercise goes higher and higher, you'll need all the support you can get. Push the jaw right down on the most difficult notes – this takes a lot of courage. Make full use of the diaphragm.

You'll need to constipate the highest notes: this exercise is so demanding that you need to use *everything*.

Keep it all entirely in the chest voice. Don't let it go into the head voice at all.

CD1, Track 38: Vocal Thunder From The Diaphragm

This is a very demanding exercise. Read the Guidance Notes on pages 66-67.

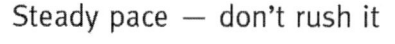 means *pull the diaphragm in hard.*

 means *shake the diapragm to produce some vibrato.*

sfz means *sforzando*. Look it up in the 'Glossary'.

Steady pace — don't rush it

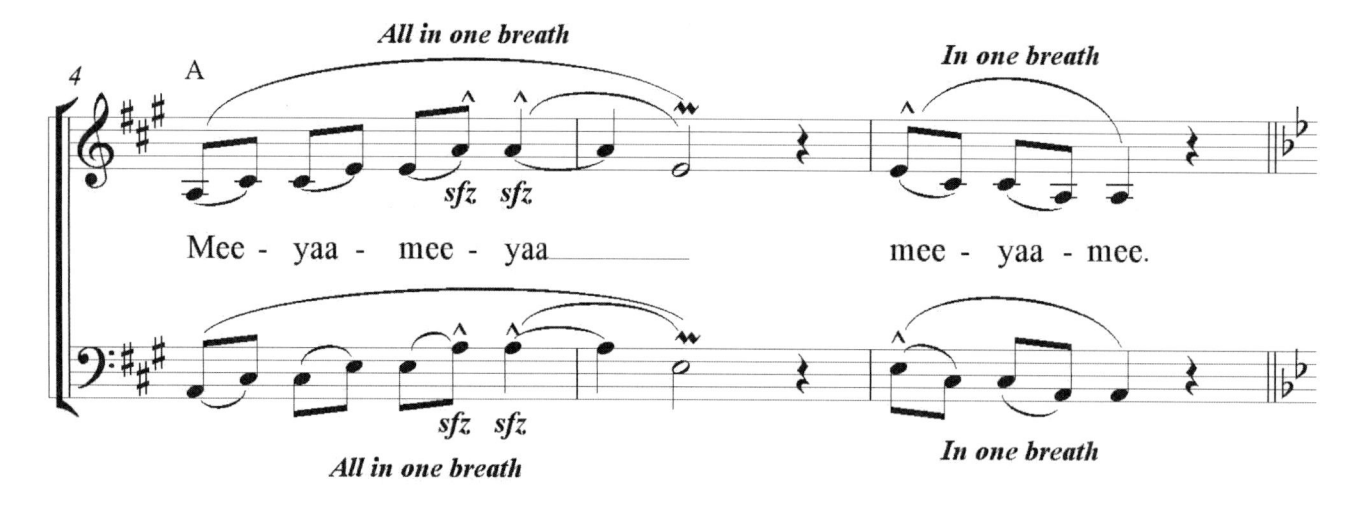

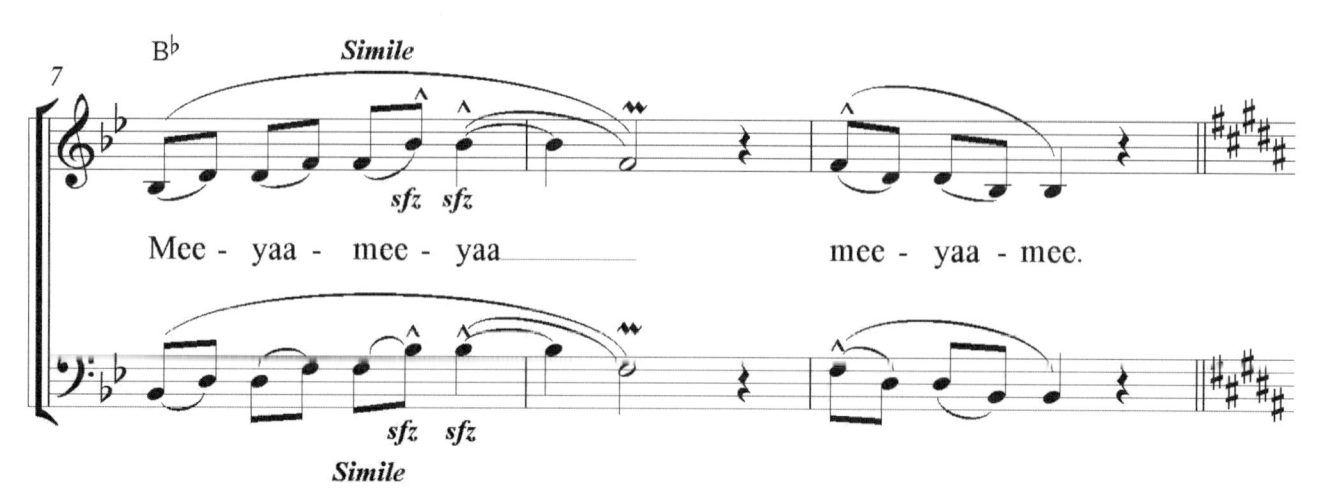

Few ladies will be able to sing as high as this without going into the head voice.
Those of you who can, continue an octave higher than the men.

This one should be really triumphant:

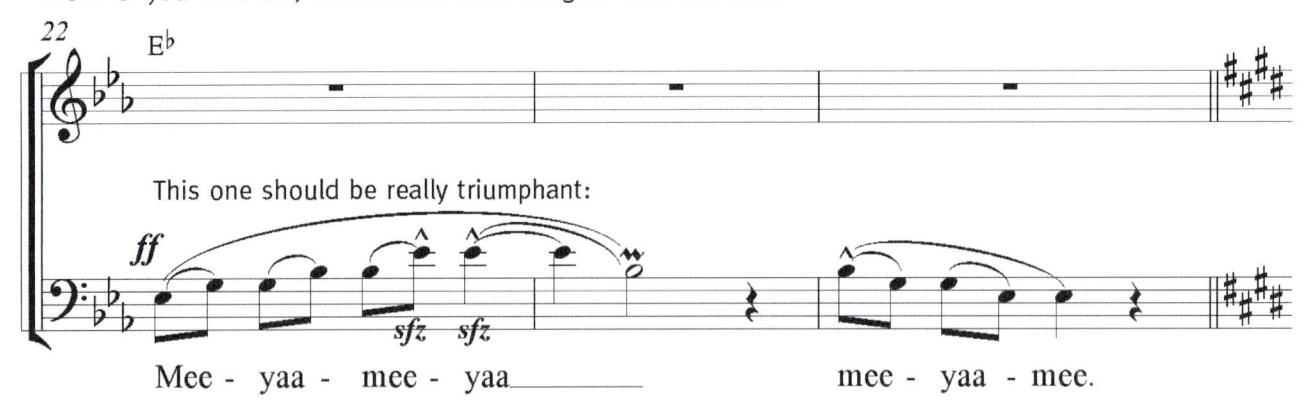

Mee - yaa - mee - yaa_____ mee - yaa - mee.

Keep your head down here, or it will go onto the throat:

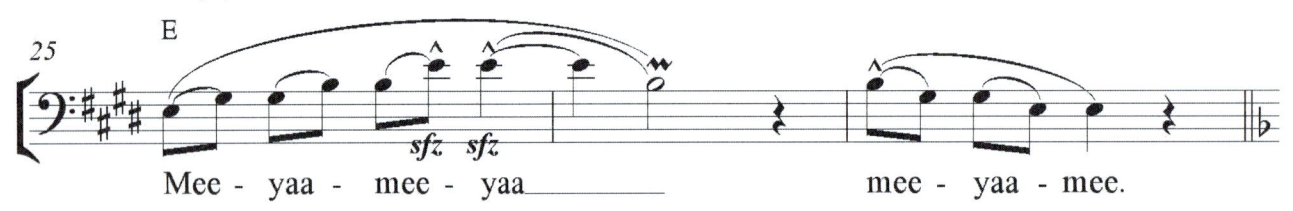

Mee - yaa - mee - yaa_____ mee - yaa - mee.

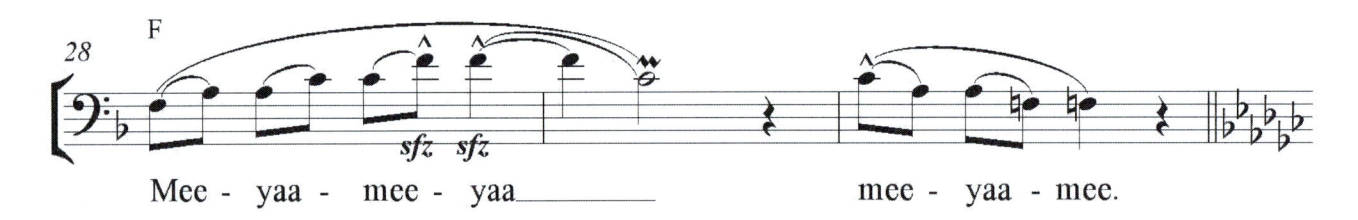

Mee - yaa - mee - yaa_____ mee - yaa - mee.

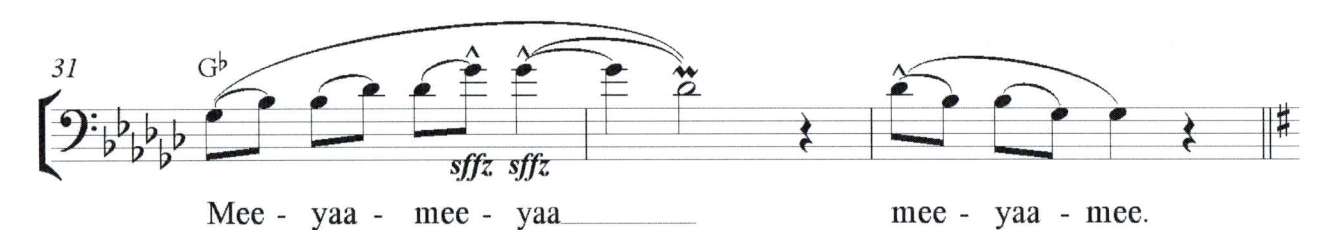

Mee - yaa - mee - yaa_____ mee - yaa - mee.

Constipate like mad for the top notes:

Mee - yaa - mee - yaa_____ mee - yaa mee.

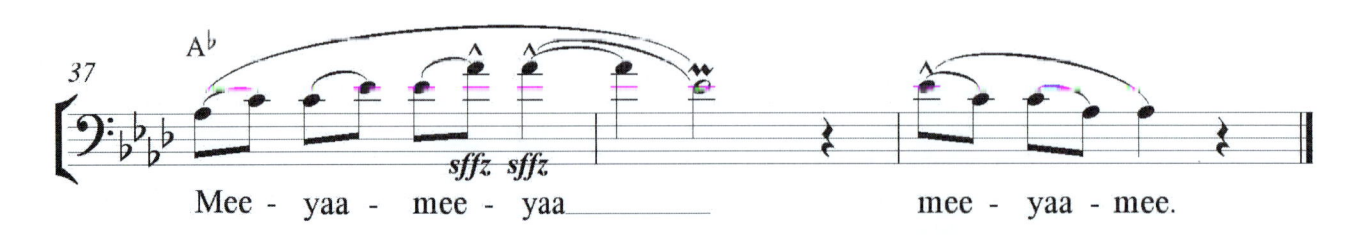

Mee - yaa - mee - yaa_____ mee - yaa - mee.

6 MAGICAL SOUNDS IN THE MALE MIXED HEAD VOICE

This is a peculiarity of the male voice. Although a similar technique is often beneficial in female voices (I shall come to that in the next section), it doesn't produce the same effect. This is because the quiet mixed head voice is the perfect mixture of the falsetto head voice and the natural head voice. The difference between these two voices (and, therefore, the possibility of blending them) doesn't occur in the female voice.

It is made almost entirely in the sinuses. Singers often go dizzy or light-headed when they do this, partly because they are intoxicated with the sounds – magical!

There are two ways of getting at your top notes: loudly and quietly. What a surprise! You need both. Until now, we've looked at the loud approach; the mixed head voice is the quiet technique. It is one of the great problem-solvers. If your voice refuses to go up to the high notes that you so desperately want, if people (including some singing teachers) tell you that you'll never get up above an F or a G, for instance, because you're a baritone or a bass, then this is the technique you need. Eventually, it *will* produce the goods. It's the most difficult technique of all for the male singer, but don't let that worry you. Persevere. Your entire voice will benefit from the attempt long before you master it, which may take years.

Most of the previous exercises in this book are about range and power; this section is mostly about tone quality, although it will also increase your range. The mixed head voice is the most valuable of all the voices available to you. It can turn a good singer into a great one, because it allows you to choose and control your sounds. Nearly all of the great rock and pop singers have relied on it for their most seductive vocal moments. You don't need to be born with a magical voice; you just need to do a lot of hard work.

However, the unfairness of it is that, while you're working your guts out to master it, there's always another lucky sod who (apparently!) gets it together without doing any work. That's life!

The quiet mixed head voice can be tackled alongside the previous exercises, but ideally you should have achieved some power in both the natural and falsetto voices before trying to join them up in these exercises. Don't try to alternate these exercises with the loud ones; do the loud exercises first – get them out of the way – and then devote yourself to the mixed head voice.

Exercise 16: Men Mixing Their Head Voices – Quiet Koos

CD 1, Tracks 39–40

This is similar in shape to Exercise 7, the loud 'koos', but with a very different style and purpose – this one is quiet. Read the guidance notes carefully. This exercise is about 300 years old, and nobody has been able to devise a better one for the purpose. The pitch is appropriate for modern rock; operatic tenors would start slightly lower.

GUIDANCE NOTES

Do Exercise 7 (the loud 'koos') first.

Ease your head right back – don't jerk it – and stick out your jaw, stretching the front of your neck and smoothing out any veins or pipes that seem determined to be tense. You don't want the carotid arteries standing out like drainpipes.

When you first do this exercise, it's likely to be a fight between your jaw and your neck, but the jaw must win. You'll gradually learn to do this without any pressure on the neck at all. Watch your neck in the mirror while you do it.

Sing the first scale quietly entirely in falsetto. Keep your tongue against your bottom teeth. The first note must be absolutely in tune – a tiny squeak, not merely an escape of air. You may need to help the first note of some scales by squeezing the diaphragm, or by constipating slightly.

In the subsequent scales, change on the note indicated by the asterisk (*) into the mixed voice. At first, the mixed voice is merely a quiet version of the natural voice, but as you persevere it will take on the smooth focus of your own distinctive mixed voice. This may take a long time. You'll know when you're getting it right: you'll hear it 'ring', and you'll be very dizzy. It is called the head voice for good reasons!

Don't try to change voices on the second note of any scale – it's almost impossible to keep it in tune.

You might need to go slightly louder on the 'change note' – that is, the first note in the mixed voice in each scale. Here is a paradox: if you sing the change note too loudly, you'll blow yourself off the note; if you are not loud enough, you won't get hold of the note at all, and that will force you into a second, unwanted change further down the scale. You want only one change of voice in any scale. Eventually, you'll develop a specific awareness of the right volume for every single note. (This is different for everybody.)

Repeat the whole exercise endlessly. Magic takes time.

CD1, Track 40: Descending Scales For Male Mixed Head Voice

Notated at the actual pitch.

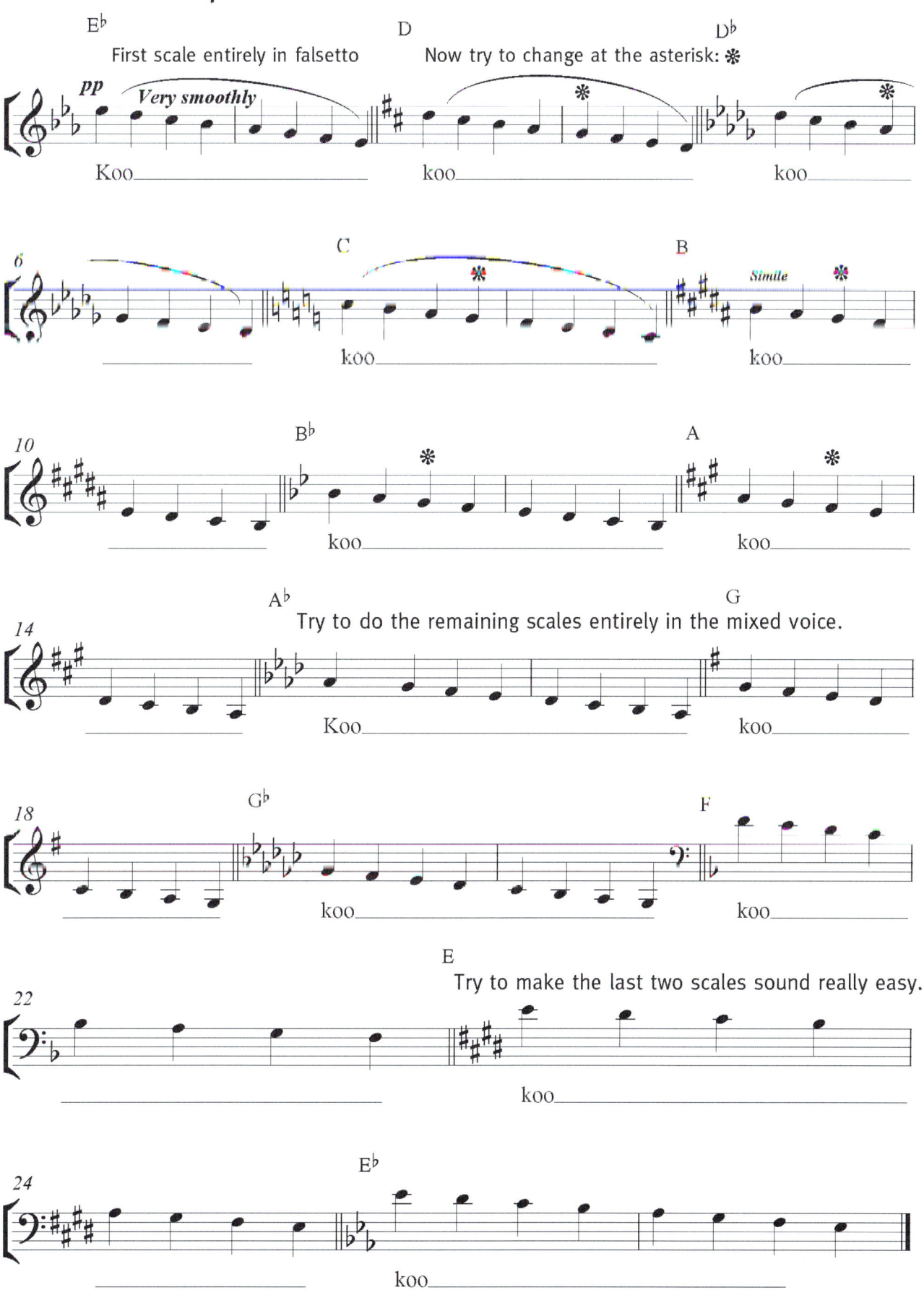

CD1, Tracks 41–42

Exercise 17–20: Looking After The Easy Part Of The Male Voice

This aspect of singing is often neglected. We're so keen to tackle the spectacular sounds that we forget about those light, pleasant, throwaway sounds, so that none of our singing ever really sounds easy; it always sounds like heavy weather. This is how to tackle it. It's particularly useful if you're finding the other mixed-voice exercises very difficult.

Don't scorn the boy-band sounds; they won't stop you from producing the dirtier sounds of hard rock, death or metal. Far from it, indeed – they'll make the transition from one type of sound to another a lot easier, provided that you do the harder sounds first. But feel free to scorn the singers who *only* sing boy-band sounds!

All the notes in this exercise are easy. They're supposed to be. Sing it a dozen times or so in quick succession, then go back to the other mixed-voice exercises. They should then be a little more accessible.

IMPORTANT: This mustn't replace the other mixed-voice exercises, particularly not Exercise 16.

GUIDANCE NOTES

Do at least one loud exercise first (Exercise 1, 'may, may may', for preference), then do Exercise 16 at least twice before you relax into this one.

Keep your head back so that the sinuses come fully into play. They are essential for producing magical sounds.

Sing very gently, but focus the sound. Go for *nice* sounds. Make them sound easy – boy-band stuff.

Change into the mixed voice wherever it feels most comfortable. This is the only difficult thing in this exercise. Don't leave the change too late, or you'll find that a nasty jolt is forced on you, but don't make the change too early, either, or it will sound difficult.

Remember that, in any phrase or scale, even when it's all supposed to be quiet, the top note is still supposed to be the loudest, so don't fall into the trap of starting so quietly that there's nowhere left to go and then being forced to go far too loud after the change. That will tell everyone that you've changed voices. No one is supposed to know. It should be so smooth that it all sounds like one continuous, smooth, easy voice – and, eventually, it will be.

Sing this exercise over and over again. If it seems to be getting worse, give it a rest and come back to it; you'll find it a lot smoother.

CD1, Track 42: Making The Male Voice Sound Beautifully Easy

Start in falsetto and finish quietly in the natural or mixed voice.

Sostenuto (very gently and smoothly). Change where it feels most comfortable.

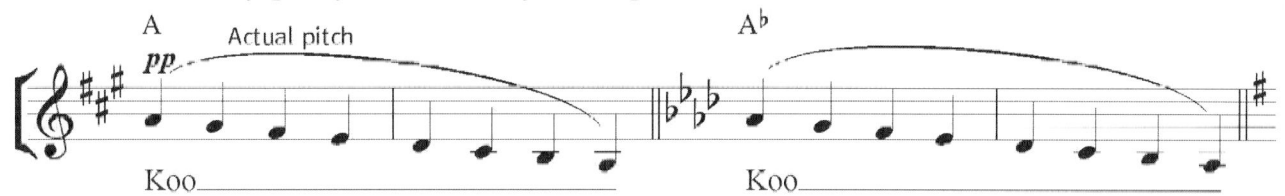

It's all very easy, except for the change note.

Try to make the change so smooth that it sounds like one continuous voice.

Keep your head back throughout, and keep your tongue against your bottom teeth.

If it hurts, you're doing too much. Keep it gentle but focused. Watch the tuning.

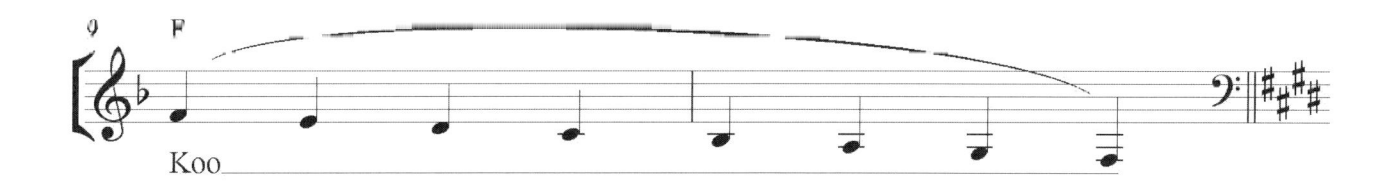

Do the last two scales entirely in the mixed voice, quietly.

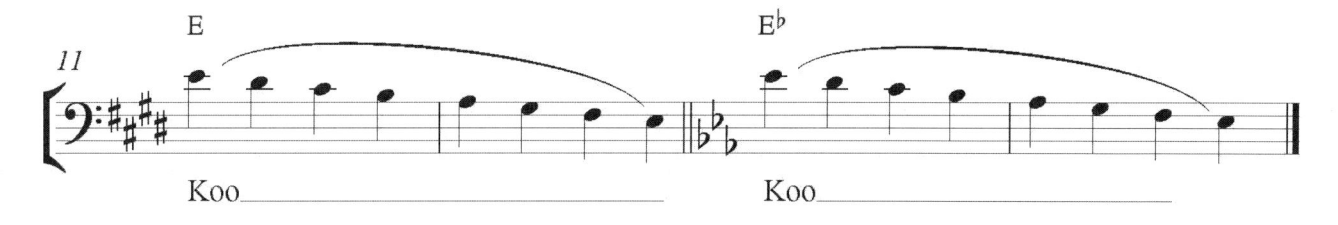

Exercise 18
CD1, Tracks 43-44: Chromatic Half-Scales In The Male Mixed Voice Descending

The same Guidance Notes as for Exercise 16, except for the falsetto, which doesn't occur here at all.

These are very good for tone and tuning. Keep your head back and your tongue against your bottom teeth. Do them quietly, entirely in the mixed voice, with no falsetto at all.

Slowly and smoothly, entirely in the mixed voice.

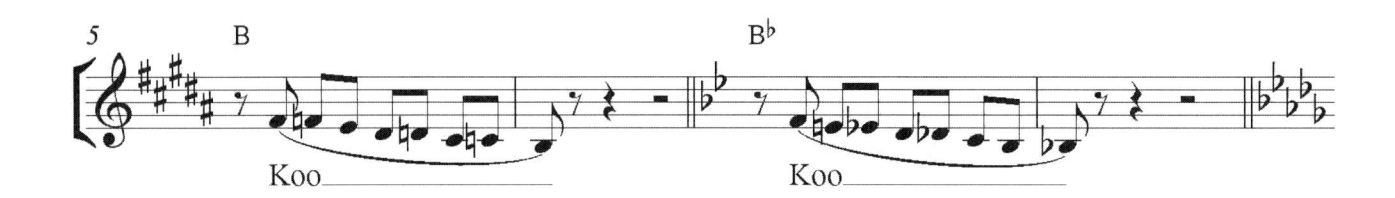

CD1, Tracks 45-46: Descending And Ascending Scales

You'll need to take a big breath for these. Squeeze the diaphragm towards the end of each rising scale.

Keep it all in the mixed voice

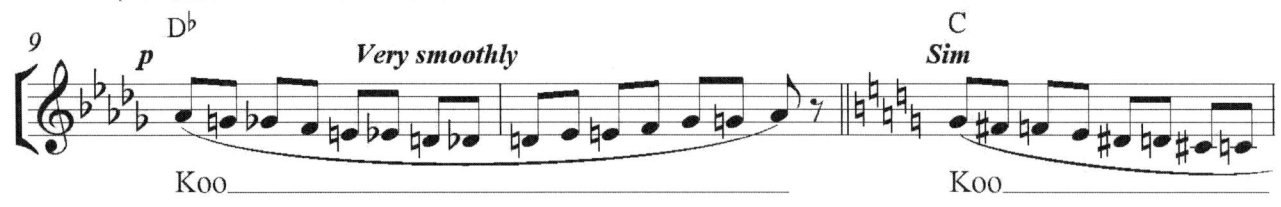

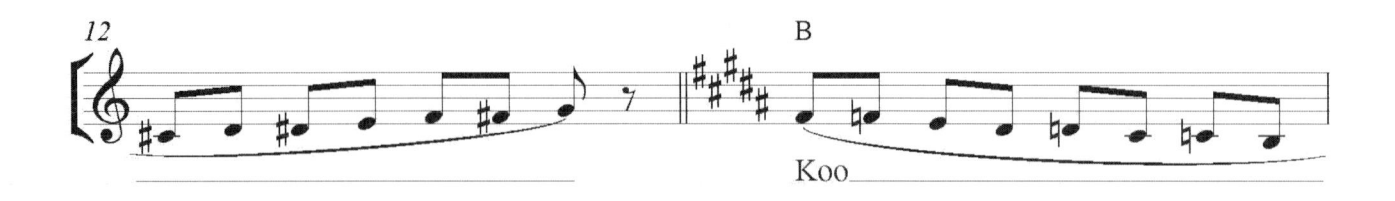

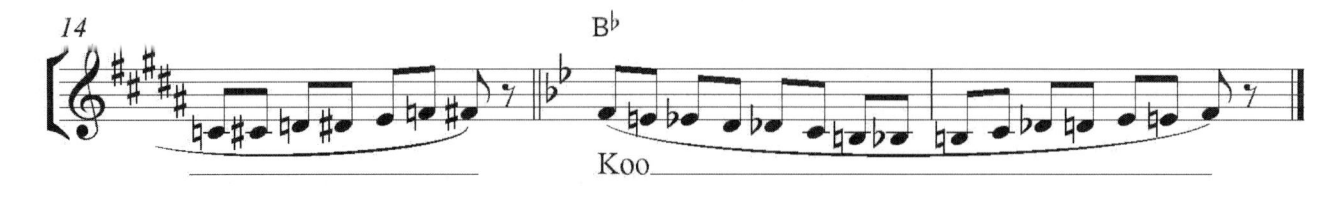

Exercise 19
CD1, Tracks 47-48: Chromatic 12-Tone Scales In The Male Mixed Voice

Ease your head back and keep your tongue against your bottom teeth.

Do the first scale entirely in falsetto:

Exercise 20
CD1, Tracks 49-50: Darkening The Sound Of The Male Mixed Voice (Octave Scales In The Reverse Order)

The Guidance Notes here are basically the same as for Exercises 16-19, plus:

i   Do this entirely in the mixed voice. Don't allow it to go into falsetto at all.

ii   As you go higher, you'll need to start each scale slightly louder than the previous one.

iii Remember to keep your head back and your tongue against your bottom teeth, or you'll go into the chest voice, which will defeat the object of the exercise.

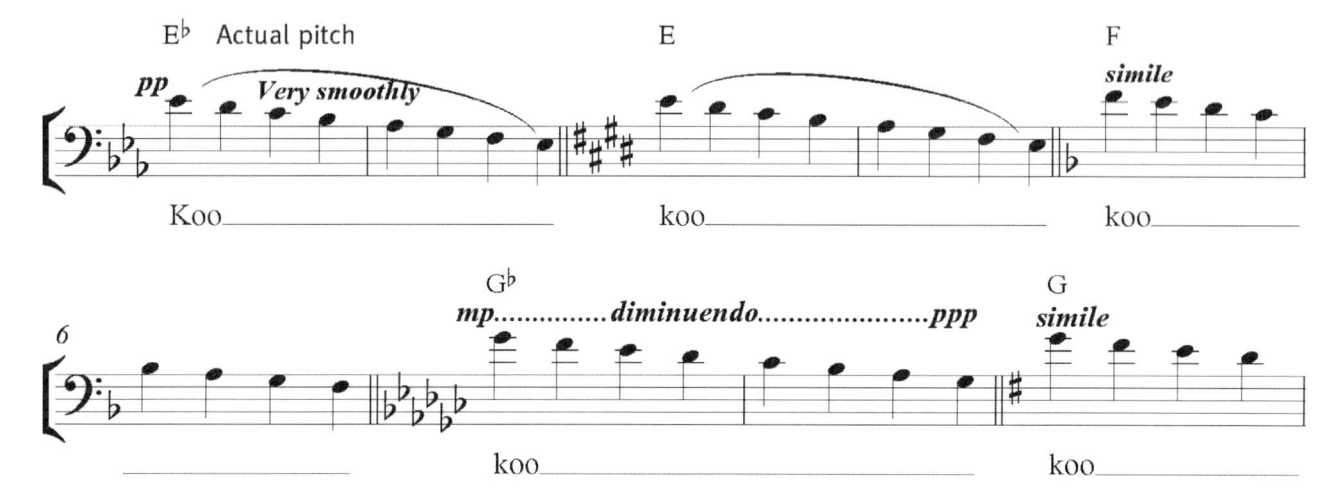

From here on you may need to go quite a lot louder on the first note — ONLY the first!

It's perfectly possible to bring the male mixed voice up to here. It usually takes about four years...and some excruciatingly hard work!

7 THE FEMALE MIXED VOICE
Quiet, Smooth Sounds

The quiet mixed voice was always thought to be the exclusive province of men, who can mix the natural head voice with the falsetto head voice. In women's voices there is really only one head voice, so in theory there should be nothing to mix. Recently, however, women have begun to produce an unmistakably mixed voice in the so-called *feigned voice*, the overlap of the head and chest voices. It is a wonderful sound and entirely new, characterised by a smooth, velvety focus. Unlike the male mixed head voice, which is by far the most difficult technique in singing, the female mixed voice is easy: you just need persistence. It's formed almost entirely in the sinuses, which means that any form of struggling for notes in the following exercises defeats it. This doesn't mean that you shouldn't continue to struggle for notes in the bigger, more demanding, exercises. You *must* do the power exercises first, stretching the range of both head voice and chest voice, or you'll have nothing very much to mix in the mixed voice.

I discovered this voice almost by accident. One of my students asked me if there was a way to soften those very loud notes at the top of the chest voice without switching into the head voice. It was obviously worth exploring, as the gentleness required precluded any risk of forcing the voice, and in any case she had developed the full range and was expert at power singing. So I devised the following exercises, some of which are adapted from fairly ancient exercises for quiet singing in the male voice. Within a few weeks, she was able to soften the high chest-voice notes without losing the focus or the tone – in fact, the tone was improving. Within a few months, it had developed into an unmistakably mixed voice. So I tried it with several other students with similar gratifying results.

Most of the previous exercises in this book are about range and power, whereas this part is mostly about tone quality. You may not notice any difference for a few weeks or even months; as with every singing technique, some people learn it more quickly than others. The quiet mixed voice can be tackled alongside the previous exercises but, ideally, you should have achieved some power in both the head voice and the chest voice before you try to blend them in these exercises. Don't try to alternate these exercises with the loud ones; do the loud exercises first – get them out of the way – and then devote yourself to the mixed voice.

This section can also be seen as looking after the easy sounds of the voice, which are often neglected. We're often so busy tackling the virtuoso sounds and techniques in our ambition to sing higher, lower, louder, etc, that we forget those crucial, gentle sounds, so that our singing always sounds like a tremendous effort. These exercises will help you when you want your singing to sound effortless.

Exercises 21–25: The Female Mixed Voice

First, be aware that, although some of these exercises look like Exercise 6 in reverse, they employ very different techniques.

GUIDANCE NOTES

First, do all the usual warm-up exercises, especially Exercise 6. Make sure that the range is fully exercised, both head voice and chest voice, or you won't have anything to mix.

Ease your head right back – don't jerk it – and stick out your jaw, stretching the front of your neck and smoothing out any veins or pipes that seem determined to be tense. All of the notes must be easy; if they aren't, you're doing too much of something and probably singing too loud.

Stick your lips out a little bit, causing a tunnel forward and back in your mouth and throat. You can't push your jaw down in this exercise. Keep your tongue against your bottom teeth or bottom gum throughout.

CD2

Think 'Chest voice!', but don't force it into the chest voice: just *think* it. Let the voice change where it wants to, but try to smoothe over the changes.

Make sure that you're absolutely in tune. The intonation here is crucial. You might need to help the first note of each scale by squeezing the diaphragm, or by constipating slightly – just on the first note. You may also need to squeeze the diaphragm again on the last two or three notes of some scales, just to stop them from fading out. Quiet singing must still be audible, so maintain the focus – quietly. It must all be easy.

There must be no jolts between the notes, particularly between the first and second notes, which is where the worst jolt usually occurs). Slide from note to note, but keep it all in tune.

If the tuning is at all difficult, even when you follow these instructions, either you're trying to sing too loudly or you need to take bigger breaths.

Repeat the whole exercise endlessly. You may not notice any difference for several weeks, or even months.

Exercise 21
CD2, Track 2: Softening The High Notes Of The Female Chest Voice

Read the Guidance Notes on pages 79-80. Sometimes you'll need to do the whole of this exercise, starting from bar 1 and going on to bar 20. At other times you'll want to concentrate on the distinctive tone of one particular part, but at first I recommend that you begin at Part 2.

Part 1

If you need to darken the voice, start here and continue up to bar 18.
Keep your head back, sing very gently and focus your voice by putting the tip of the tongue against your bottom gum

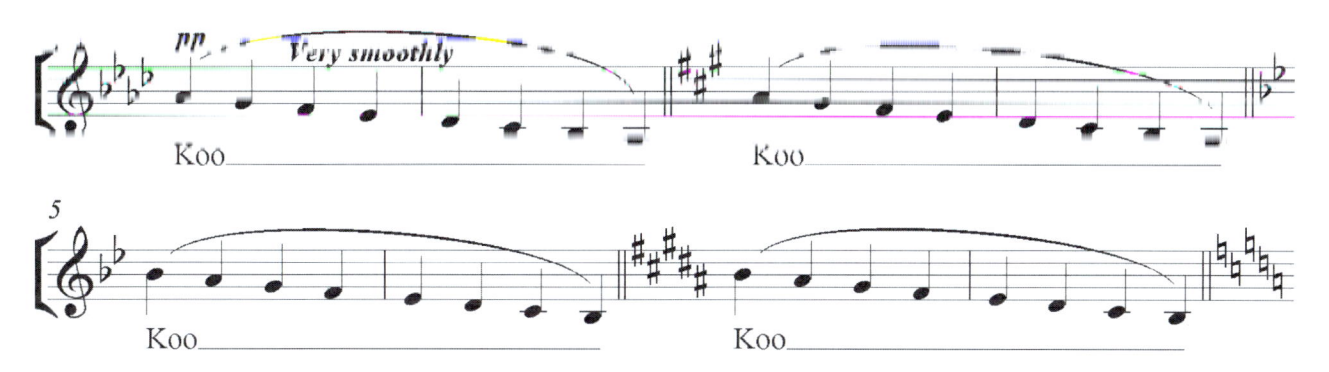

Part 2

Start here. This is the section you need to do most.
Keep your head right back, and do this very quietly.

Let the voice change where it wants to change, but try to smoothe over the jolts.

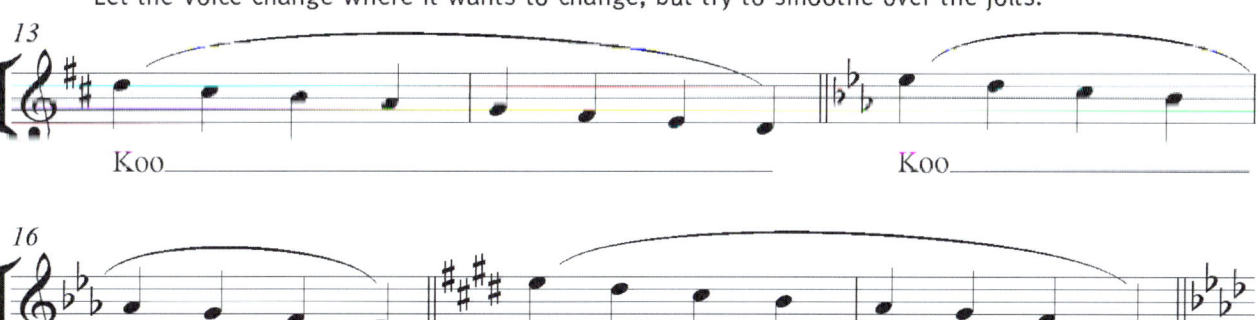

Part 3

This section should be used very sparingly, but it's useful if the voice feels a bit stiff or difficult in Parts 1 or 2. Continue up from bar 18, semitone by semitone, until you get to here. Keep it all very easy.

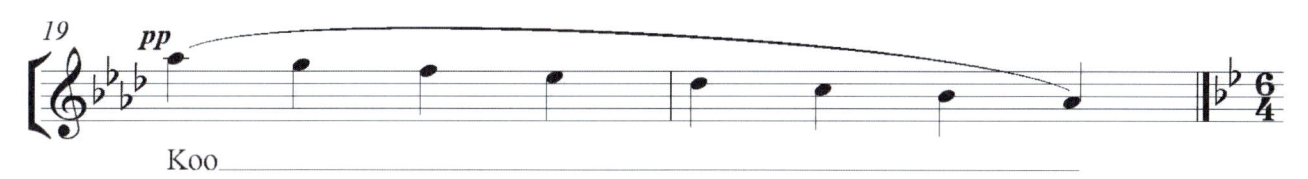

Exercise 22
CD2, Track 4: Crossing Between Female Head Voice And Chest Voice

Read the Guidance Notes on page 79-81.

Note: *port* is short for *portamento*, which, musically, means slide.

There must be no gaps, jolts or silences between the notes here. Keep it very smooth and quiet. Don't worry about what voice you're in or try to keep it all in one voice. Let it change where it wants to. Just keep it all very easy.

Chromatic Half-Scales In The Female Mixed Voice
Exercise 23
CD2, Track 6: Descending

Chromatic Half-Scales In The Female Mixed Voice
Exercise 24
CD2, Track 8: Descending And Ascending

Read the Guidance Notes on page 79-80.

Squeeze the diaphragm for the last few notes. You may need to bend over slightly to squeeze out the last drop of air. You may also need to increase the volume slightly for the last few notes.

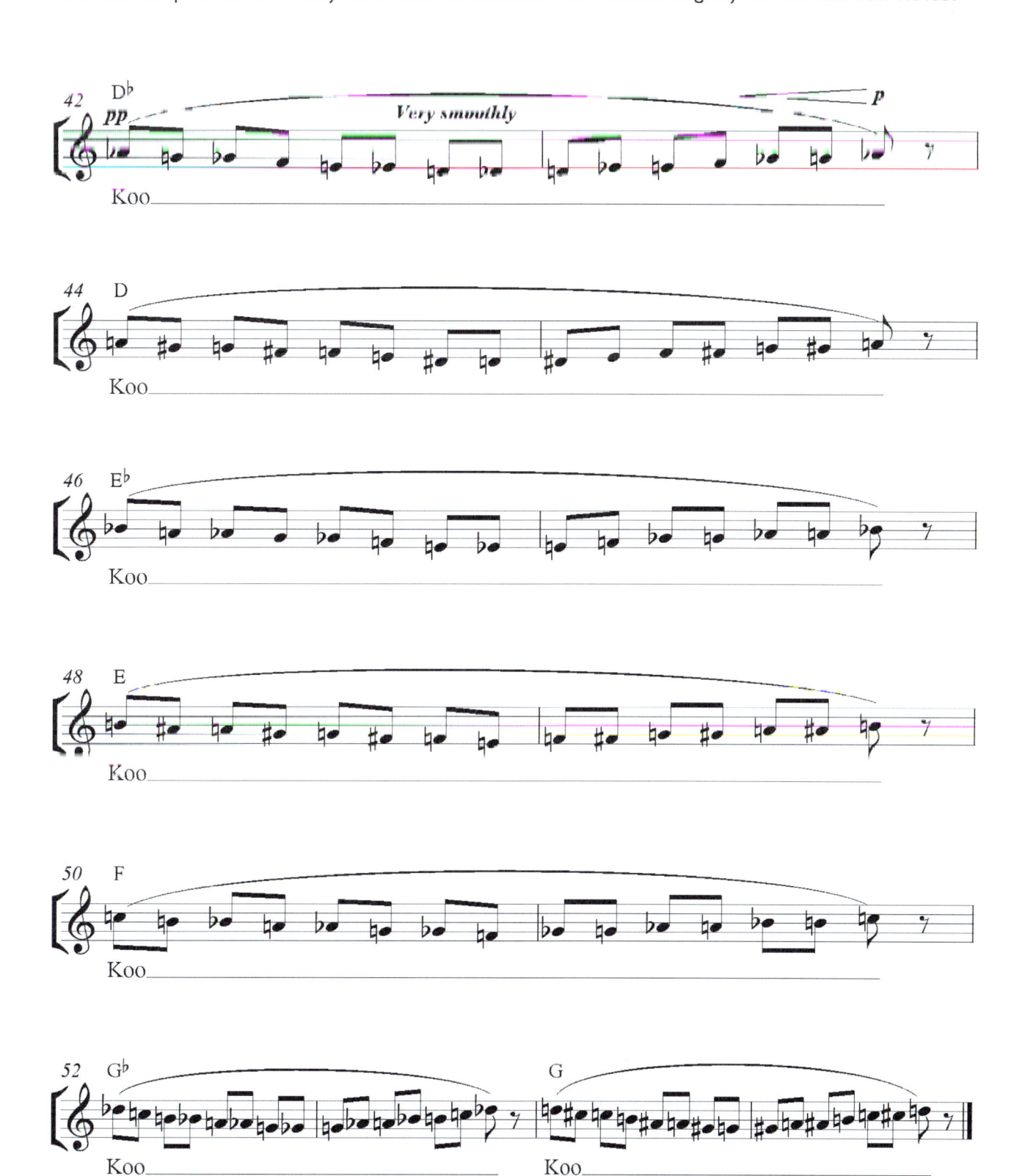

Exercise 25
CD2, Tracks 9-10: Chromatic 12-Tone Scales In The Female Mixed Voice

Read the Guidance Notes on page 79-80.

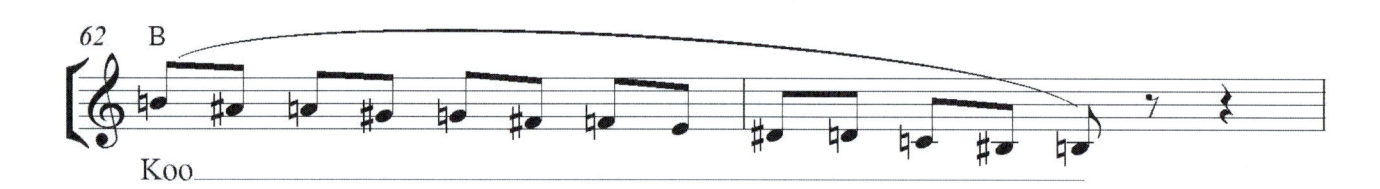

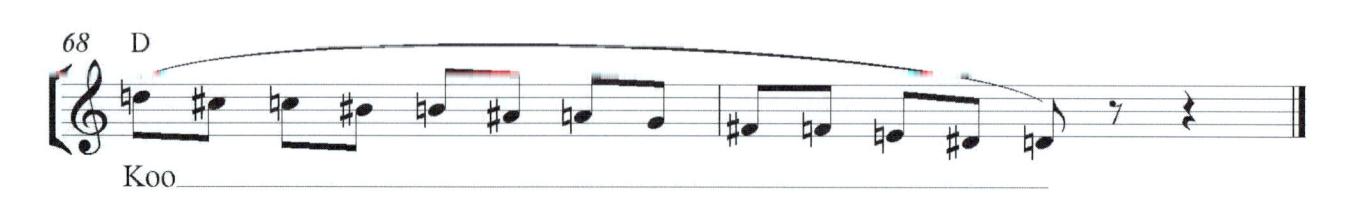

8 THE EXTREME MIXED VOICE

Screaming Into Natural Voice

This section is aimed largely at men, who need to be able to join up their screaming with the natural head voice. If women want to tackle it as well, that's fine by me. Screaming is an extension (or extreme form) of the falsetto head voice, so for women – whose head voice is entirely falsetto – there is no exceptional joining-up to be done. For men, on the other hand, it's very difficult yet very rewarding. This section isn't essential to everyone, but if you *do* want to scream, this section is essential to you and these exercises will produce incredible improvements throughout your entire voice.

The extreme mixed voice is an extension of the quiet mixed head voice, which mixes falsetto with the natural head voice (Exercises 15–19). The extreme mixed voice takes it a stage further, mixing screaming with the natural head voice. The extreme mixed voice really came into its own with the advent of heavy metal, although many of the singers who were so good at it would probably class themselves as rock singers now. It's particularly suited to riding over or cutting through the music of the loudest and heaviest bands.

With the extreme mixed voice, essentially the two voices blend into one – this is the way to technical brilliance. It is a colossal sound, very open and very flexible, giving an enormous range. (See Chapter 1, 'The Range'.) You can get an amazingly rich, smooth sound with this technique, switching between the smooth and harsh voices expertly. It will always be hard work, but it's also exhilarating.

You should exercise all parts of the voice – head, chest and quiet mixed head voices – systematically before you tackle this demanding area. You don't need to have mastered them, but you need to have at least tackled them thoroughly. In any case, you'll find that all areas of the voice loosen up and grow as you work these exercises. So, if you're in a hurry to get on with these sounds, don't wait until everything else is perfect; just have a go.

The two basic rules in this section are:

1 Go loud enough to hold the sequence of notes together (in other words, to stay in tune);

2 Any notes that you can't sing in the natural voice should be screamed (in other words, do whatever you must to stay in tune).

Exercise 26: Spoilt-Brat Sounds

The object of this exercise is to use the screaming voice to extend the natural voice. It's the only exercise in this section that starts in the natural voice.

GUIDANCE NOTES

The phrase 'It's mine' should be sung like a crying child: 'It's mi-yi-yine'. You might find it helpful to imitate the sound of Axl Rose in such phrases as 'Sweet child o' mi-yine' or 'You could be mi-yine', etc.

This is a loud exercise – any quiet notes will make it almost impossible. Keep your head down throughout the entire exercise. You'll need very big breaths for this, and make sure that you puff up the diaphragm as you take them.

The pronunciation is crucial: 'Maa-yaa-yaa-een' – screaming child, not grand opera. Push the jaw right down to give yourself as much space as possible on the three open sounds, taking your time over them. Close and open on the 'Y' sounds – you need to do both fully. You can always afford to make a meal of 'Y' sounds, as they focus the voice wonderfully. Let the 'it's' take care of itself, but don't separate it from what follows; join it all up in a fine legato.

Sing the first phrase entirely in the natural crying voice. (You should be able to manage this if you do it loudly enough.) Then do the same on the subsequent phrases if you can. When you reach a pitch where you can no longer sing the top notes in the natural voice,

CD2, Tracks 11–12

switch into the falsetto screaming sound, as convincingly like a crying child as you can. Start and finish every phrase in the natural voice.

Don't worry if your voice won't yet allow you to follow these instructions in their entirety. If you can't sing the notes you are supposed to do in the natural voice, scream them!

Do the usual four things when making huge demands on the voice: push the jaw right down on all the open sounds, keep the tongue against the bottom teeth, pull in the diaphragm on the highest note in each phrase, and constipate for the most extravagant sounds. And remember, the object is to join up the two voices in a coherent phrase.

Finally, don't forget the acting. You're supposed to sound like a spoiled brat in this exercise.

CD2, Track 12: Spoilt-Brat Sounds

Try to do the first few phrases entirely in the natural voice.

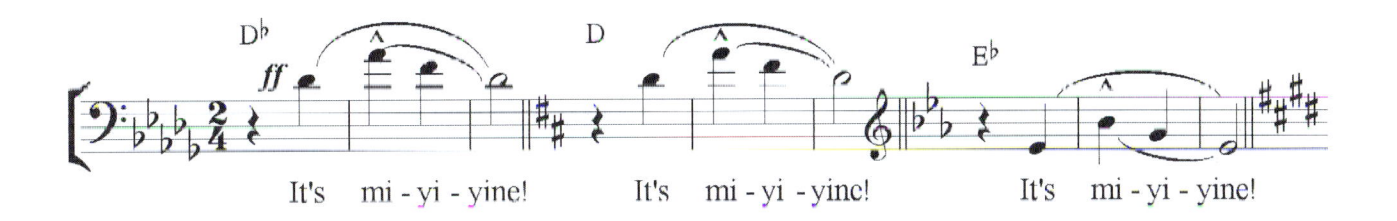

Let the top note go into screaming if you have to.

Try to keep the first and last notes in the natural voice.

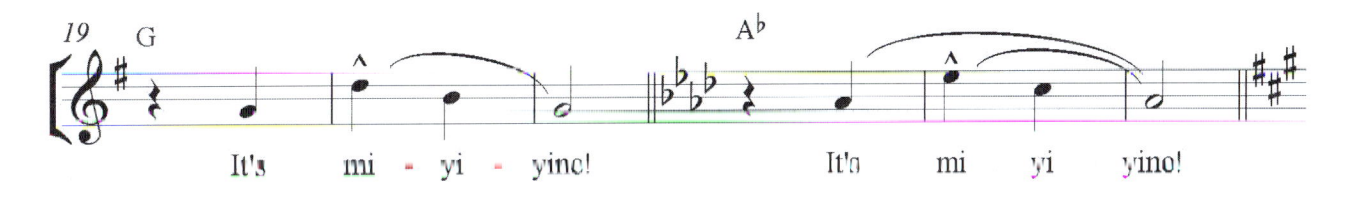

Exercise 27: Wow-Yeah! – Male Glam Rock

This is a simpler exercise, consisting of only two notes, and designed to join up the screaming voice with the natural voice. It's also good for extending the range of the natural voice. This exercise is only of use if you can do the second note, 'yeah', in the natural voice for the first two phrases, at least.

GUIDANCE NOTES

This is a screamers' paradise! Here, you're joining up the two loudest sounds a human can make, and at this pitch the power is colossal! You can choose whether to be raunchy and deafening or beautifully smooth – and deafening. Think of Sebastian Bach's sounds.

Start by singing the first note, 'wow', in falsetto, and 'yeah' in the natural voice. The falsetto voice has no power at this pitch, so 'wow' won't be very loud yet, but 'yeah' is very high in the natural voice and so must be very loud indeed. The object is to join up the two voices, which at this pitch are very different.

Don't force the falsetto at this pitch, and don't rush – give yourself enough time to revel in great sounds. Keep your head down throughout the exercise, pushing your jaw down on every single note but wallowing in the Y of 'yeah'. In fact, overdo the Y.

As soon as you can, turn the 'wow' into a full scream. Scream it in tune and still keep the 'yeah' in the natural voice if you can, but if you can't, scream both sounds.

Constipate the screams. Use all your technique. As one great heavy metal singer once said, 'Put your ass into it!'

Coming back down, try to get the 'yeah' back into the natural voice from as high as you can.

There must be no gap, no silence, between the 'wow' and the 'yeah'. Join up the screaming and the natural voices as smoothly as you possibly can, making them sound like one voice. This might take a couple of years to achieve, although some singers achieve it in a couple of weeks.

CD2, Track 14: Wow-Yeah! — Male Glam-Rock Smooth Scream Mix

Join up the two voices smoothly, and very loudly. Screaming is the loudest sound you can make. If you try to scream quietly, it will hurt.

All at actual pitch.

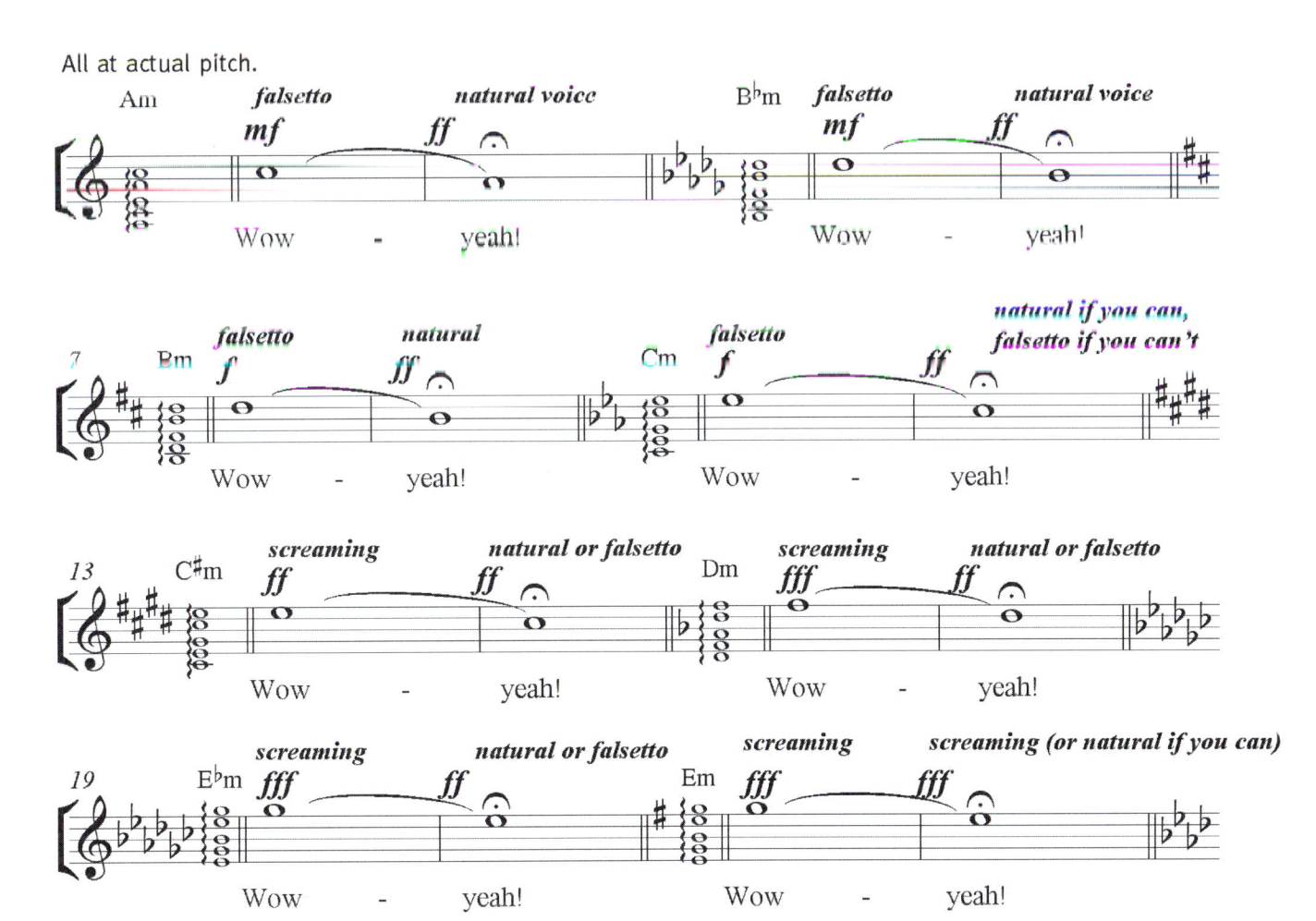

Scream both. If you can get the second note into the natural voice, you've cracked this exercise.

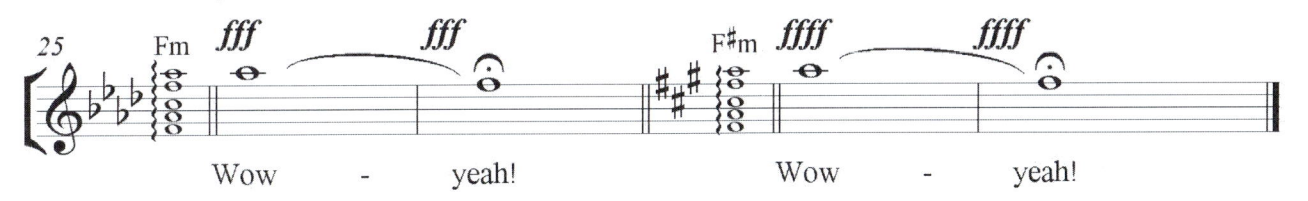

Continue in the same way, going as high as you can, then come down, doing the phrases in the reverse order.

Some singers can take it up to here, eventually:

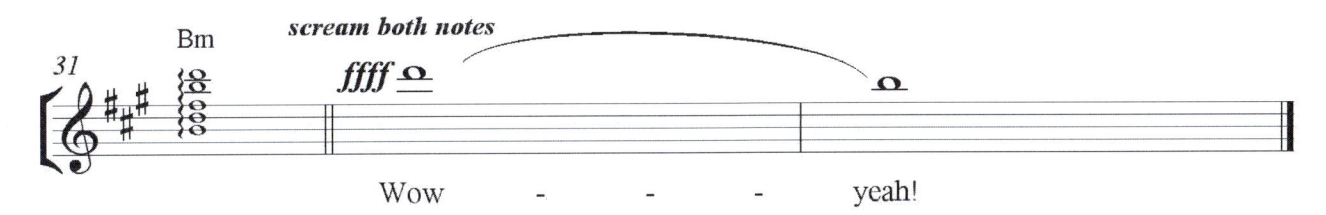

Exercise 28
CD2, Tracks 15-16: Male Blending On A Grand Scale — Screaming Into The Natural Voice (Downward Scales)

This is the big one. The object of this exercise is to bring the screaming voice down into the natural voice, eventually achieving a perfect mixture of the two.

Because this is so demanding, it is wise to lead into it with some 'koos'.

In falsetto, and at actual pitch.

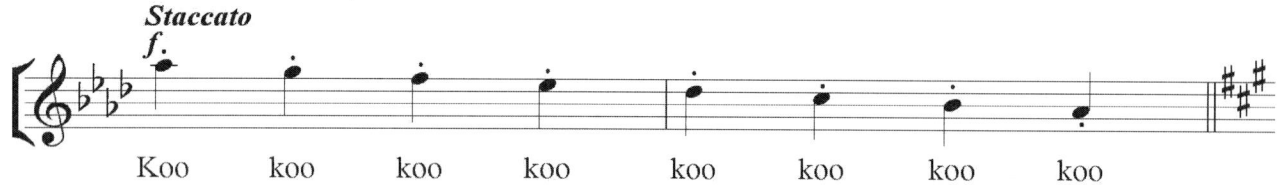

Now try the 'koos' progressively higher and louder.

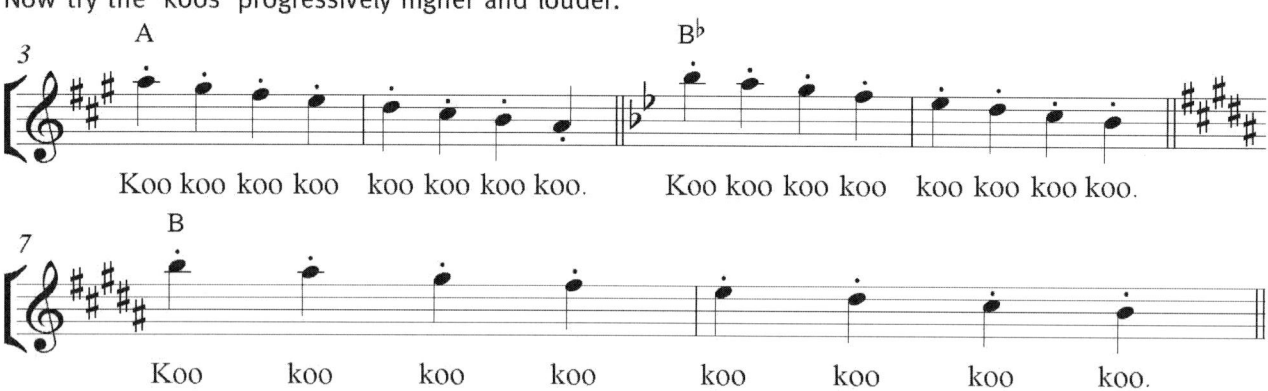

When the 'koos' become difficult, change to screaming. This will enable you to go louder and, therefore, higher.

Keep your head down. Push your jaw down with your tongue. Your throat must be open.

Constipate. Take all the strain with your bottom.

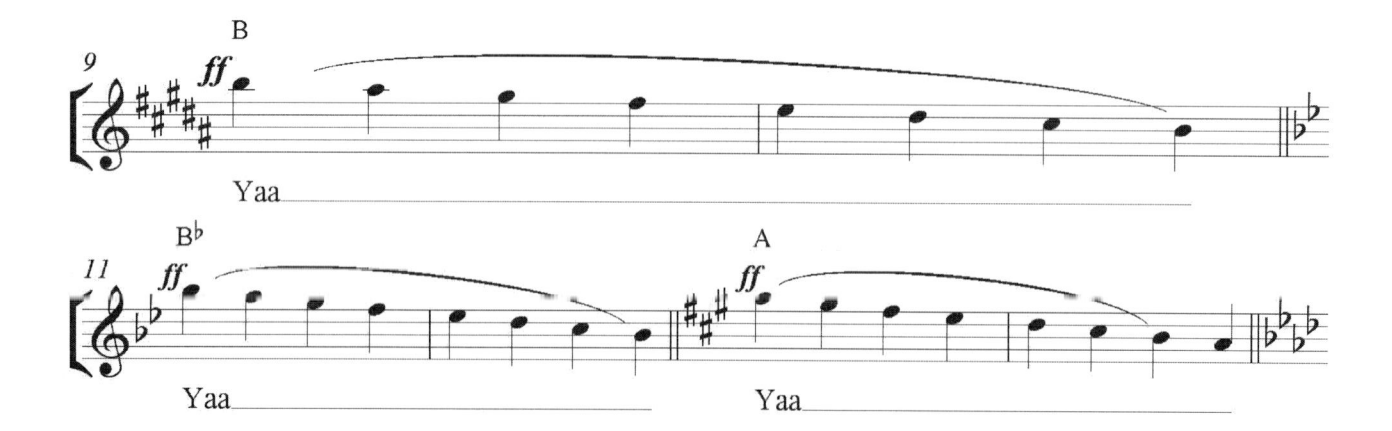

Now, this is where it gets *really* difficult. You'll need all the technique you've learnt for these particular tough vocals — and they don't come any tougher.

Do the first four notes in falsetto screaming, and the last four notes in the natural screaming voice. The join must be as smooth as possible. There must be no gap between the voices.

Keep your jaw down throughout, especially at the change. It requires an incredible effort of will. You will feel a great urge to close your throat at the change. Resist it. Constipate as you have never constipated before. That will help you to keep the strain off the throat.

Don't go quiet at the change. Keep it loud and open.

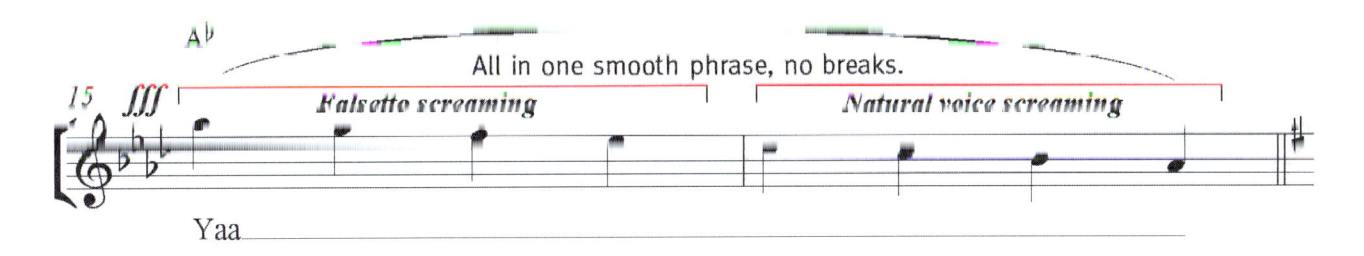

Don't worry if you found the change impossible. Do all the notes as well as you can and then move on to the next exercise, which is *slightly* easier.

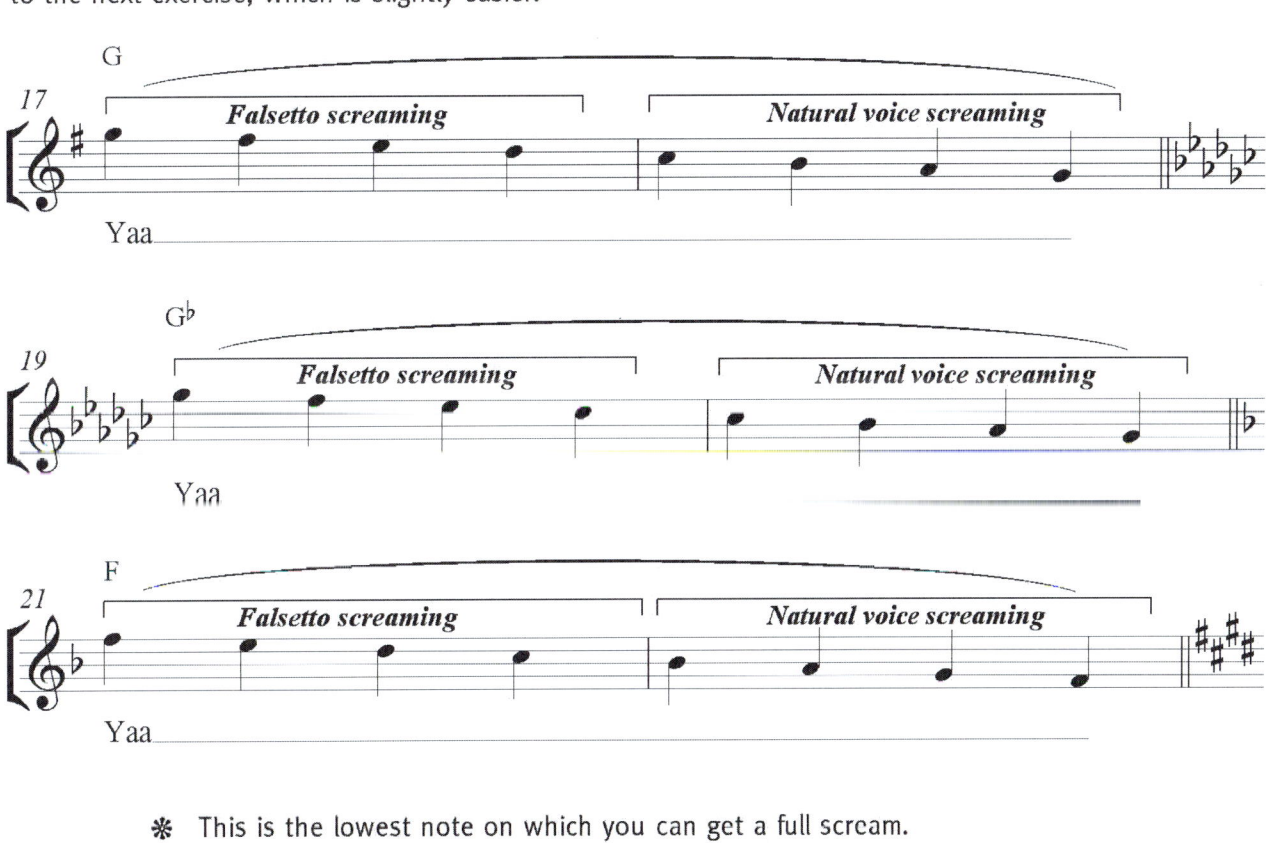

✳ This is the lowest note on which you can get a full scream.
Don't try to take this exercise any lower than this.

9 JOINING UP THE LOUD VOICES

When you've worked extensively on both halves of the voice, doing lots of exercises that focus on the different aspects of the head voice, and you've explored the large variety of purposes of the chest voice, you might feel that you'd like to do some exercises involving the whole voice all at once.

This is advanced stuff. You need to make sure that both halves are working really well. We've already done some work on this with Exercises 14–15, and it might be a good idea to do one of those again before you tackle the exercises in this section.

Exercise 29: 'Nee-yaa-vaa-ee'
GUIDANCE NOTES

CD2, Tracks 17–18

Take a big breath, big enough to support the last three notes of this huge phrase. The diaphragm won't support you without such a full breath.

Keep the tongue firmly against the bottom teeth throughout, from the introductory breath before you sing onwards.

There must be absolutely no movement at all in the throat or on the outside of the neck – no pipes, no outside plumbing, and no appearance of the carotid arteries. If any of this happens, you haven't taken a big enough breath with the diaphragm. (I make no apology for banging on about taking big breaths with the diaphragm here, as this is where you're going to pay for any shortfall in diaphragm control or breathing technique.)

Push the jaw right down on 'yaa' and 'vaa'. Close the jaw on the 'ee' sounds on the first and last notes. The way in which you handle the difference between the very open and very closed sounds will determine whether you get through the exercise without hurting yourself.

The voice will change during 'yaa'. Don't be tempted to close the jaw or the throat at this point – and it is a very strong temptation. Keep your jaw open and take all the strain with the diaphragm as you ease the huge voice through the change. This is the crucial part of this exercise.

Start loudly enough to give you a good start. Crescendo to a massive climax on the top note (be triumphant about it – go for a big, beautiful sound!) and fall back with an erotic, slightly slower, still loud, sustained ending.

CD2, Track 18

Exercise 30
CD2, Tracks 19-20: 'Signorana bella'

This isn't nearly as demanding as Exercise 29. It's very old and has a great many variations: 'Senóra bella', 'Sengorina bella', etc. This version is the most fun and is quite a good substitute for Exercise 1.

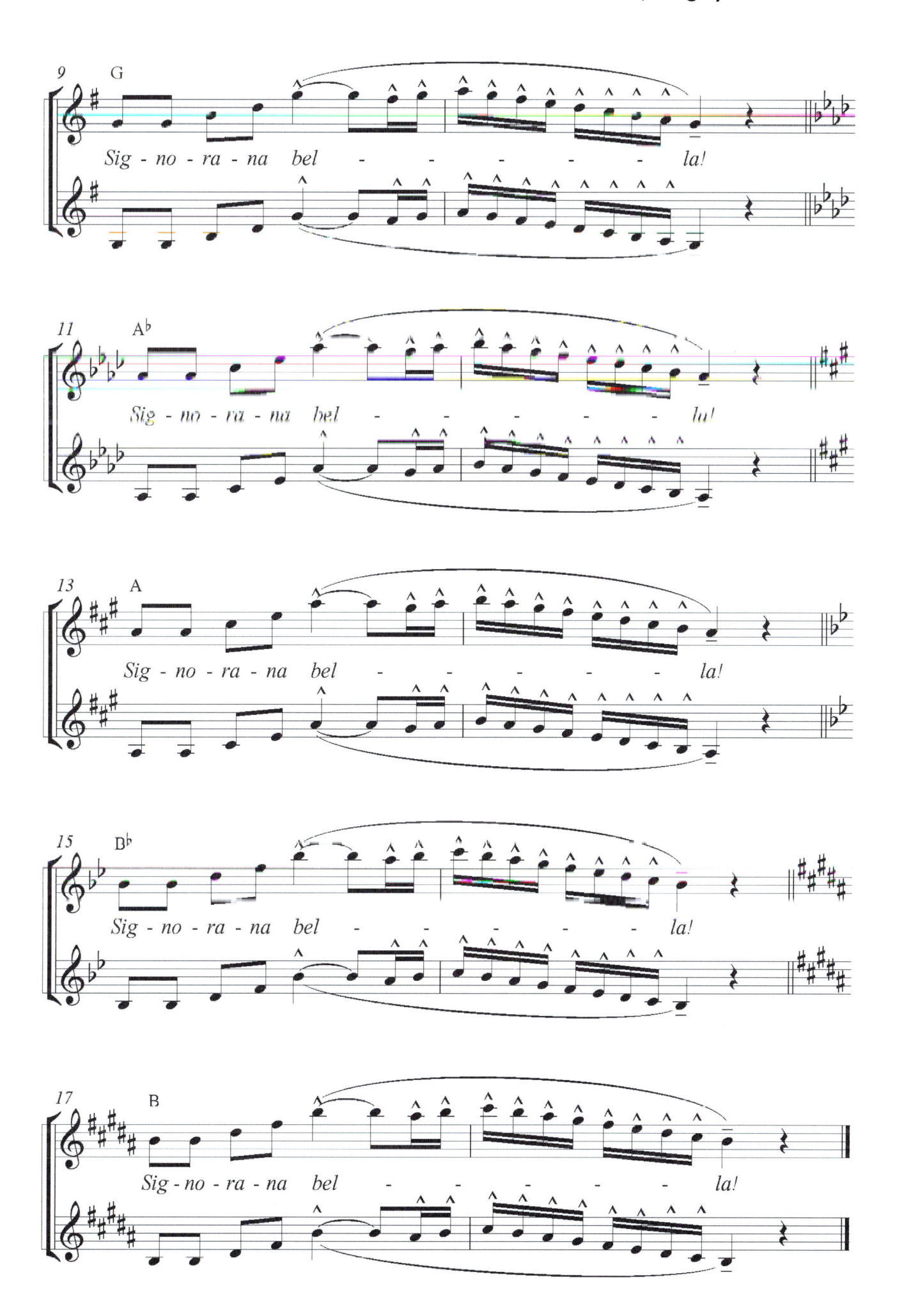

10 ULTRA-LOW SOUNDS

Death Metal, Grunge And Thrash

Death metal, grunge and thrash – call it what you will, it's great fun to sing, and so are the exercises. It's not a particularly difficult style of singing; it mainly requires persistence. The deep, deep notes open up with practice and dry up when neglected. The important thing is not to force them. Even if you don't intend to sing any death or thrash metal, you'll still find these exercises useful for extending the chest voice downward and generally darkening your sound – a very good antidote for those with voices that have a tendency to sound trivial or shrill.

Warming Up For Exercises On Ultra-Low Sounds

There are two contradictory schools of thought here:

- To improve the bottom end of your voice, you should work on the top end.

- You should work on the weakest end of your voice to bring it up to the standard of the stronger end.

In fact, both of these contradictory statements are true, so you need to compromise. Start with the head voice. Begin with:

i   Exercise 1, 'May, may, may';
ii Exercise 3, 'Ha! Ha! Ha!';

(Screaming is a very good warm-up for death, grunge, etc, but if you don't want to scream, go on to vi.)

iii Exercise 4, 'Too-wee';
iv Exercise 5, crying and screaming;
v   Exercise 10, 'Too-wee-yaa';
vi Exercise 11, crying sounds in the chest voice.

Now you're ready to get the best out of the exercises in this section. Don't try to force these low notes or you'll be wildly out of tune. Not only this, but they will also hurt.

Exercise 31
CD2, Tracks 21-23: Repeated Death-Metal Notes —
Diaphragm With Attitude

First, here are some Guidance Notes:

Don't force these low notes, or you won't get down to them.
Get a good hard edge on every note in both verses.
First verse: staccato dots apply.
Second verse: diaphragm accents ^ without silences. Move the diaphragm on every note.
If in doubt, reread the Guidance Notes for Exercises 12 and 13.

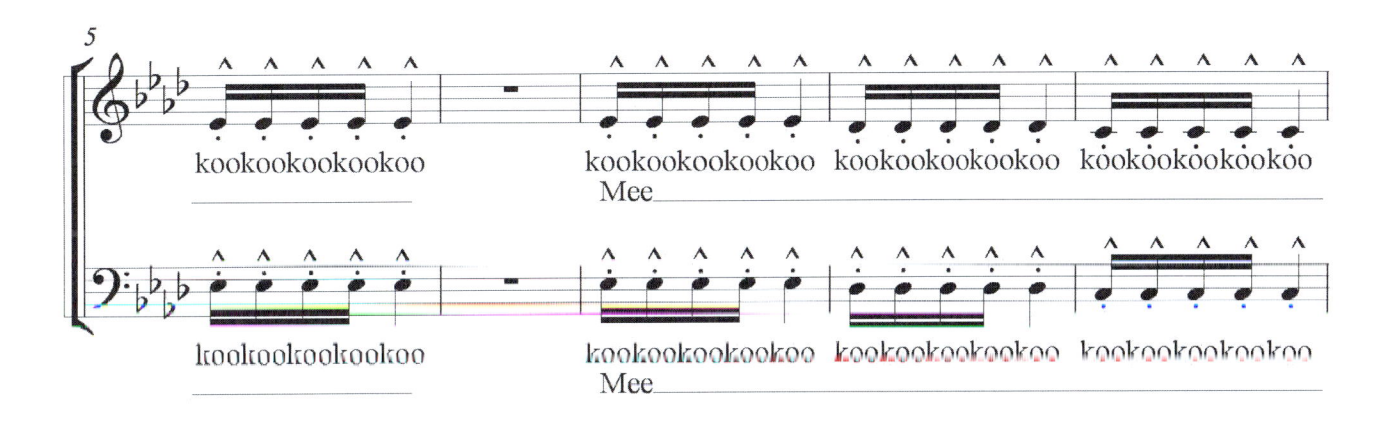

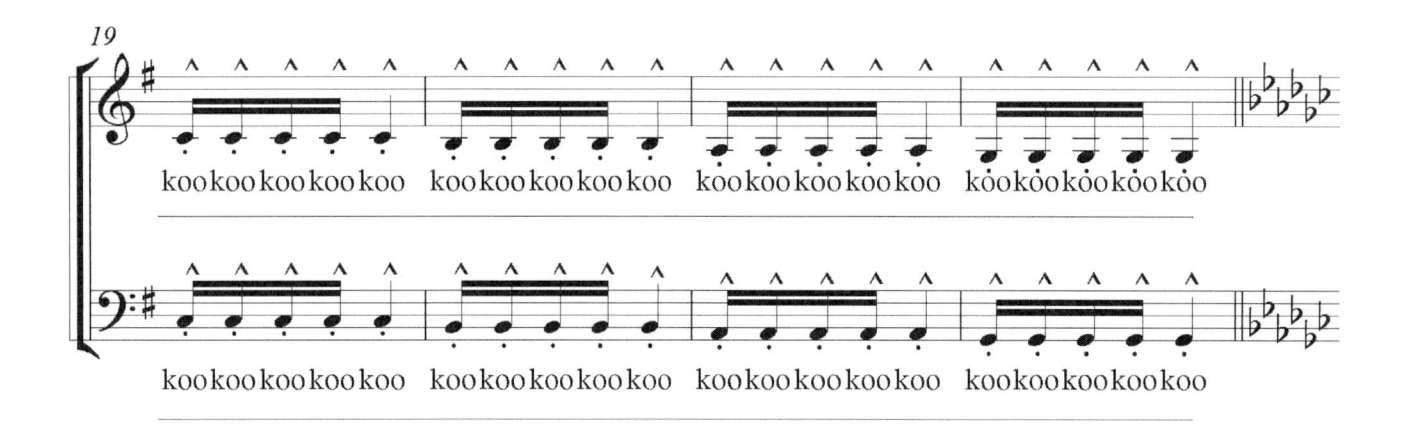

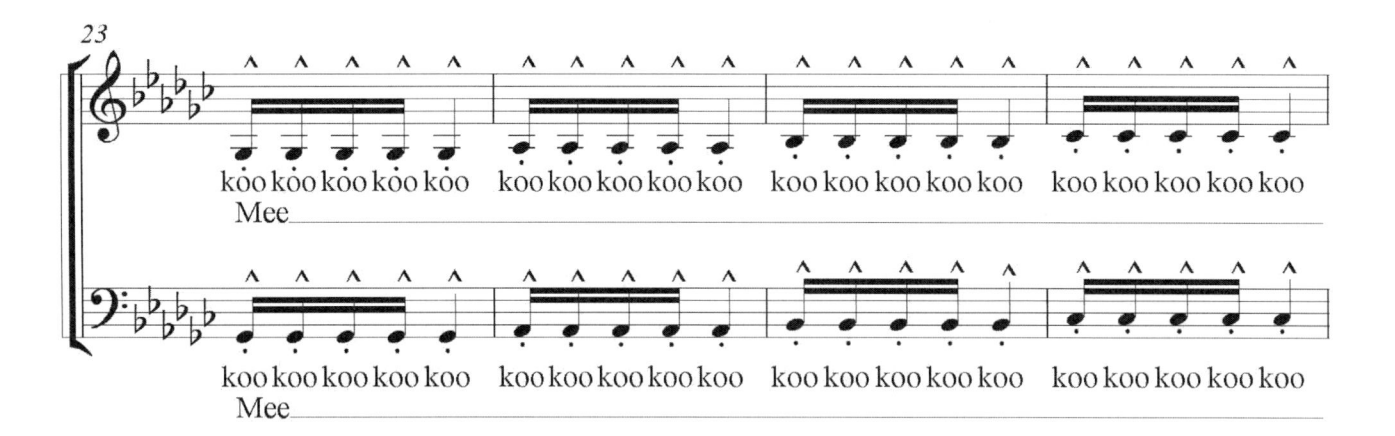

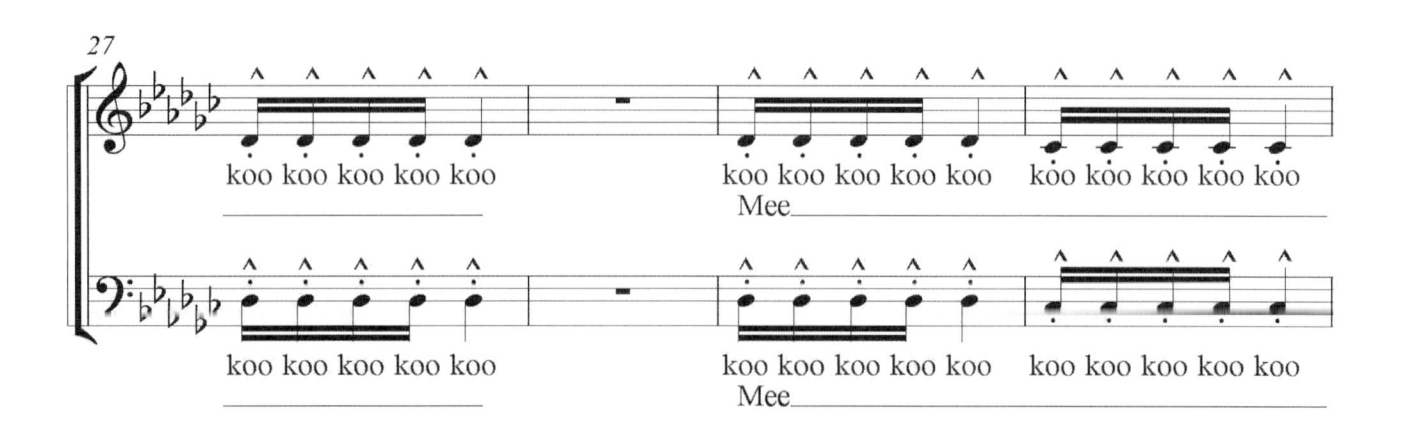

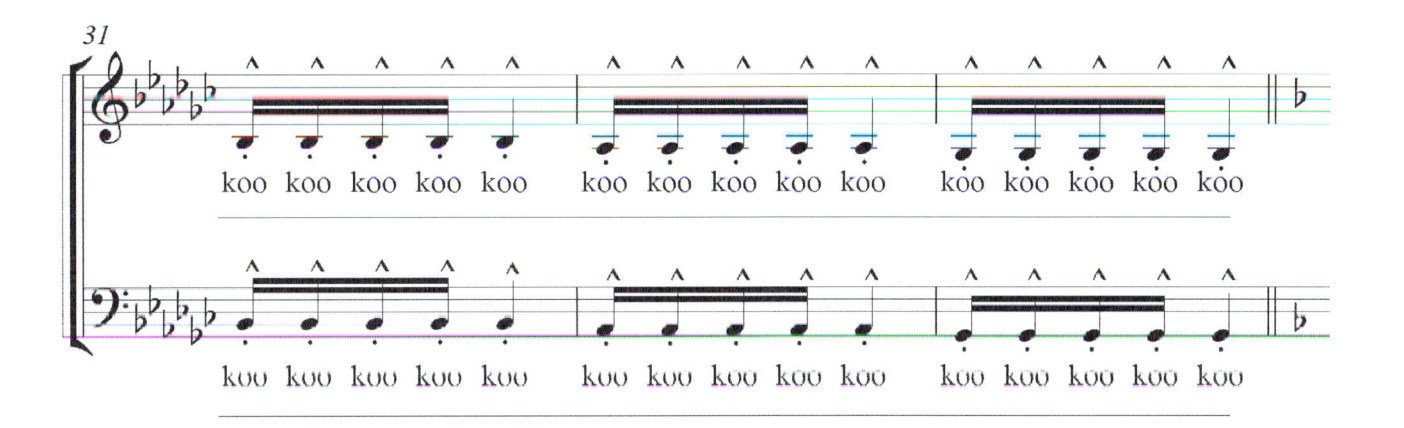

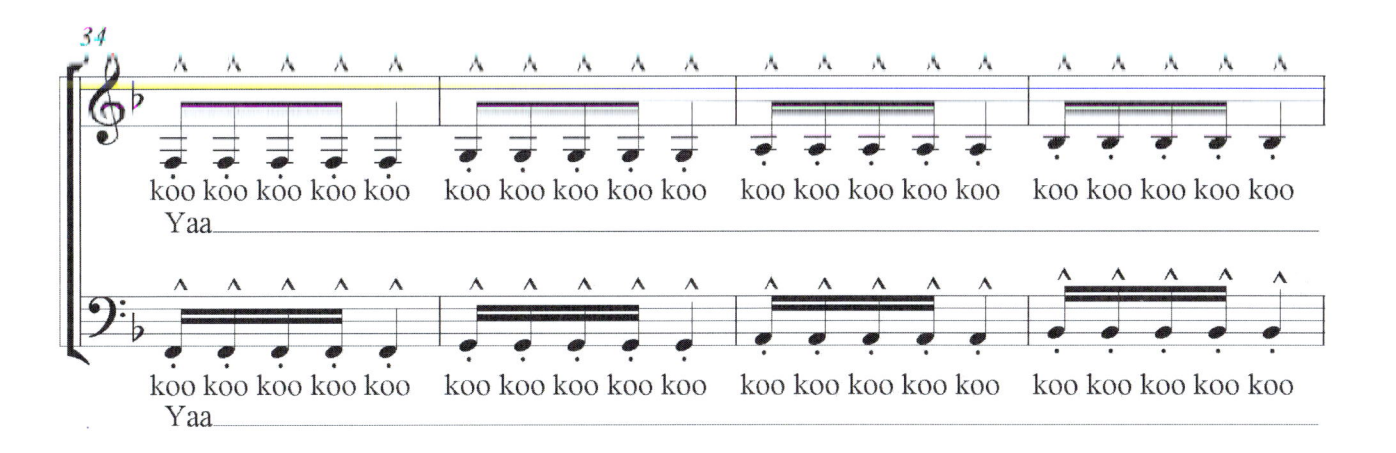

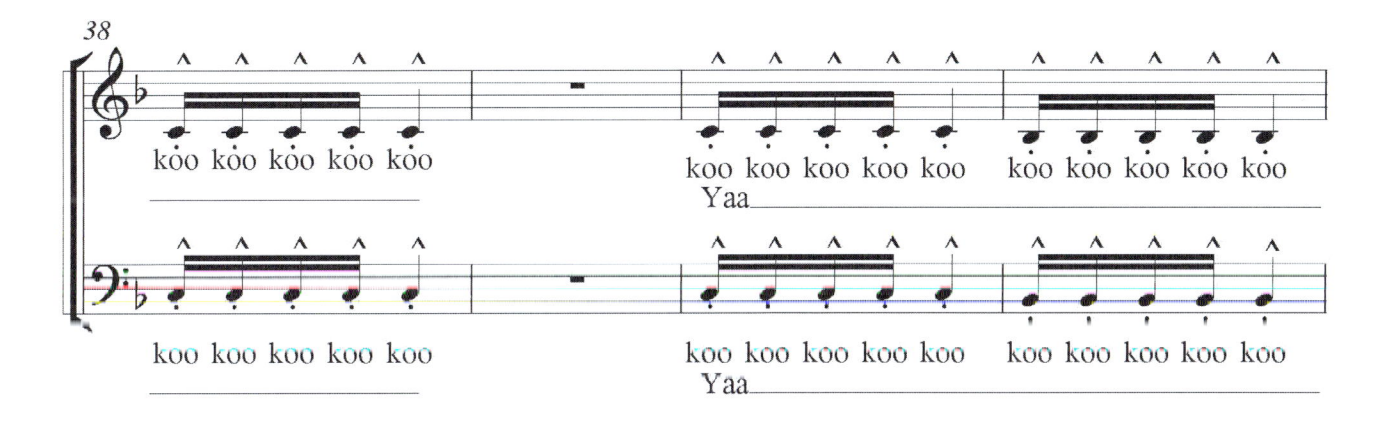

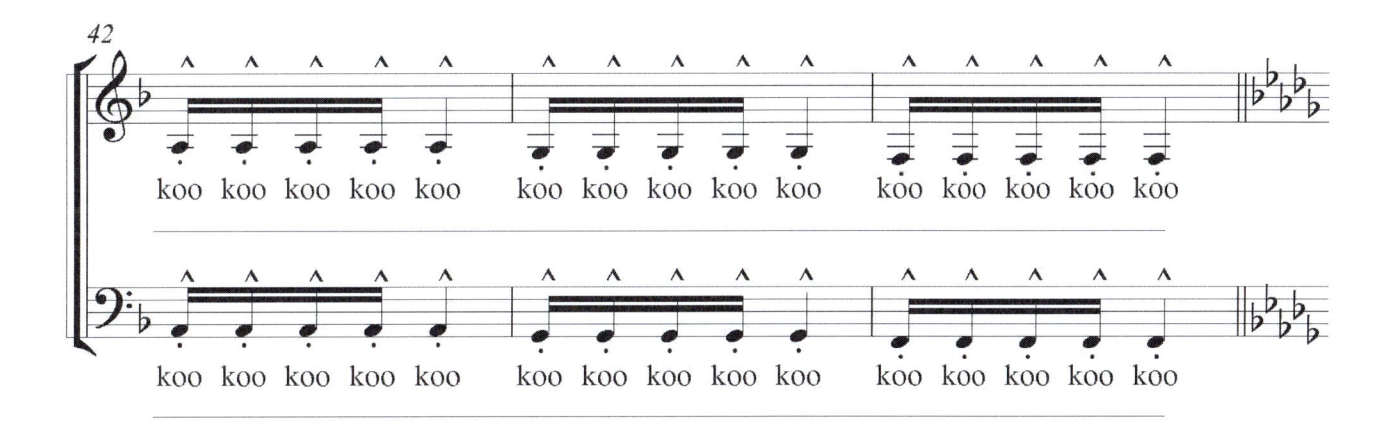

Continue in the same way, dropping each phrase by a semitone, until you get down to here:

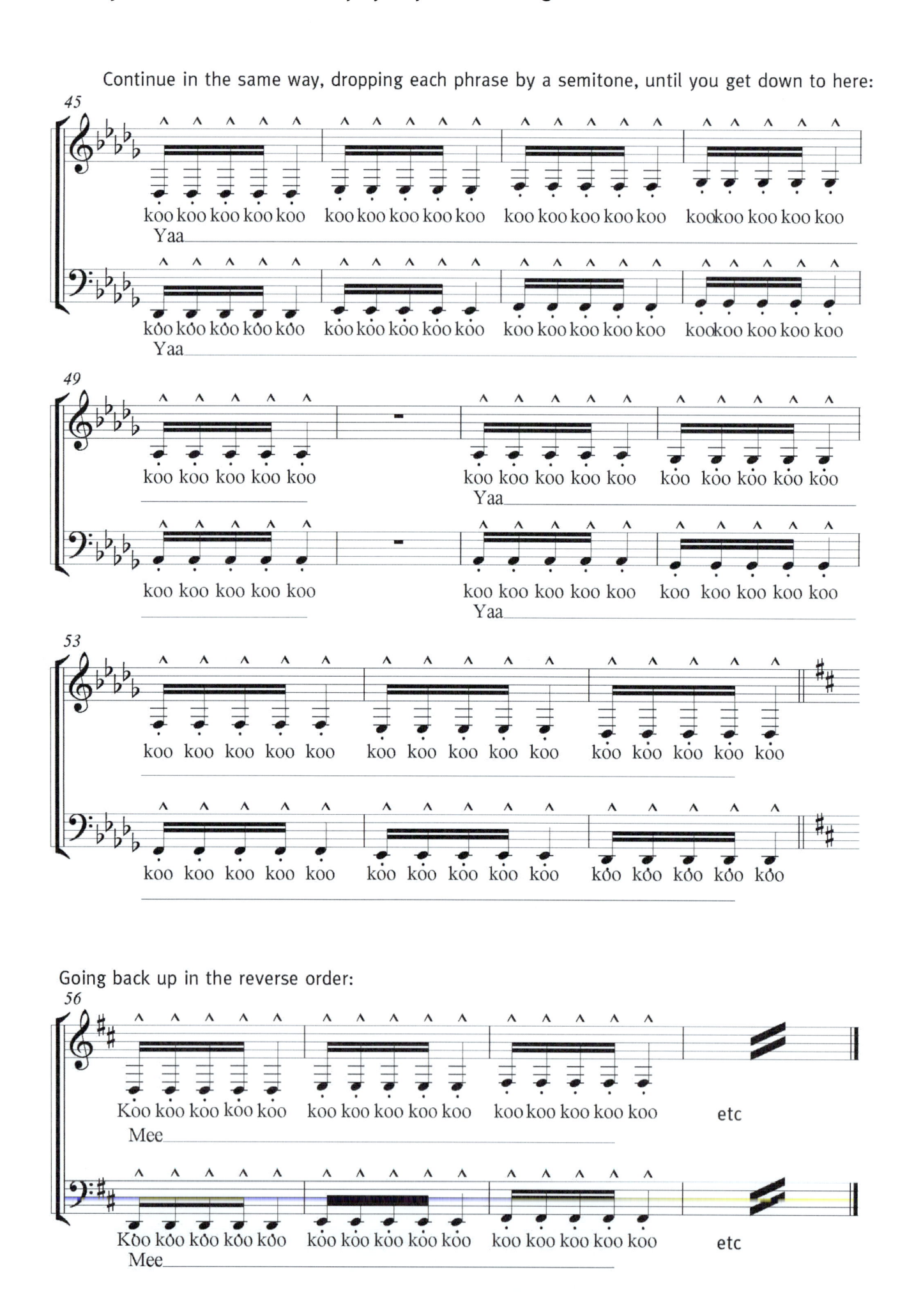

Going back up in the reverse order:

Exercise 32
CD2, Tracks 24-25: Death-Metal Five-Note Scales

In this exercise, you should sound as if you're vomiting.

The speed isn't critical; try it fast and slow.

Move the diaphragm on every single note and keep a good hard edge on the sound.

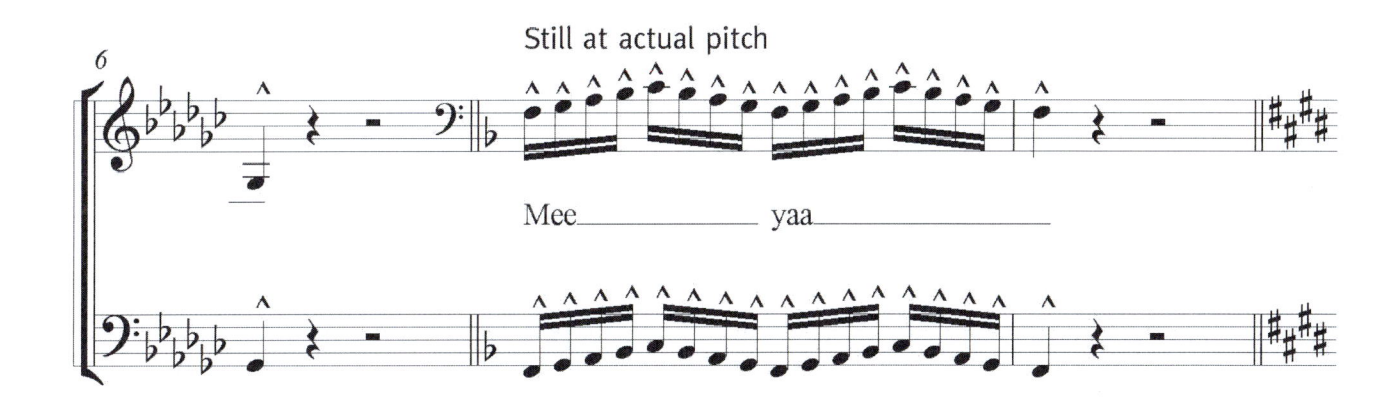

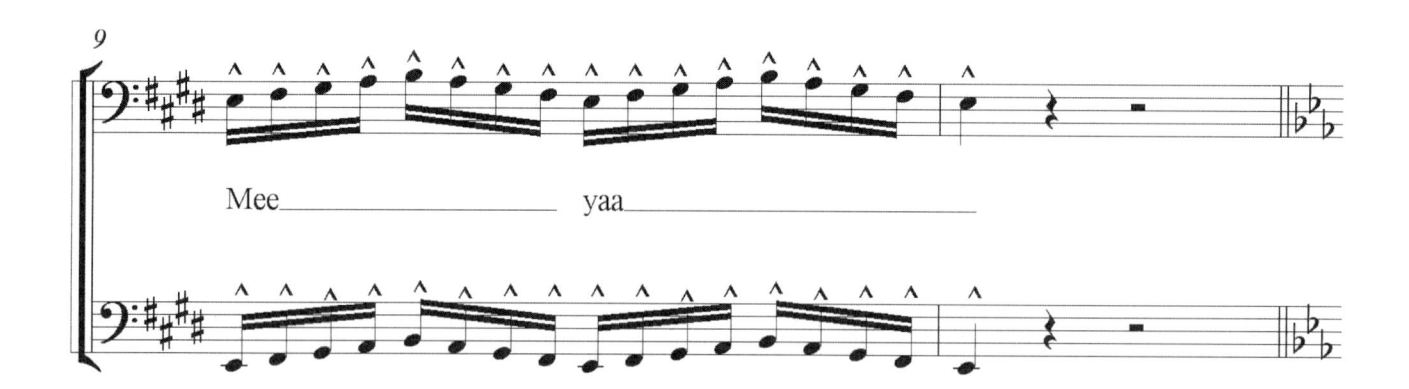

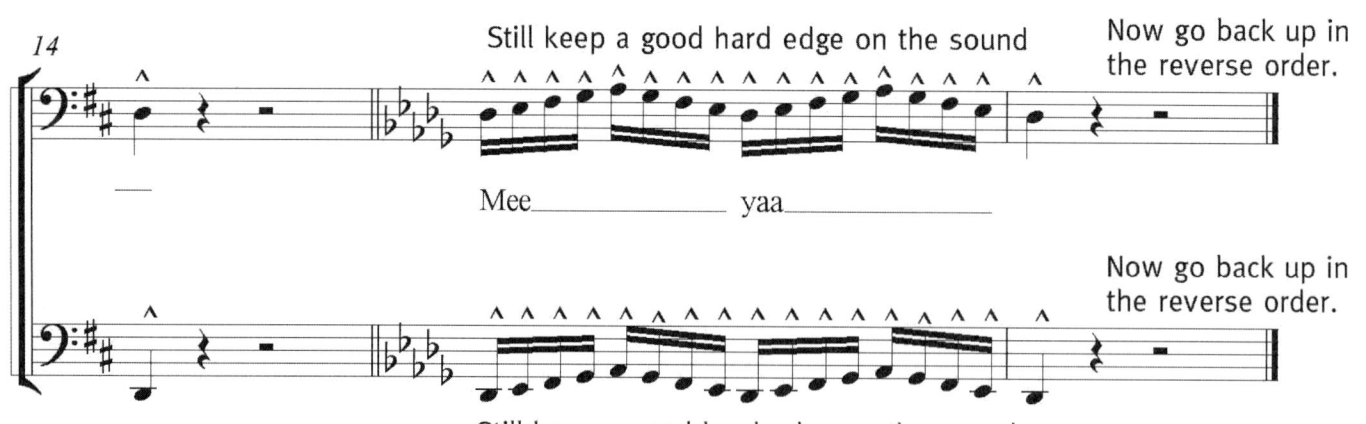

CD2, Tracks 26–27

Exercise 33: Sustained Death-Metal Sounds

This is fun. Do it after you've warmed up with Exercise 10.

GUIDANCE NOTES

Whenever you're going to work on these sounds, begin your workout with some of the high exercises – particularly some of the screaming exercises – in order to stretch the soft palate. The connection between screaming and death-metal sounds is obvious.

For this exercise, keep your head down. You'll soon discover why death-metal singers always look deadly serious: the facial expression is part of the technique for producing that sepulchral voice, and inevitably it will give you the giggles.

Almost close the front of your mouth and open up a huge cavern at the back of your throat. Stick out your lips, this causes a tunnel forward and back down your throat. Hunt for the resonance, which you should find after a bit of experimenting, it will develop into a big sound fairly soon.

Pronunciation

- **Too-ee-yaw** – Let it rattle around the back of your throat and focus in your nose. Try changing the third syllable to 'yeur', making it quite dirty. Squeeze your diaphragm as if you're vomiting from your stomach. Keep practising until it gets disgusting, shocking and loud. Don't force it, or you won't be able to keep the sounds down at this pitch.

Exercise 33
CD2, Track 27: Sustained Death-Metal Sounds

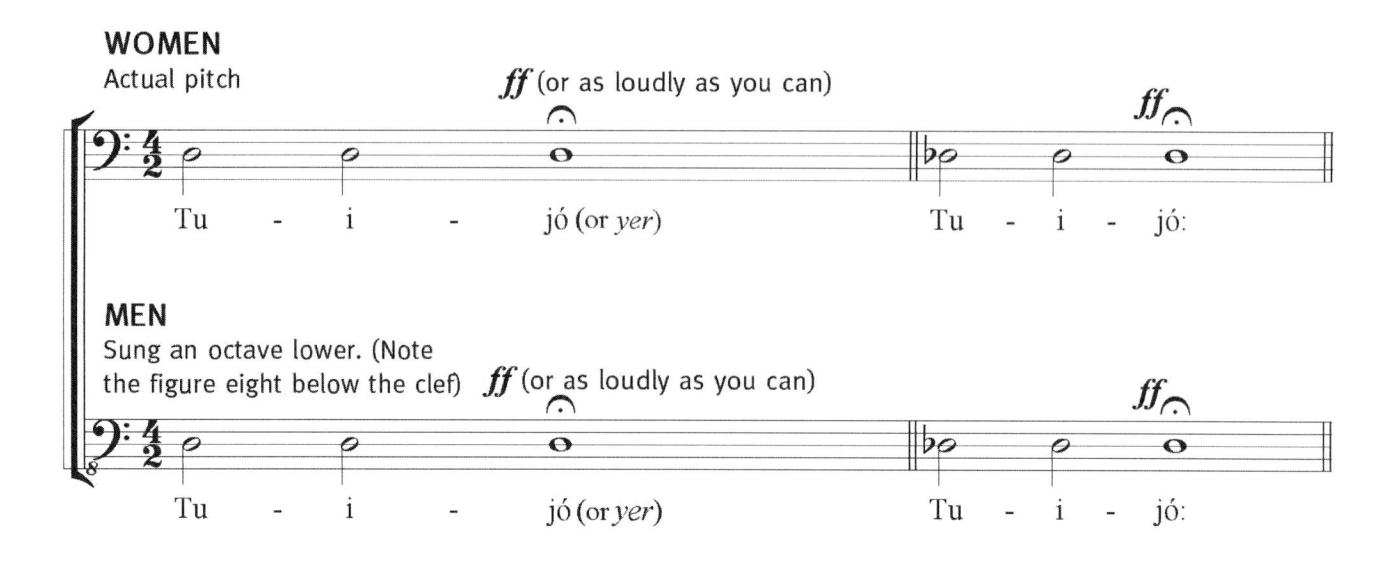

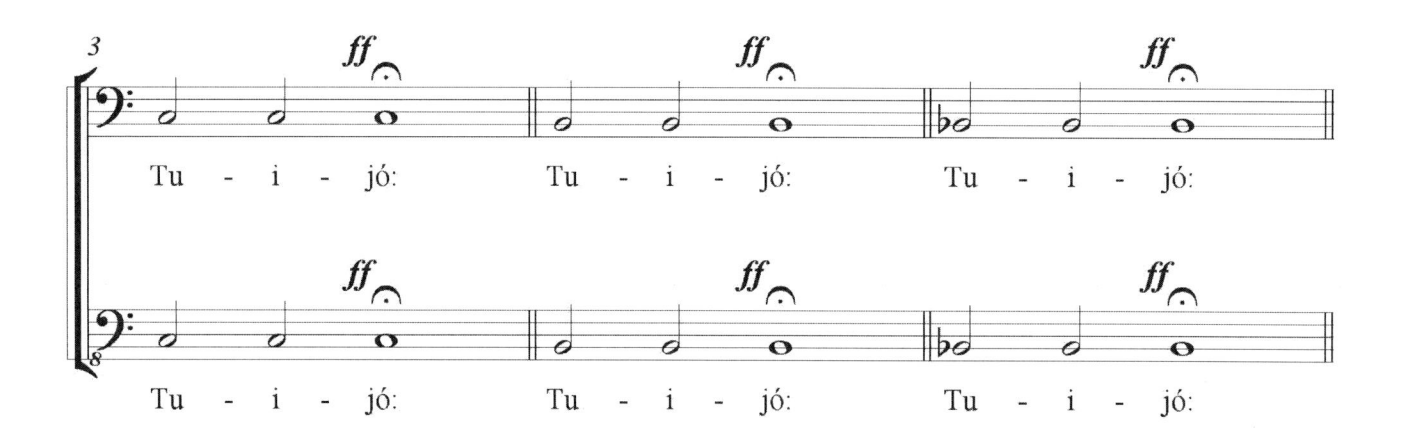

Now go back and do it again.

Etc etc. Continue as low as you can go.

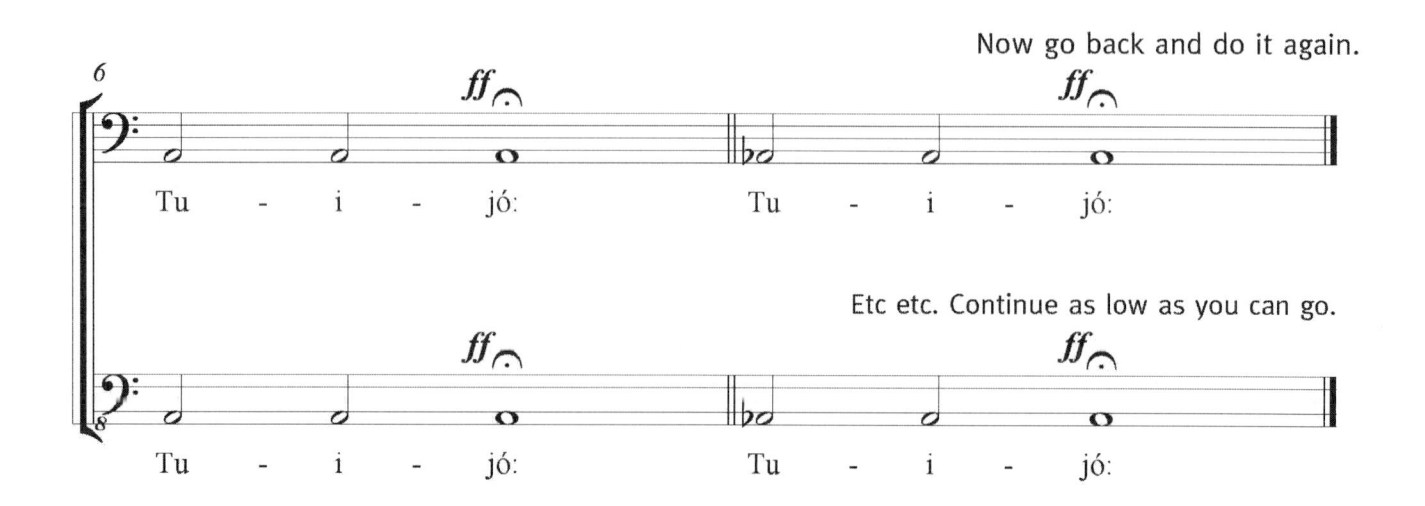

11 SOLVING PROBLEMS

The obvious answer to most of the problems listed here is to go to a good teacher, but this is not always possible, either for financial or geographical reasons, or because you can't find a good teacher!

Voices come in a great variety, and so do vocal problems. In this section I've tried to cover every eventuality. Whatever problem you have, you should find help for it somewhere here. Remember, every singer who has ever lived has had problems with his or her voice – you're not the only one. But problems don't come singly; you probably have a small collection of them, all of which you can solve eventually – it just takes time and hard work. You may also discover that your problems are contradictory and so are the solutions, so you may have to tackle them systematically – for instance, concentrating on loud high notes today, on chest voice and diaphragm tomorrow, on mixed voice the day after, and back to the beginning on the day after that. Read this entire section, not just the bit that you think applies to you, as you might find that your problems aren't the ones you thought they were.

Problem 1: I Get A Sore Throat Every Time I Sing

This is probably the most common complaint among singers. It may be caused by a number of things. For instance:

Problem 1a
The top register (particularly the falsetto part of the male voice) might not have been exercised enough.

Answer
Practise the various 'koo' exercises. For women, these are Exercises 6, 21–25 and Appendix 5; for men, Exercises 16–20 and Appendix 4. Falsetto (in women's voices, the falsetto means the head voice, particularly the highest notes of it) is the healing part of the voice. If you can get the falsetto working, you can usually recover the rest of the voice. Men should practise it a lot.

Problem 1b
You might not be getting the jaw down far enough, or often enough, or you might be allowing it to close into the halfway position. This will cause the jaw to lock at the hinge, which is approximately under the ear.

Answer
Practise some of the exercises containing the sound 'yaa', ie Exercises 10–11 and, if you're into screaming, Exercise 5. Make sure that you do a really good 'Y' at the start of each 'yaa'; that will release the locking mechanism in the jaw.

Problem 1c
You might be doing all of the work in the throat, instead of supporting the voice with the power muscles, such as the diaphragm, leg muscles, etc.

Answer
Practise the breathing (Exercise 2) and also Exercises 7–12, taking care to follow the Guidance Notes.

Problem 1d
Instead of breathing properly from the diaphragm, you might be breathing from the upper part of the chest, probably by raising your shoulders to take in the breath, which will also cause various veins and arteries in your neck to clench and stand out like drain pipes. You can check this by looking at your neck in the mirror when you sing.

Answer
Go back and do the first 10 exercises in this book (leaving out Exercise 5 if you don't wish to scream), taking great

care to follow the Guidance Notes, especially those about breathing and the diaphragm.

Problem 1e

You may be trying to force the sound in the middle of the range to give it a bit of 'edge', without having developed sufficient chest voice.

Answer

Work on Exercises 10–15, leaving out Exercise 14 if it's too exhausting. Exercise 15 is more important.

Problem 1f

You may just be suffering from an early-day sore throat or early-day cold (my terms for it). It's quite usual for singers to go down with a cold or a sore throat in the early stages of learning to sing. In addition to the probable causes mentioned above, there is the shock to the system of doing more with the voice than you ever thought possible. All that stretching of the soft palate and jaw to make the wider range accessible is bound to cause some slight physiological changes.

It's very similar to taking up a new sport, such as running, football, tennis, weightlifting and martial arts, which a lot of my students do. For the first few weeks of a new or renewed sport, you can hardly walk. You've stretched muscles to a greater degree than they're used to being stretched; you might even damage ligaments and hamstrings, which will recover.

Under new physical demands, most people go down with colds. The body is out of practice at coping with such demands, so the resistance isn't there. But once you've shaken off these dreaded lurgies after a few weeks (sometimes a few months), you'll find that you can engage in all of these athletic pursuits without the suffering – or, at least, without so much suffering!

Stretching the range also causes physiological changes.

- You're stretching the muscles. Well, that's all right; muscles are supposed to be stretched.

- You're changing the shape of the sinuses minutely in order to make a good tone. However, you won't be able to change them faster than nature will allow.

- You're working the leg, buttock and front-abdominal muscles. They will come to no harm; they're the strongest muscles in the body and will do all the work you can put on them. The more you demand of them, the stronger they will become.

All of this is natural, and therefore the changes are *somatic*, not *psychosomatic*. Stretching the range, like stretching anything else, makes demands on the defence system in the human body, so your resistance drops and you go down with a sore throat and a cold.

Sore throats can also be caused by nervousness, fear, or self doubt. Have you ever had that lump in your throat when you knew you had to sing in front of people? Well, you're the one who put it there. It usually goes away when you start to sing. Unlike the sore throats that are caused by physiological changes, these *are* psycho-somatic – and they are important.

That fear or self-doubt is essential to a singer. I've never met a great singer who was truly self-confident. Oh yes, for the television cameras they can put on a breathtaking show of arrogance – it's a professional skill, like acting – but you should see some of them before they go on stage. You *need* that sensitivity, or you're unlikely to make the type of sounds that people will want to listen to. But that fear, that psychological threat which undermines your confidence, adds to the somatic problems, particularly in the early stages, and is likely to be another cause of colds and sore throats. This is why so many singers go down with colds and sore throats immediately before they're about to perform at important gigs and auditions.

Answer

There is no answer to this problem – it's called 'being human'. It is a fear, and the only thing you can do with fear is either live with it or outface it. Work on your technique so that colds and sore throats don't stop you singing, and do lots of gigs so that you get used to them. That way, you have a good chance of overcoming the fear.

Pressure, and the technique of overcoming pressure, has to be practised as much as any other technique, and the best way of practising it is to do lots of gigs. If that doesn't work or, for some reason, is not an option for you, you need to find a teacher who can help you deal with pressure.

The most interesting thing about singers' colds is that singers usually come out of them singing better than they ever did before the cold, just as athletes perform better after the initial shock. I can't absolutely guarantee this, but it's what normally happens. This suggests that something intriguing happens during a cold, and as nobody really knows what causes the common cold, let me put forward a theory.

Think of what actually happens when you catch a cold. All the damageable parts of the throat are covered with a protective layer of mucus. We usually try to cough it away, but it often comes back. Maybe a cold *protects* you while physiological changes are happening. That is certainly indicated by the evidence. I suggest that the common cold (as if all colds fell neatly into two categories) is a tool of the auto-repair system of the human body.

Ultimately, a cold isn't necessarily a bad sign. It's not a particularly good sign, either – it's a fact of life. But everyone gets colds and sore throats, not just singers. You can't expect to go through life without ever getting a cold or a sore throat just because you've had a few singing lessons.

Problem 2: I Can't Get The Power

The human voice is enormously powerful. A good singer in full voice can be deafening in a small room, even without a microphone. Power gives you the focus (the edge on the voice) which enables you to sustain long passages on a single breath. Paradoxically, it can work the other way around, too: the edge gives you the power. It also enables you to sing very quietly without losing vocal quality, which is often necessary for singing with a microphone.

There are four basic reasons for being unable to produce power in the voice:

Problem 2a
You're not using the diaphragm enough. (See the *diaphragm* in the 'Glossary'.)

Answer
Practise all of the diaphragm exercises until it becomes a habit to use your diaphragm for everything. Every time you see the accent ^ over or under a note, pull in the diaphragm and make sure you sing louder on that note. If you find that you're singing that note quieter than the other notes, or almost going silent on it, then you're probably doing something with the throat as you work the diaphragm. You should always try to do nothing with the throat, but this isn't always possible. You might need to *act* the connection between the diaphragm and the voice (that means singing louder and pretending that the additional volume is coming from the diaphragm) until it becomes automatic.

Problem 2b
You haven't opened up an important part of your range. Power usually comes from the top register (the highest notes in a man's natural voice), but many singers have difficulty in getting into this register. The fact that you

find high notes difficult doesn't mean that you can't sing them.

Answer
For help in tackling this problem, see 'Problem 3: I Can't Get The High Notes'.

Problem 2c
Conversely, the high notes might come quite easily to you, even if they are a bit weak. Your problem might be a lack of chest voice – that is, you have no deep notes, or, if you have, they aren't resonant or strong enough. This can cause a serious lack of power in the voice as a whole and may sometimes make your voice strident or too piercing on the high notes.

Answer
For help in tackling this problem, see 'Problem 8: I Can't Get The Low Notes'.

Problem 2d
You're not taking big enough breaths, or you're not breathing in the right place.

Answer
You need to breathe from the diaphragm. However, the diaphragm won't support your most demanding notes unless you've taken in sufficient air. (See the *diaphragm* in the 'Glossary'.)

Problem 3: I Can't Get The High Notes

The following problems deal with five different types of high note. I'll attempt to deal with them one at a time, but here are a few general points that apply to all of them.

Not being able to reach high notes is a very common problem. The cause might be that you are simply not going loud enough when you attempt a high note. Like many singers, you might get into the habit of 'holding back' (which usually means *strangling* the voice) for fear of disturbing the neighbours; after a while, you do not *realise* that you are holding back. This could be disastrous. Find somewhere that you can practice without anyone hearing you; or where you are not *bothered* whether anyone can hear you or not.

You shouldn't expect the high notes to be easy. They might be easy, but don't count on it. For most singers, high notes are very difficult to reach until they've opened up the appropriate register and discovered the knack or trick of singing high notes. All singing is really a trick.

Problem 4: Ladies – I Haven't Got A Head Voice/My Head Voice Sounds Awful

This can be a very distressing area for sensitive singers, who simply may not like the squeaky sounds they make every time they attempt notes in the head voice, but it is important. Exercising the head voice stretches the soft palate and resonates in the sinuses in a way that the chest voice doesn't, and it will make the chest voice a lot more flexible and wide-ranging. Otherwise, you're likely to be a one-volume singer, going flat-out all the time for the power at the top of the chest voice, scared stiff of singing quietly in case your voice breaks up – except on very low notes, which will often be inaudible and out of tune.

This is the crucial point: you're *exercising* the head voice; you don't have to sing songs up there if you don't want to. Don't worry about the squeakiness, the silliness or the girliness of these sounds – that really doesn't matter. Squeaking your way to the very highest notes is perfectly all right; it will do the necessary work just as well as it would if you sang it like an operatic diva. You don't have to do it all at once, either – each day, or each time you do the exercises, try to go one or two notes higher than you did before. Don't worry about the quality; worry about whether or not you're in tune and whether or not the strain is in the throat or on the power muscles. And there *will* be strain, but the throat should feel stretched but not sore.

There are two ways of opening up the top registers:

1 **Loudly** – For this you must use the diaphragm to support your voice as you attempt to sing notes you haven't reached before. Singing loudly is generally the way by which most women first manage to get hold of their top notes.

   Do Exercises 1, 4 and 10. If you want to scream, add Exercise 5. Pay particular attention to the Guidance Notes on all these exercises.

2 **Quietly** – Women can sing their top notes quietly, which men cannot. For stretching the range and controlling the tone, singing quiet downward scales is generally the best method. You'll need to support the voice very firmly with the diaphragm for this. Don't think that quiet notes need less technique than loud notes; they need just as much diaphragm technique, often more. Start from the highest note you can. Don't worry about the quality; instead, concentrate on the support and the tuning. Good tuning is crucial here, but again don't worry if the

tuning or the tone are difficult; get them as good as you can today and try to sing them better tomorrow. A squeak will do if it's in tune.

First do Exercise 1, 'May may may', to get the voice started. Then do all the 'koo' exercises, particularly the quiet ones for the mixed voice, including those in Appendix 5.

Problem 5: Men – I Can't Get High Notes In The Natural Voice

There are two ways of opening up the top register, both of which require a lot of work on the falsetto voice:

1 **Loudly** – In the male voice, high notes are louder than low notes, this is entirely natural. If you cannot manage the high notes of U2 or Aerosmith, for example, it might be that you're simply not going loud enough. For this, you must use the diaphragm to support the voice when you attempt to sing notes higher than those you've ever sung before, and you probably need to constipate as well.

   Do exercises 1, 4, 8 and 9. If you want to scream, add Exercises 5 and 26, but pay particular attention to the Guidance Notes on all of these exercises. When you've done these (or some of them), move on to the quiet method:

2 **Quietly** – This is the most reliable way of opening up the top register. It involves using the falsetto as a way into the high notes of the natural voice and eventually joining up the two voices. Falsetto is essential here – this technique won't work without it – but be prepared for it to take a long time (four years, with some singers): endless, painstaking work. You'll also need to use the diaphragm for this. Sing some loud, high exercises first, even if they go wrong – and they probably will; they go wrong for everyone at some time or other, but you still need to do the loud stuff before you can get full value out of the quiet, smooth aspect of the voice.

   For this method, you need the exercises devoted to the quiet mixed head voice (Exercise 16–20) and those in Appendix 4. Do them endlessly, hour after hour, week after week. For variation, sing Exercise 19 very, very quietly (ignore the Guidance Notes for once), starting and finishing in the key of F (starting at bar 3), letting the voice choose its own sound – falsetto, mixed or natural.

   It's essential always to keep it in tune. The object is to retrain the voice in order to focus it easily. This is, in fact, the most difficult thing you will ever have to do as a singer, but try to make it *sound* easy. Your jaw will ache badly and you'll feel as if your tongue doesn't fit any more. If the hinge of your jaw becomes painful, give it a rest for an hour, a day, a couple of days and then come back to it, but persevere for however long it takes.

You can vary the exercise by changing the 'koo' to a *gentle* childlike crying sound on the scales, letting the voice choose its own sound easily. At the beginning of each session, to get the voice started, you might find it helpful to warm up with 'May may may' (Exercise 1) loudly, possibly following it with Exercise 6. If the chest voice is all right, leave it alone; if not, you may need to devote an occasional session to that. Obviously, if you have gigs to perform, you can't leave any part of the voice alone entirely. But your all-consuming task is to make the mixed head voice perfect.

You might find that alternating the loud method and the quiet method will suit you best – trust your instinct – but if alternating them doesn't seem to be improving matters, devote yourself almost totally to the quiet method for several months, possibly a couple of years. It works for nearly all male singers eventually, but you might need an expert on the mixed head voice to listen to you. Unfortunately, not enough singing teachers *are* experts on the mixed head voice, or at listening.

A word of warning: Don't abandon loud singing altogether. That would be disastrous.

Problem 6: Men – I Can't Do Falsetto

Also read Problem 7. For a lot of singers these are the same problem.

This problem is almost certainly due to a psychological block and is surprisingly common. There is no technique for getting into falsetto. It's a crying sound – you practised it a lot when you were a toddler, so you should be good at it by now! But when you grew up and your voice broke in your teens, you were glad to get away from all that wimpish crying and childish squeaking, so you lost it. Well, now you have to get it back, and this can prove difficult, mentally.

Answer

Falsetto is the childish sound that never leaves us. Try some gentle whimpering sounds. In other words, act like a child. Try whimpering the downward scales on Exercise 7. Pronounce it as 'yaa', with your jaw down and your tongue touching your bottom teeth, giving yourself plenty of space in your mouth and throat. Start

where you can, or where it feels comfortable. Gradually expand the falsetto range.

Another possibility is to find a teacher who knows about acting techniques. Or you could join an actors' improvisation class.

Problem 7: I Can't Scream

Screaming is an extreme form of falsetto, and the answers to the problem are very similar to those associated with Problem 6. If you can't scream, it's probably because you're not going for it enough. It's fear that stops you screaming. That doesn't mean that it isn't a problem, particularly for men. Physically, we can all scream from the day we're born to the day we die, but screaming can be very difficult, mentally; you're afraid of looking or sounding like an idiot, and that could stop you. You might also be afraid that the neighbours can hear you. You need to throw away your dignity – you can always get it back if you really miss it.

There's a slight confusion with the female voice because many women can sing very quiet notes right at the top of their screaming registers, which a man can't do. With women's voices, there is far less difference between falsetto and screaming than with the man's voice. The main distinctions are in the volume and acting.

Answer

Women should do all the head voice exercises, and for the screaming exercises you should make sure that you give the voice all the muscular support you can (use the diaphragm and legs and constipate like mad). Follow the Guidance Notes fully.

Men, you won't be able to scream quietly – it will hurt if you try. You might need to alternate the quiet falsetto exercises with the loud screaming exercises. Don't try to sing loud (*f* or *ff*) exercises quietly or quiet (*p* or *pp*) exercises loudly; you won't be able to get the notes.

You might need to tackle Problems 6 and 7 together.

Problem 8: I Can't Get The Deep Notes

This is often more of a problem for women than for men and is usually easy to deal with. Low notes are easy; they just take a long time. Please don't be put off by some idiot saying that you'll never sing low notes because you're a soprano or a tenor – this is nonsense. If it were true, it would mean that only mezzos and contraltos would be able to sing rock or pop and only basses could sing death metal, both of which are clearly not the case. Everyone has a chest voice, and everyone can get down to the lowest notes of it, as long as they don't force them.

Answer

The entire chest voice – including the power notes at the top of it – depends on your deepest notes, which tend to become weak when they're not used very much. Building up the chest voice will take nothing away from the head voice as long as you don't sing from the throat (that *will* reduce your ability to sing the high notes), but it does need quiet, painstaking work. For a while, you might have to sing your deepest notes in a whisper in order to get down to them.

Relax on low notes or they won't happen. Let the hard edge develop patiently and in its own good time, and eventually you'll build up a lot of deep resonance.

Start with Exercise 1, 'May may may', followed by Exercises 6 or 7, 'Koo, koo, koo', in order to stretch the soft palate, *making sure that you don't use the throat.* Then sing all of the chest-voice exercises, including all the 'Utra-Low' exercises, and the diaphragm exercises, following the Guidance Notes implicitly for each.

You might find that your breath runs out quickly on your deepest notes, so make sure that you take bigger breaths than you think you'll need. Use the diaphragm to control the breath, expanding it fully before you sing. Be grudging about how much air you use up and then squeeze the last drops of air out at the end. You may need to bend over to pull the diaphragm in enough.

Don't worry if the lowest notes refuse to 'click in' immediately; just be gentle enough to keep them in tune and persevere. On the very physical diaphragm exercises, go for a hard-edged sound. If you focus the sound in your nose, you'll find that using the diaphragm fast and loud on very low notes will make a surprisingly good sound. If, however, you produce the sound in the throat, it will all go wrong and the diaphragm will lose its effect. Make a conscious decision: 'I WILL NOT USE THE THROAT AT ALL.' Make the sound go straight from the diaphragm to the nose, bypassing the throat altogether.

Above all, keep the tongue against your bottom teeth and push your jaw down on all of the open sounds, such as 'yaa' and 'all', or the throat will take over and you'll never get the deepest notes to work in a month of Sundays.

For the death-metal sounds, open up a huge cavern at the back of your throat (you can help this to happen by sticking your lips out, causing a tunnel to form forward and back down your throat), almost close the front of your mouth and hunt for the resonance. Experiment. This technique get better with practice – a *lot* of practice.

A Special Note About Problem 8

There are two special reasons why some singers have problems with the chest voice: psychological barriers and medical history. Some of the men I've taught arrive unable to use the chest voice even when they speak. (Speech is produced predominantly in the chest voice.) Psychological problems are tackled in Problem 15.

The medical-history problem, however, is generally due to childhood illnesses in the chest – asthma, pleurisy, pneumonia, etc – causing the child to avoid using the chest for the voice because it is irritating or painful. Assuming that the medical problems are resolved, or that the doctor has agreed to the singing, opening up the chest voice is largely a matter of patience and ambition.

Problem 9: Men – I Can't Get Any Power In The Middle Of My Voice

This can be quite a serious problem for men, particularly in the early stages of singing. It's usually caused by a lack of development in one half of the voice, which can be either high or low. In other words, it is a problem of range. A lot of men have said to me, 'I'm quite satisfied with my range; I just want to improve the tone in the middle of my voice.' This is self-contradictory – being too easily satisfied with the range *causes* feebleness in the middle registers. Traditionally, this area of the voice is called the *feigned voice* because, for many singers, it has to be manufactured by building up other parts of the voice, ie the head voice and the chest voice. (See Chapter 1, 'The Range'.)

The mid range isn't a naturally powerful area of the male voice. You can't *force* these notes or you'll be in real trouble, so you need to borrow some tricks from other parts of the voice. The basic principle is that you should concentrate on the half of the voice that works least well until you've brought it up to the standard of the other half, which it will probably overtake. Then work on the other half to bring it up to the standard of the half on which you've been working. This begs the question 'How do I know which half is better?'

My advice is to start with the high notes. This will stretch the soft palate, without which the tone of the mid voice will always remain dull. Stretching the soft palate will always focus and brighten up the entire voice, as long as you don't try to sing from the throat; instead, focus in the nose – it's much safer. Go for a bright sound in the natural voice, which at this pitch should be loud. Don't try to produce high notes quietly; they're naturally louder than low notes. However, make sure that they don't go into falsetto, which is too easy at this pitch;

the top of the natural voice is much harder. If you go into falsetto every time it gets difficult, you'll never solve the problems in the mid range.

However, if you can get a decent sound on the high notes but the mid-range and low notes sound woolly (or you can't get the low notes at all), work mostly on the low notes – I mean the *really* low notes – until they improve. It might you a while to work your way down to them. A whisper is enough to start with. Let it grow in its own good time. Continue to exercise the deep, deep voice until it becomes resonant and reliable – this will lend an edge to the middle registers. You need both high and low. This will certainly convince everyone that you have a powerful voice.

But don't force the low notes. Have patience. You'll find that the mid range will improve a lot with them.

Answer 9a: Difficulty With The High Notes
Treat this in the same way as Problem 5.

Answer 9b: The Deep Notes
If the high notes are good, treat this in the same way as Problem 8.

Problem 10: Women – I Can't Get The Chest Voice Up Very High
This is crucial in modern singing. It's generally the problem of not singing loud enough to get hold of these notes, so they break into falsetto and it all remains weak and feeble. This is the most powerful part of the female voice, but be prepared to have to do some hard work.

You need to work on the sustained exercises of the chest voice, going right down to the death-metal notes. You might have to be patient with them – just persevere. Then you need to build up your diaphragm control until the notes are really loud. (Make sure that you don't allow the voice to break into the head voice when it passes the dreaded A♭ in the middle of your voice. If that happens, it means that you're not going loud enough to keep these notes in the chest voice.) You'll then be ready to work the diaphragm exercises up to the top of the chest voice.

Always start your workout with at least one exercise to take you right up to the highest notes of the head voice so that you stretch your soft palate, even if you're never going to use them in songs. This pays dividends, improving the control right through your entire voice.

Answer
Treat this in the same way as you would Problem 8, then do Exercise 15 (arpeggios). Then, if you're feeling very brave, do Exercise 4. You'll have to do Exercise 15 loudly in order to stop things from breaking into falsetto. There is no quiet way of getting hold of these high notes in the chest voice. Take a good breath with the diaphragm, keep your head down, be brave, determined and loud – and constipate for all you're worth. When you've made these notes secure (and it might take a while), then, and only then, you can turn your attention to softening them off.

Problem 11: Women – I Can't Soften The High Notes Of My Chest Voice Without Going Into Falsetto
This is virtuoso stuff. Effectively, what you need to do is join up the two halves of the voice by mixing and blending the voices in the middle registers. For this to happen, you need to get both head voice and chest voice working fully. This is much more difficult than in classical singing, where the head voice predominates and the middle voice is expected to be 'prettified' by the head voice. In modern singing, the chest voice predominates. It is powerful, but you need to be able to soften it when you want to without it sounding too girly.

Answer
First, exercise the head and chest voices fully. You would be wise to start with Exercise 1, but the crucial exercises are 14 and 15. Even so, don't exclude other chest-voice and diaphragm exercises.

Then, after the chest voice, concentrate on the female mixed voice (Exercises 21–25). Do them endlessly, but keep them easy and effortless. No pressure!

Problem 12: I Make A Horrible Sound When I Sing
We all do. I'll tell you a secret: very few singers actually like the sounds of their own voices. We struggle with this malicious thing called The Voice. We train it, pamper it and have blazing rows with it. We actually shout at our voices, while other people abuse our voices, too: 'Why don't you stop making that bloody horrible racket?!'

We record it. We play it back to ourselves. We think, 'This is going to sound dreadful,' and it sounds even worse than we expected. In fact, it doesn't even sound like us. That wasn't what was going on in our heads when we sang it. Recordings are cruel – they tell the truth without pity. Then one day we play our latest efforts back to ourselves and we think, 'That's not as bad as I expected.' Then you *know* you're improving. If you can please yourself on a tape recorder – even if only slightly – you're making progress. In the meantime, however here are a few tips.

Answer

First, keep your tongue down. Try to make the tip of it touch your bottom teeth or bottom gum when you sing. This will usually get you out of trouble if you're using most of the other singing techniques mentioned in this book. However, if you let your tongue wander around aimlessly, the singing is likely to sound rough or tuneless. You can push the tongue quite hard against the bottom teeth and gums – you won't do any harm, although it might make the words difficult to pronounce at first. When you become accustomed to this, though, it will seem quite natural and easy – and you'll like the sound.

Also, keep your head down. Many singers make the mistake of lifting or tipping their heads back too much. There are certain effects at certain dynamics at certain pitches (notably in the mixed head voice) which can be helped by lifting the jaw and stretching the front of the neck. However, if you're getting a rough sound (and, probably, a rough throat) while lifting your head, this is generally a sign that you should bring your head down. For most singing, in fact, it's best to keep your head down.

Keep your shoulders down, too. Under pressure, many singers raise their shoulders in their anxiety to do better or take bigger breaths. This can be disastrous – it puts pressure on the neck, and you don't want that.

Look at your neck in the mirror when you sing. Are the veins and arteries standing out like organ pipes? You must transfer all of that enormous pressure to the diaphragm. The neck can't take it – it's the weakest part of the body – yet the diaphragm can. Take a deep breath with the diaphragm, puff it up like a balloon and use it to support your singing. Taking the strain with the diaphragm must become a habit, which means that you must lose the habit of straining the neck. Replacing a bad habit with a good one takes time – old habits die hard, as the saying goes.

You should try to exercise the entire voice, but don't be alarmed if you can't sing the very highest or the very lowest notes. Check the exercises in this book to see if there's a part of the voice that you haven't yet opened up. If there is, that might be the part which holds the secret of the individuality in your voice. Screaming isn't essential, but it would still help.

Also, remember that this book isn't magic and the exercises aren't foolproof spells; you still need to use your ear and work on the acting part of singing. Although I've tried to cover every eventuality, providing exercises for every sound and type of singing in rock, ultimately *you* are responsible for your own sounds. You must keep trying.

One last point worth mentioning on this subject: read the Guidance Notes for each exercise carefully, just to make sure that you haven't missed something crucial.

Problem 13: How Do I Find A Good Teacher?

Answer

There are two ways to tackle this problem: look at the classified ads in the music press or on web sites, or ask a singer to recommend a teacher.

The best way is to go to a lot of gigs. If you're impressed or excited by a particular singer, ask him or her who their teacher is. Most singers are happy to be told that they were good, but they will usually tell you that they've never had a lesson in their lives – they're just innate geniuses! But you might be lucky and get the name and telephone number of a good teacher. It's worth a try.

Beware of teachers who tell you that opera is the best training for rock – it isn't. I was trained as an opera singer and have sung both opera and rock professionally. Operatic training doesn't encompass the necessary range for rock singing, and the sound is too 'covered'.

Problem 14: Have I Damaged My Voice?

This is a very common question, and it comes in a number of guises:

Problem 14a: Have I Damaged My Throat?

First, if you're in pain, you *must* seek medical advice. However, it's difficult to damage your throat permanently by singing. You might give yourself a sore throat, and if you're singing from the throat, with no technique or support, you're likely to add to the damage. If you're seriously worried, give it a rest for a day or two and see if the trouble clears up. Nine times out of ten, it will turn out to be a cold.

Answer

When you come back to singing, you *must* pay attention to your technique: when to keep the head down, getting the jaw down enough and not letting it lock in the halfway position, keeping the tongue down, taking big enough breaths, supporting it with the diaphragm and other power muscles, etc.

Problem 14b: Have I Damaged My Vocal Cords?

Your vocal cords, which should really be called vocal folds (see *vocal cords* in the 'Glossary') are well protected, very small (about a quarter of an inch long), very thin, flat and invisible from the outside. If you can see pipes standing out on the side of your neck, these aren't the vocal cords; they're probably the carotid arteries, and they usually stand out because you haven't taken in enough breath. Again, if you think you have problems with the vocal cords, seek medical advice.

Problem 14c: Will Screaming Damage My Voice?

The answer to this question is no – not if you do it correctly, the way you did when you were an infant. First of all, you must really *want* to scream, because screaming can't be half-hearted. It is the loudest vocal sound a human can make. The only way to scream quietly is to allow your defence mechanisms to strangle your voice, and that will hurt. You need to recognise that some registers in the voice are naturally quiet while others are naturally loud. If you try to force a loud sound in the quiet registers, it will hurt, but equally if you try to sing quietly in the loud registers, that too will hurt. Keep your head down, your tongue firmly against your bottom teeth and take the strain with the power muscles – the diaphragm, buttocks and leg muscles. If they don't hurt or ache a little, they're not taking the strain.

Problem 14d: My Last Singing Teacher Told Me That You Can't Sing Both High And Low

You can, as long as you don't use the throat. The evidence is overwhelming: singers who stretch their ranges just keep getting better and better (see Chapter 1, 'The Range', and also the 'Glossary'). This applies in every field of singing, from Steve Tyler to Dame Joan Sutherland, both of whom have been stars for a very long time. Those who exercise both high and low keep going far longer than those who don't. This is also why so many of the early heavy-metal singers are still going strong.

Problem 15: Coping With Nervousness, Fear And Pressure

I could write an entire book on this subject, and indeed I probably will! Singers, like most performing artists, are usually introverts – what they display on stage is the opposite side of the coin. On stage they can become the people they want to be. They have a 'handbook' telling them what to do in order to be extrovert: it's called the *script*, the *songs* or the *set list*.

However, at an earlier stage, when they go to their first singing lessons, they are nervous about what is expected of them. They may be frightened about singing high, low or loudly. They are almost certainly ashamed of the sound quality and whether it will come up to their singing teachers' expectations. In fact, you never need to worry about this – the singing teacher has heard far worse than you. A lot of this will be solved by constant repetition of the exercises listed here. You become used to singing high, low and loud. Familiarity is very reassuring, and with repetition you'll get very good at these exercises.

But then you come up against another effect of pressure: sabotaging yourself. Just as you are about to reach that golden note, that hard-worked-for climax…you chicken out. You strangle it by clenching the throat, or you change voices, probably collapsing into falsetto.

Then there's the fear of singing in front of people, particularly in auditions. Having paced backwards and forwards past the door, afraid to go in, you're unable to show what you can do when you finally do go in, and afterwards you tell your teacher, 'I didn't like their music,' or 'They didn't like my music.' You'll say anything to avoid meeting the challenge. Don't worry – you're not alone in this.

There are many solutions to this particular problem depending on the type of fear and the circumstances involved, but here are two that apply to most fears.

1 Fear is something to face down. Confront it as much as you can. Some singers and musicians cope with it by being outrageous, stripping off on stage, smashing up their kits, whipping each other with belts, drumsticks, etc, exposing themselves physically and emotionally, leading to a terrific rush of energy and, probably, a release of adrenalin. Most of us might find the thought of that more alarming than the fear we are trying to confront.

2 Singing under pressure must be rehearsed. Coping with it needs to be practised as much as the numbers and the set. For this, I recommend the techniques of drama training and improvisation. You need a teacher who will put you under a bit of pressure so that you learn to cope with it and, perhaps, forget to be frightened by it.

APPENDIX 1

30-Lesson Plan

This section is designed to coincide with the academic year, although it should be understood that reaching the standard required for modern commercial singing takes more than a single year. This section is geared towards the students singing all together or in groups – sometimes the whole class, at other times the boys all together and then the girls – thus avoiding the problem of most students doing nothing for most of the time while they wait their turns and the danger of individual exclusion. The sheer volume of an entire class (even a small class) singing these exercises and songs will be extremely good for morale. There is no need to hear them as soloists until the mock assessments.

As male and female voices climax and soften at different pitches, male songs in male keys don't stretch women's voices, and likewise female songs in female keys don't stretch men's voices. It is therefore important that men are given songs *for* men, either in the original key or in the key of the best male version. Similarly, women should be given exercises at the women's pitch and songs in versions expressly *for* women.

With rock and pop songs, it's generally best to use the original track as a backing or accompaniment. Trying to accompany them on keyboards, apart from being extremely difficult, diverts the teacher's attention from the students, who should be watched like hawks if they're to lose bad habits, such as clenching the throat. Backing tracks are fine, as long as the students know the songs very well, although they often have peculiarities in their introductions so that nobody knows where to come in, and sometimes they're downright incomprehensible! Also, when students lose their way with a backing track, it can be difficult to pick up the song from a few bars earlier when one bit of the track sounds much like another. All in all, it's easier to use a famous, or standard, recording.

In group lessons, it's probably best for teachers to use this book rather than the accompanying CD.

Lesson 1: Opening Up The Voice

Basic exercises for the natural head voice, Exercises 1–7, possibly leaving Exercise 5 until Lesson 3. In a large class, it's not always possible to hear everybody individually, but it is easy to see them – to see pressure on their necks, and to see the diaphragm being worked. As this cannot be over-emphasised, the diaphragm is the ideal thing on which to concentrate, particularly as it makes use of the natural competition between students in a class.

The strongest tool in the teacher's armoury is the ambition of the students. It's therefore important to satisfy some of this ambition at the outset. Songs that encapsulate all of the techniques in this lesson are (for the men) 'Prayer' by Claytown Troupe (Island, 1989) and 'What's Up' by Four Non-Blondes – demanding, but within reach at Lesson 1.

Lesson 2: Opening Up The Chest Voice

Warm up with Exercises 1–9.

Lesson 3: Recapitulation

A great deal of practical music-making involves repetition of the basic exercises, so the warm-up should be established at this point.

The Basic Warm-Up: Exercises 1–9

This should remain the basic warm-up, although it will need to be tempered by the individual requirements of both the students and the lessons.

Screaming should certainly be introduced by this time, as the students will be desperate to tackle the most demanding songs of Bon Jovi, Skunk Anansie, Aerosmith, Sebastian Bach and so on, all of which require a range that can be achieved only by practising screaming skills. Add Exercise 5, if it isn't already included.

Lesson 4: Building Up The Chest Voice (Women) And The Mixed Head Voice (Men)

Now is the time to work on the beautiful, smooth sounds. Do the basic warm-up, omitting the screaming exercises. Extend Exercise 6 as high as possible for women and add Exercise 16 for men and Exercise 10 for women. In the end, this difficult exercise for men will prove to be the most valuable, so spend a lot of the lesson repeating it. The 'ace' song for this sound in the male voice is Queen's 'Love Of My Life', while for the girls, anything by Whitney Houston.

Lesson 5: Diaphragm Articulation

This is very demanding and should be combined with chest-voice work. It is ideal for a class because it can be *seen*. Do Exercises 1–7 and 10, then introduce Exercises 11–12. For the men, perhaps follow this with a song using a lot of chest voice – something by The Crash Test Dummies, Pearl Jam, The Verve, etc. Most women's songs are in the chest voice anyway. Finish off with some mixed-head-voice work for the men to smoothe everything down.

Lesson 6: Intonation And Academic Considerations

It's tempting to leave the academic side of music out of singing lessons, but this is a mistake. The students won't make the connection between theory and 'real music' unless they sing them or play it. This is the time to introduce minor-key versions of familiar exercises (to be found in Appendices 2 and 3 – these are not on the CD). Alternate the major- and minor-key versions, paying particular attention to their intonation.

Lesson 7: Stretching The Range

The students will now be ready to make big, extravagant sounds. Do the screaming exercises, including Exercises 26 and 27. Try the men with the Bon Jovi song 'Santa Fe' (from *Blaze Of Glory*); they probably won't get past the first verse at this stage, so switch to a U2 song – 'I Still Haven't Found What I'm Looking For', perhaps, which will have become relatively easy after the Bon Jovi. The women will do very well with something by Skunk Anansie.

Lesson 8: Dealing With Individual Singers' Problems

At this point, your students can perform as soloists, perhaps in songs of their own choice. In practice, this is usually when they start to worry about forthcoming assessments and want to use this lesson as a preliminary mock exam. Let them have their way. They should have been given the test pieces by now, at the latest.

Lesson 9: Mock Assessments

One of the advantages of a class situation is that it has a built-in audience. The mock assessments should be in front of the class, even if the actual assessments will be in private (which is not essential until the finals). The students should be expected to clap loudly after each solo. It is perfectly acceptable at the mock assessments for the tutor to give instructions/guidance such as 'Now, take a big breath!' 'Diaphragm!' 'Tongue down', 'Jaw down', and to indicate *louder* or *quieter* by hand gesture. Many of them won't yet have grasped the connection between volume and range, that in order to go higher you often (but not always) need to go louder, or that in the male mixed head voice you sometimes need to go quieter to go higher. This is the appropriate lesson in which to deal with this thorny problem – briefly.

Lesson 10: Assessments – End Of Term 1

There are two questions here: What are the elements being marked and how are they to be assessed?
It is easiest to mark ten elements. For instance:

1 Tuning
2 Range and power
3 Tone
4 Dynamics
5 Diaphragm control/flexibility
6 Breath control
7 Is there any evident pressure on the neck?
8 Legato
9 Clarity of words
10 Controlling the *passaggio*, or being in the right voice at the right time.

Your students must be given a written breakdown of these elements and the marks they scored for each, even at the mock assessments. A mere set of tick-boxes – 'distinction', 'pass', 'fail', etc – is of no help to anybody.

At this stage, it's wise to offer a choice of two songs: one highish, one lowish. If you're teaching a large class, limit the time to two and a half minutes or so, which is generally two verses. After that, most songs go into a solo, which wastes time.

There's no need to set extra tests for specific elements; all you want to know is whether they can sing more difficult songs than if they hadn't come to your classes.

Lesson 11: Dealing With Weaknesses Revealed In The Assessments

As a general guide, a student should work on the weaker half of his or her voice to bring it up to the standard of the stronger half.

In the second term, problems of volume need to be tackled. As mentioned in 'Lesson 9: Mock Assessments', higher notes are generally louder than lower notes, and in order to get hold of them you usually need to take a bigger breath to support more volume. If mid-range notes are too loud, it makes high notes much more difficult. Your students must be aware of this.

Lesson 12: Death-Metal Sounds

These are fun. They require no force, merely searching for that enormous resonance. Here, use Exercises 32–33, particularly Exercise 33. Most death-metal singers can produce good screams, so it might be helpful to include a screaming exercise in the warm-up. Follow the death-metal exercises with Exercises 14 or 15, although probably not both – that might be a bit cruel. End with some 'koos' to lighten everything.

Lesson 13: A Fine Legato

This is the most prized ability in every field of singing. It takes long, painstaking work. Begin with the warm-up, leaving out screaming, and then spend most of the lesson on the quiet 'koos' – Exercises 16–25 – doing them all at least three times. Exercises 17 and 21 can be done in rapid succession at least a dozen times, possibly with a break of a few minutes.

Introduce your students them to the Dorian mode (Appendices 4 and 5). This needs to be done several times to make it familiar. Few singing students will have grasped it from their theory classes, but it makes an ideal exercise for the mixed voices.

Lesson 14: Focusing On The Mixed Head Voice

Repeat Lesson 13, adding the Phrygian and Lydian modes. In terms of songs, the men could sing 'Hotel California' by The Eagles, while the women could try Céline Dion's cover of Ewan McColl's 'The First Time Ever I Saw Your Face'. These songs are essential for their technical demands.

Lesson 15: West End Musicals

Bearing in mind that, at the end of the course, the students will need to earn their living, it's a good idea to prepare them with audition pieces. An audition piece for a west end show requires two virtues:

1   It must show off the voice

2   It must be something that the audition pianist has a fighting chance of sight-reading.

Songs that most fit these requirements are Andrew Lloyd Webber's 'Love Changes Everything' and 'Memory', both in the original keys. Make certain of that male top B♭ at the end of the latter – this can make or break a debutante, while all men can sing the piece without it! Do Barbra Streisand's version of 'Memory', making sure of that low middle section. Begin with the warm-up, including a recap on the three modes they've done.

Lesson 16: Hard Rock

Don't forget the need for the students to stretch their voices. It's high time to be outrageous – Aerosmith, Skunk Anansie, whatever. Guns N' Roses' 'Paradise City' is still good in a class for both sexes. Make them practise the fast enunciation.

Lesson 17: Opera

This depends on the tutor and his or her assessment of the students. But, in order to have an all-round music education, the students need to know something of the history of singing. They should, at least, be familiar with the classical style of singing – and after all, singing is only acting.

Begin with an abbreviated warm-up, changing the sound from the rocky style to the operatic style. Suggested arias: 'Non piu andrai' and 'Voi che sapete', both by Mozart, and, if someone's feeling brave, Giordano's 'Caro mio ben', all to be sung in Italian. Yes, they can do it! These are standard beginners' pieces, and they don't have to take them too seriously.

Lesson 18: Revision

Lesson 19: Mock assessments

Lesson 20: Assessments – End Of Term 2

Follow the pattern of Term 1 assessments, but with more demanding songs. 'Hotel California' (at the original pitch) and 'The First Time Ever I Saw Your Face' (Céline Dion version) should be two of the options at this stage, with their difficulty reflected in the marking.

Lesson 21

Term 3 should be devoted to dealing with shortcomings highlighted in the previous term's assessments, so a rigid programme of lesson titles is probably not very helpful. A certain amount of playing by ear is required. However, in a large class of men and women, it's likely that the male ranges will have been neglected. This is partly because women in their late teens and early 20s tend to support each other more than men of that age. They will all know that this is the last chance to stretch the students' ranges, and they will be ready to tackle the most demanding songs.

Lesson 22: Softening Off In The Male Mixed Head Voice And At The Top Of The Female Chest Voice

These criteria will certainly need to be tackled this term. For a woman, it means softening the high notes of the chest voice, while for a man it means starting a high note or phrase loudly and quietening it down very smoothly. These are very important and require great skill. Do the 'koo' exercises, using the modes. It is advisable to devote several lessons of this term to softening off.

Lesson 23: Jazz And Crooning

Crosby, Sinatra, Ella Fitzgerald, Billie Holiday, etc.

Lessons 24–27

In practice, these will all be revision of some sort. And they should be fun!

Lesson 28: Revision

The test piece(s) for the Finals should be known to the students by now. These must be memorised.

Lesson 29: Mock Exams

Lesson 30: Final Exam

This must stand up to scrutiny, so it's best to choose well-known songs, the demands of which are obvious, as test pieces. They should, for instance, each encompass a range of about two octaves so that there will be no doubt about the standard that has been reached.

APPENDIX 2
Exercises In Minor Keys (Men)

See the Guidance Notes for Exercise 1.

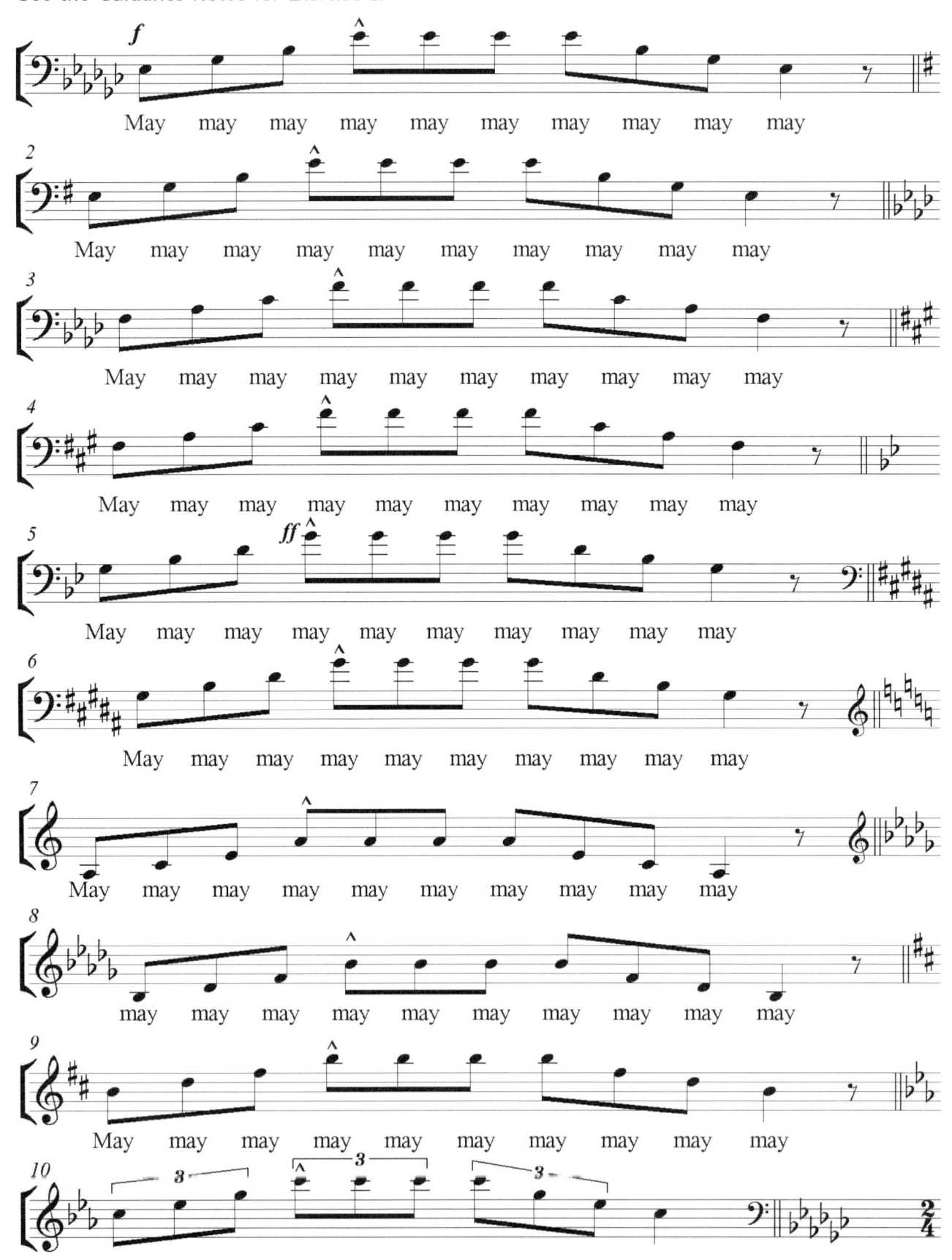

118

See the Guidance Notes for Exercise 4.

Note that, in the melodic minor scale (which is what singers generally sing), the leading note is often sharpened to make a satisfying cadence. This sometimes means that you sing a different note going down the scale from the one you sang going up.

See the Guidance Notes for Exercise 16.

Sostentuto (very smoothly and quietly)

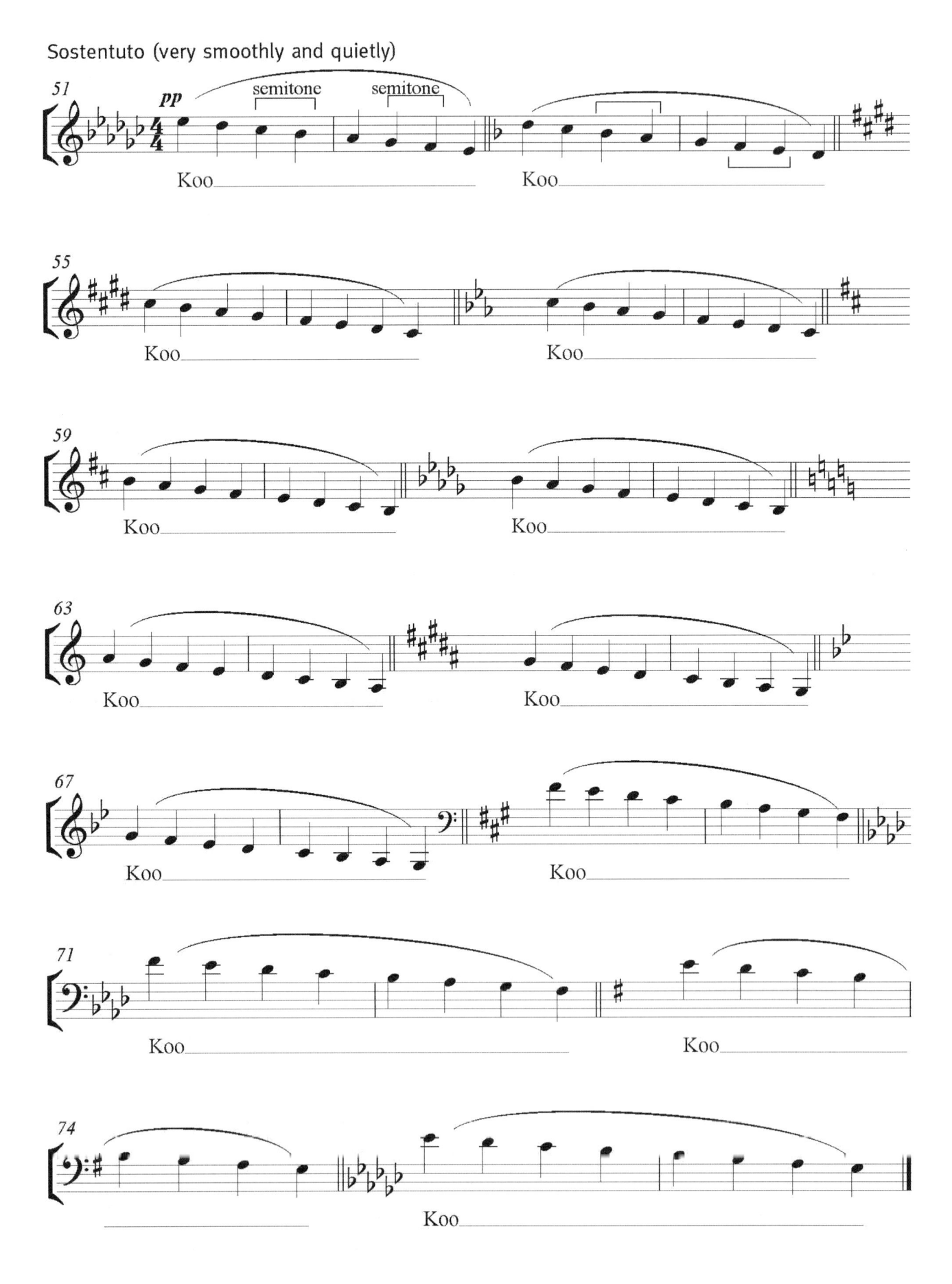

APPENDIX 3

Exercises In Minor Keys (Women)

See the Guidance Notes for Exercise 1.

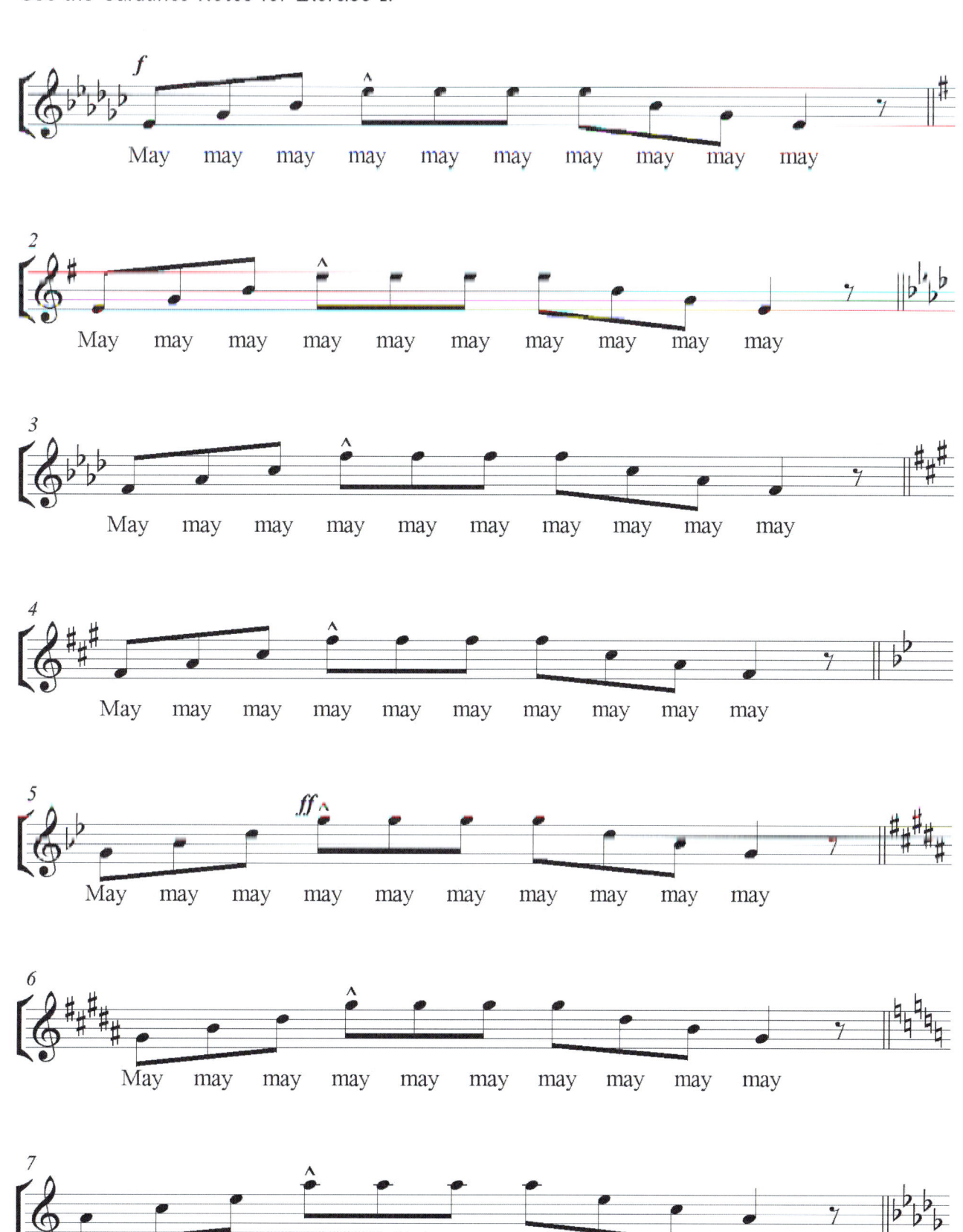

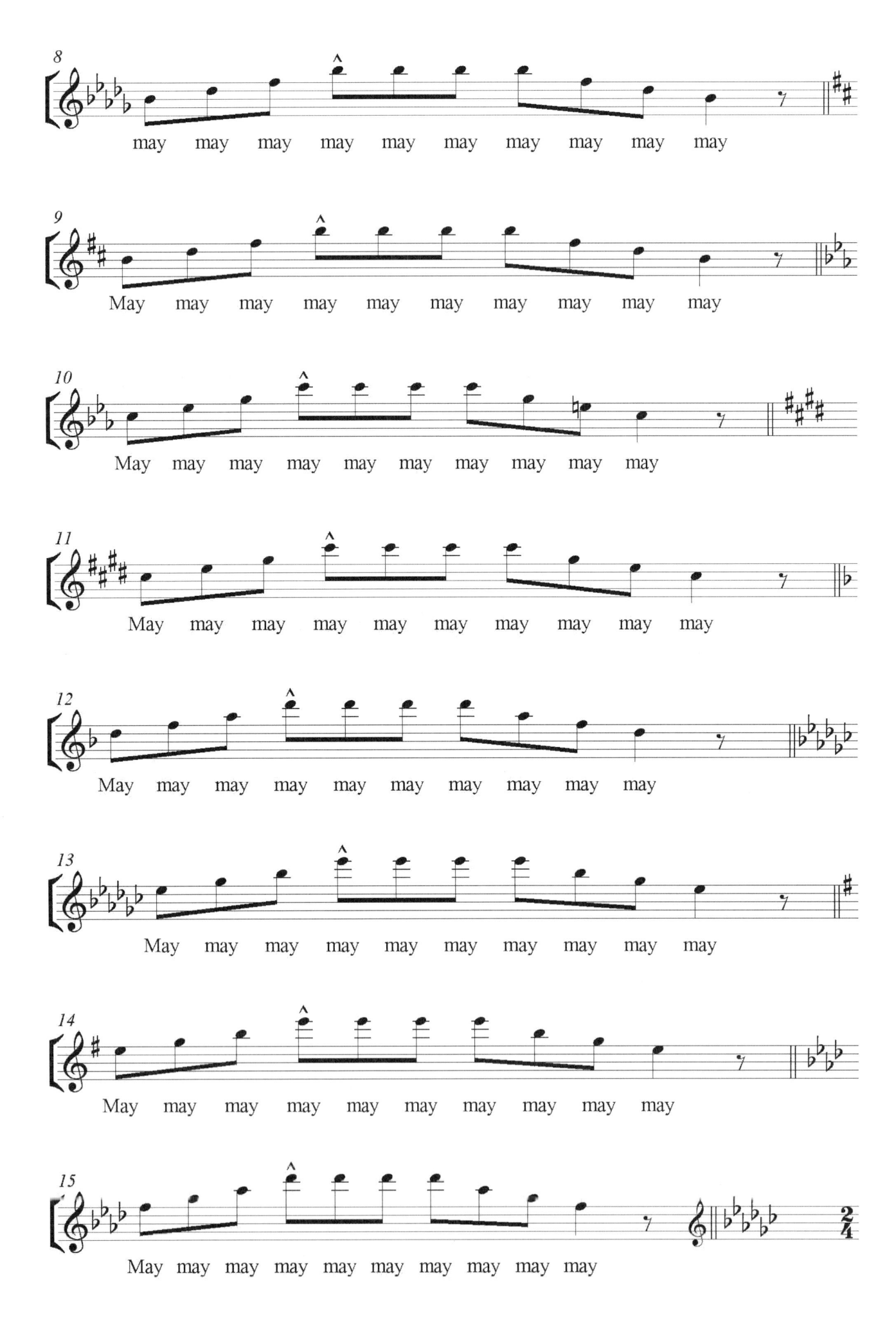

See the Guidance Notes for Exercise 4.

Note that, in the melodic minor scale (which is what singers generally sing), the leading note is often sharpened to make a satisfying cadence. This sometimes means that you sing a different note going down the scale from the one you sang going up.

Too wee_____ Too- wee_____

Too - wee_____ Too- wee_____

_____ Too wee_____ Too

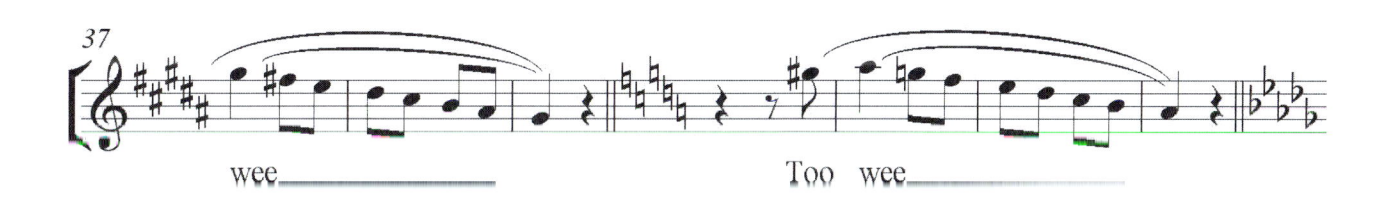

wee_____ Too wee_____

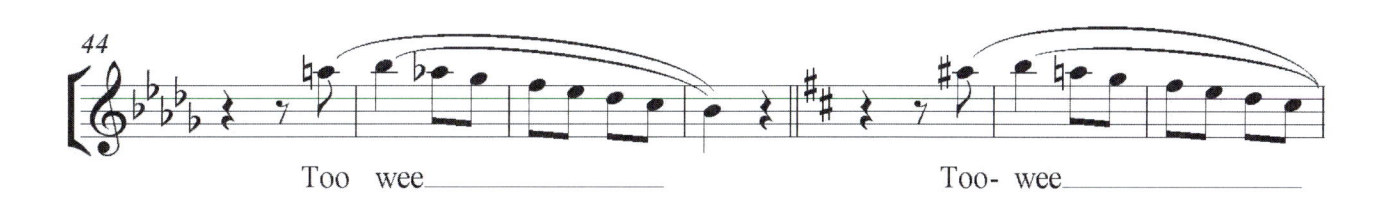

Too wee_____ Too- wee_____

Too - wee_____

See the Guidance Notes for Exercise 21.

Sostentuto (very smoothly and quietly).

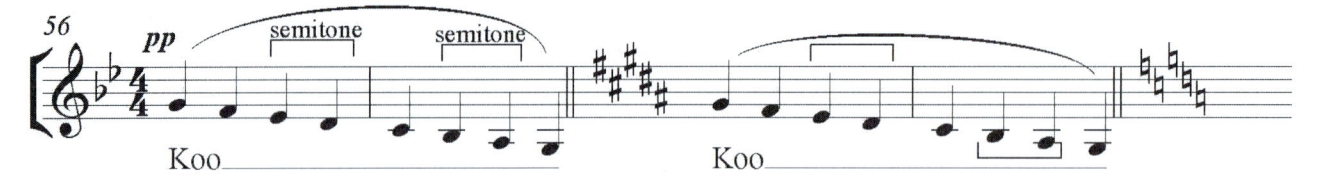

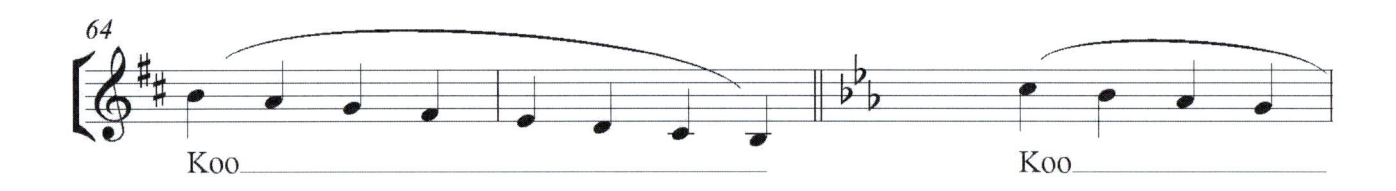

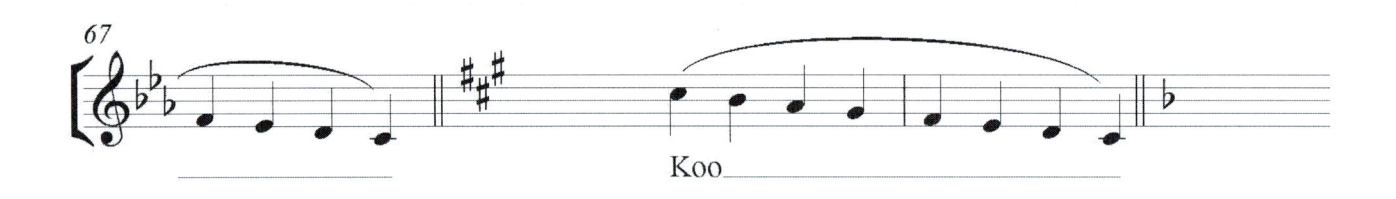

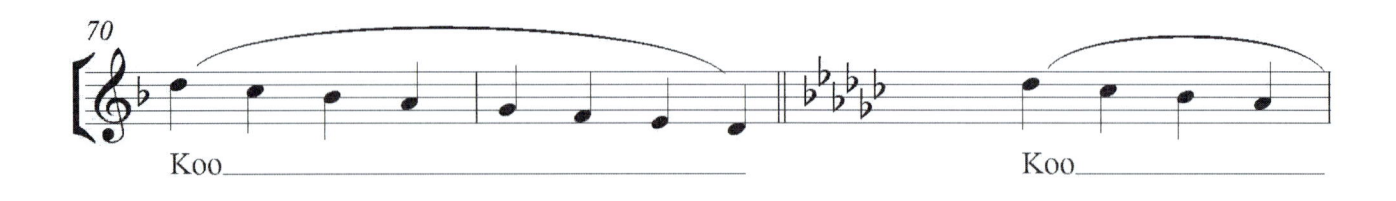

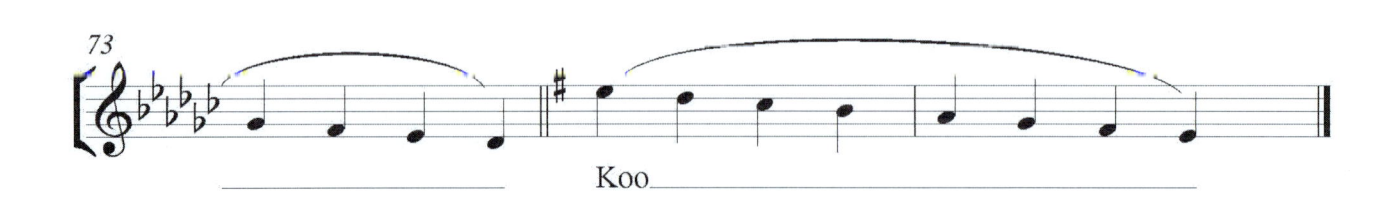

APPENDIX 4

Using The Major Modes To Enhance The Male Mixed Head Voice

1 The Ionian Mode
This is exactly the same as the major scale (see Exercise 16).

2 The Dorian Mode
Starting and finishing on the second note of the major scale.

I haven't written in the key signatures. You can see what they are from the scales.
Write them in for yourself.

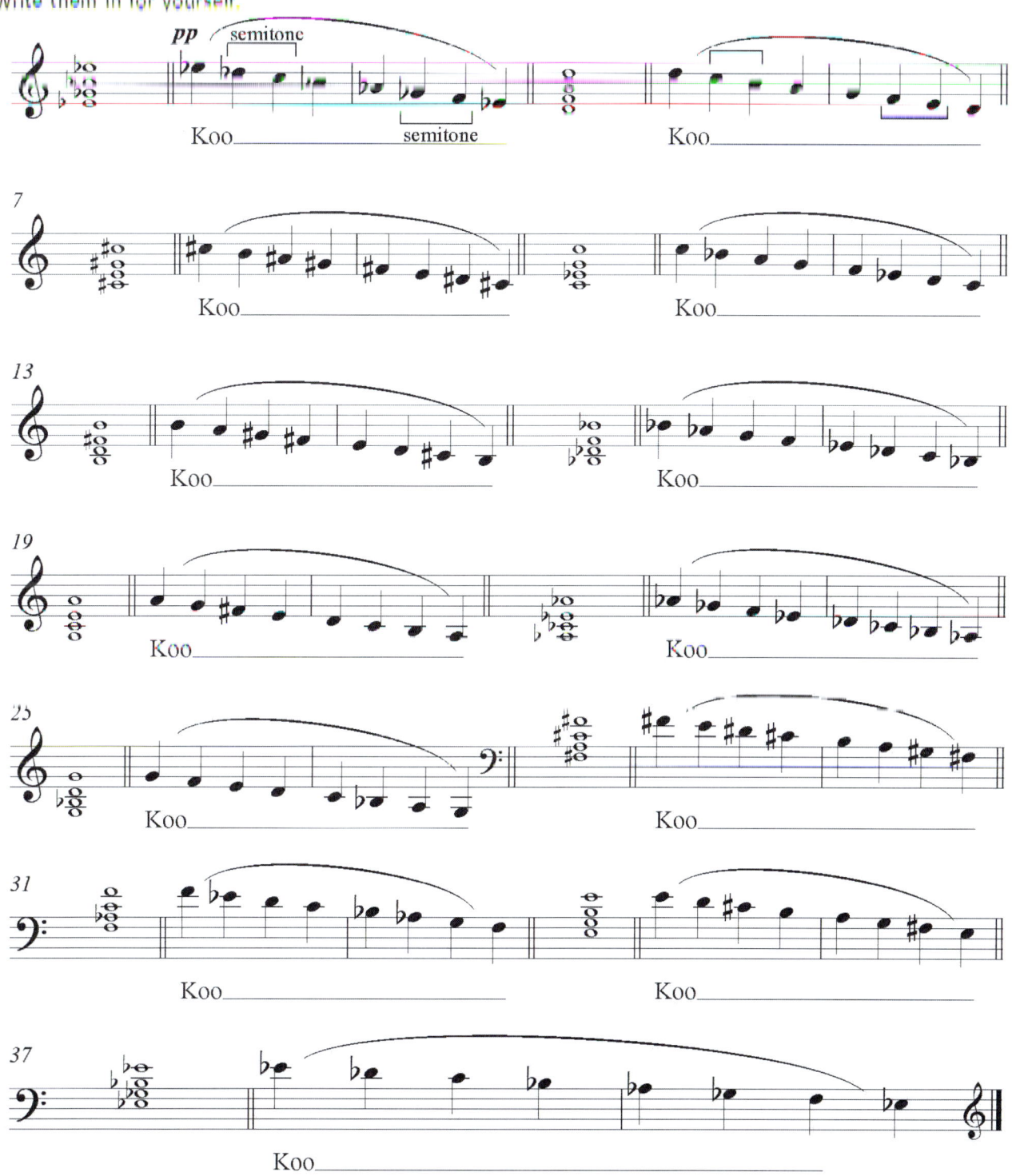

3 The Phrygian Mode
Starts and finishes on the third note of the major scale.

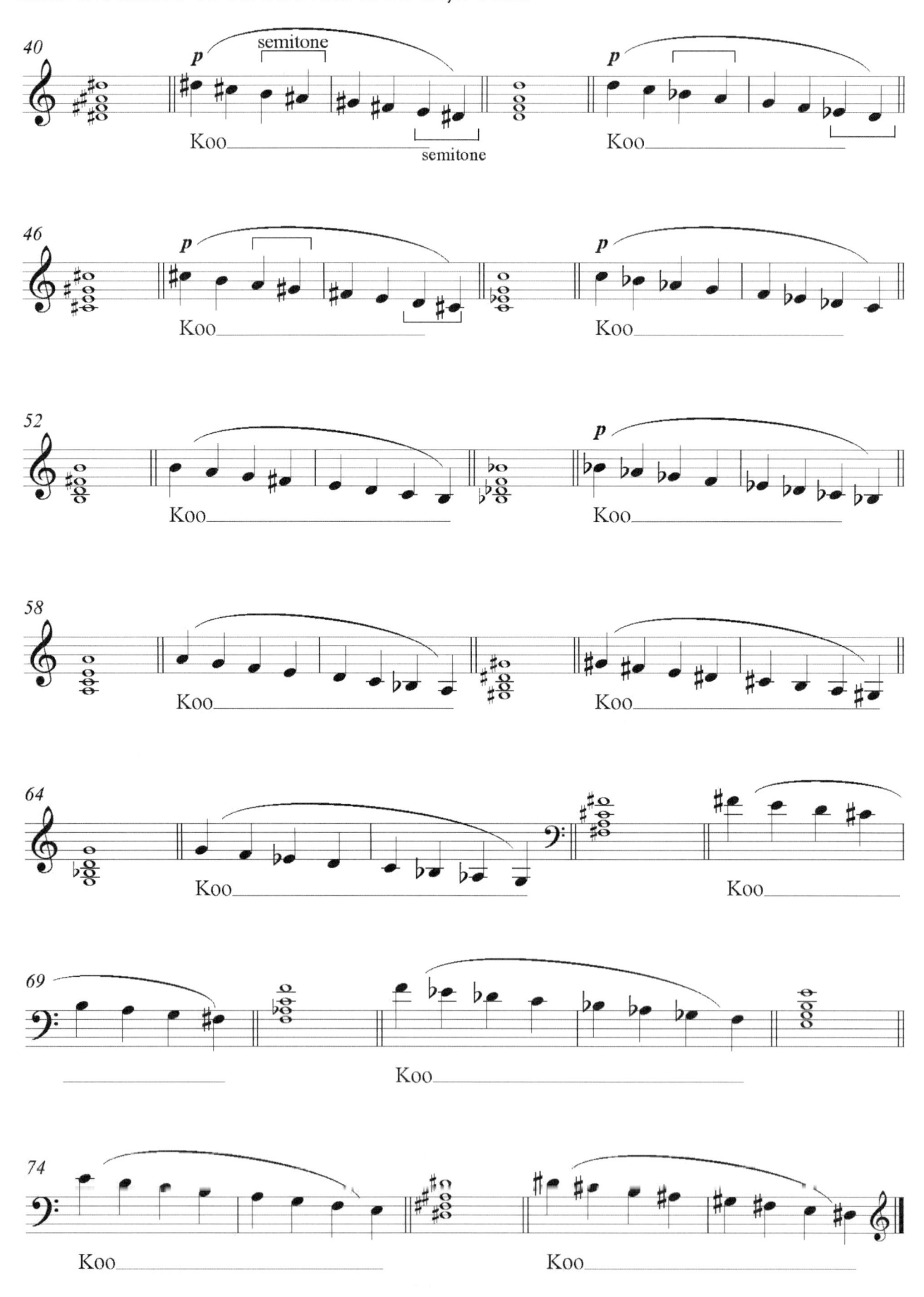

4 The Lydian Mode

Starts and finishes on the fourth note of the major scale.

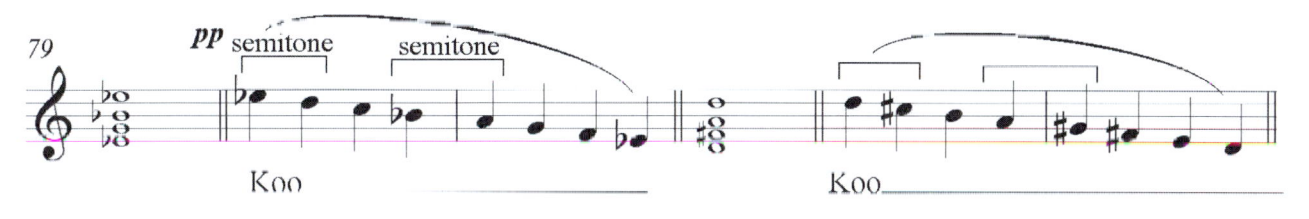

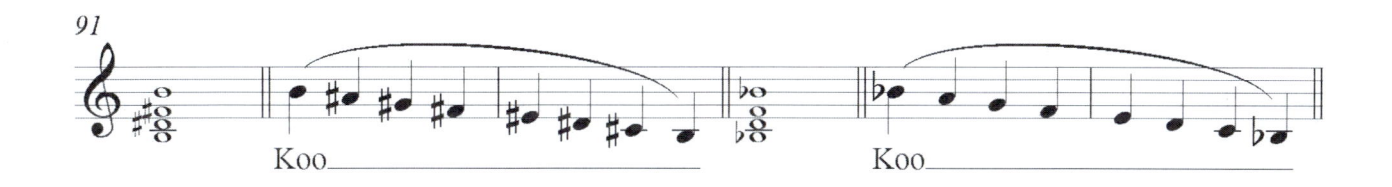

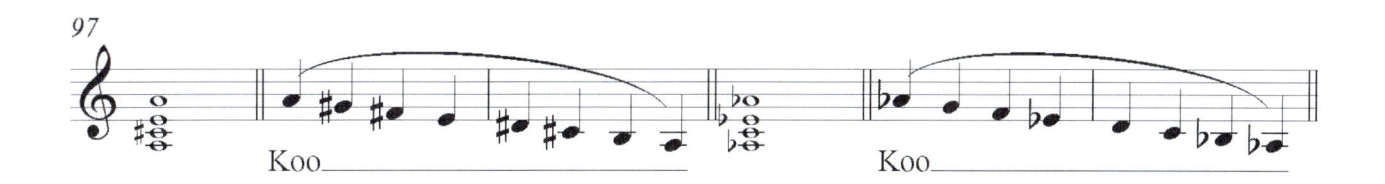

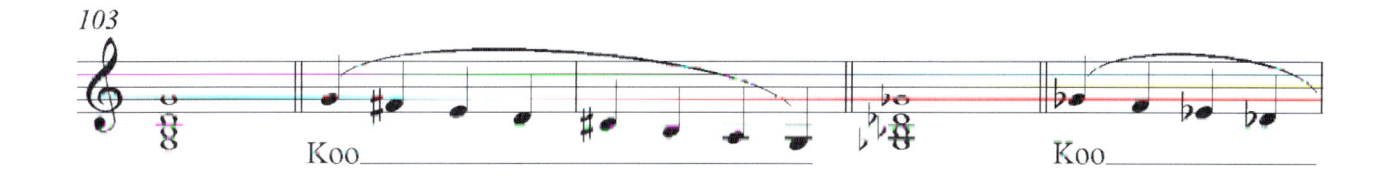

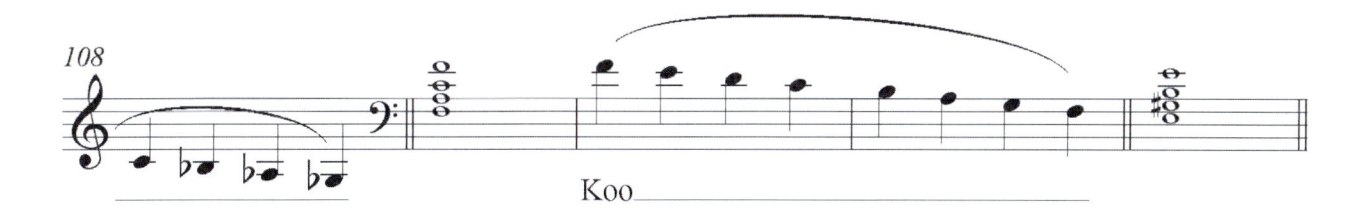

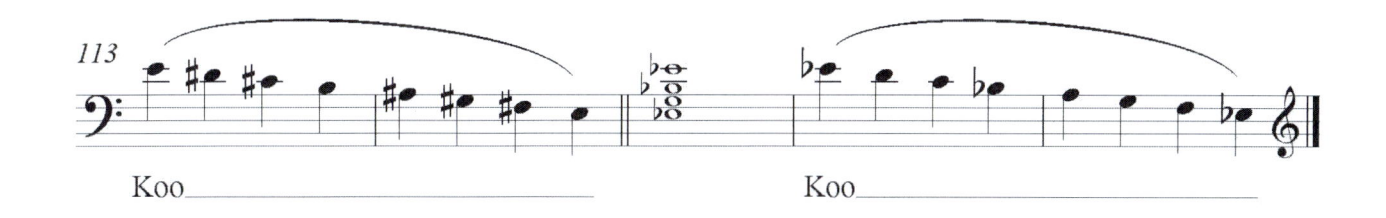

5 The Mixolydian Mode

Starts and finishes on the fifth note of the major scale.

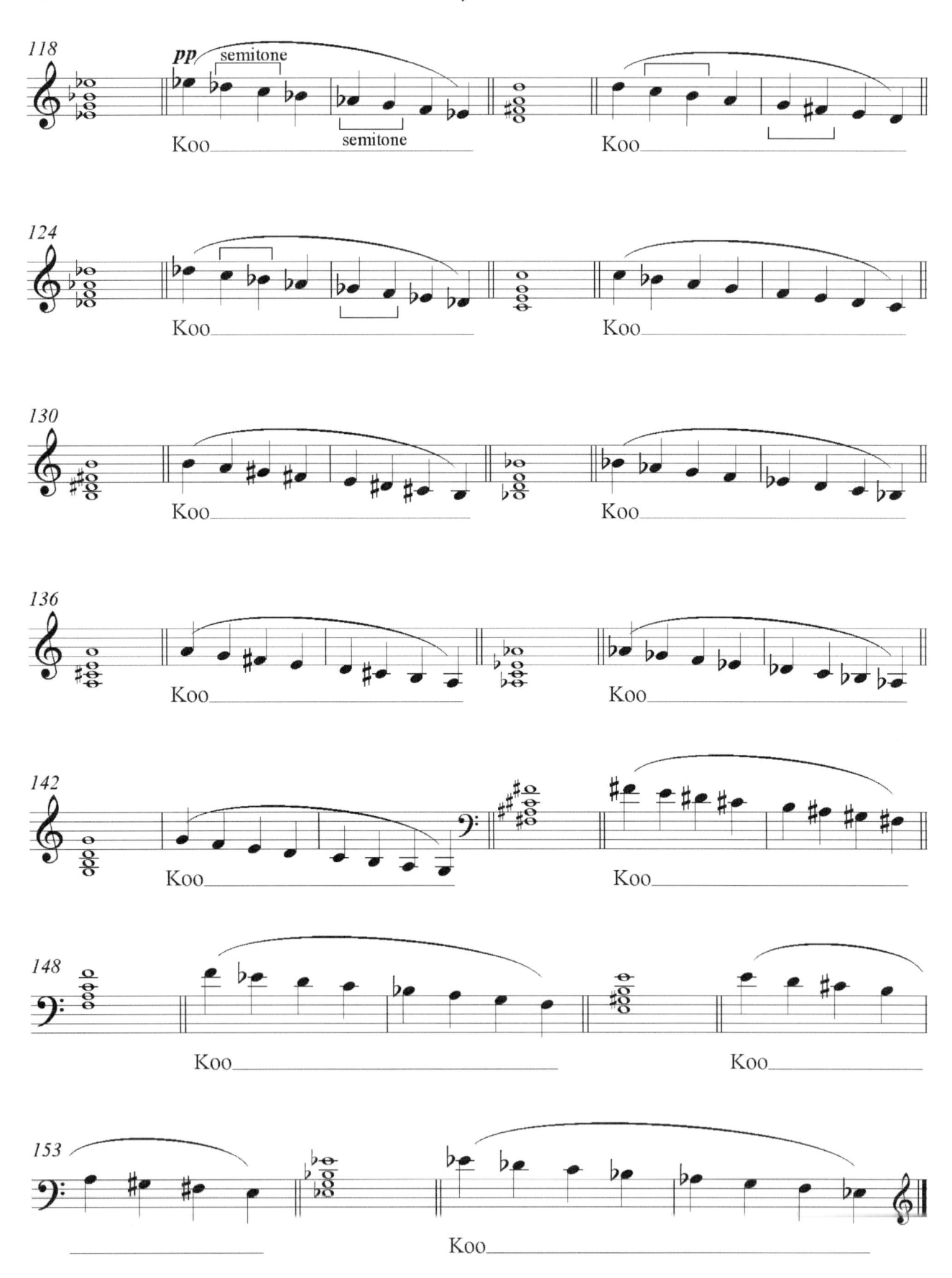

6 The Aeolian Mode

Starts and finishes on the sixth note of the major scale. This is also known as the natural minor, as if it was more natural than any other scale, or that other minor scales were unnatural!

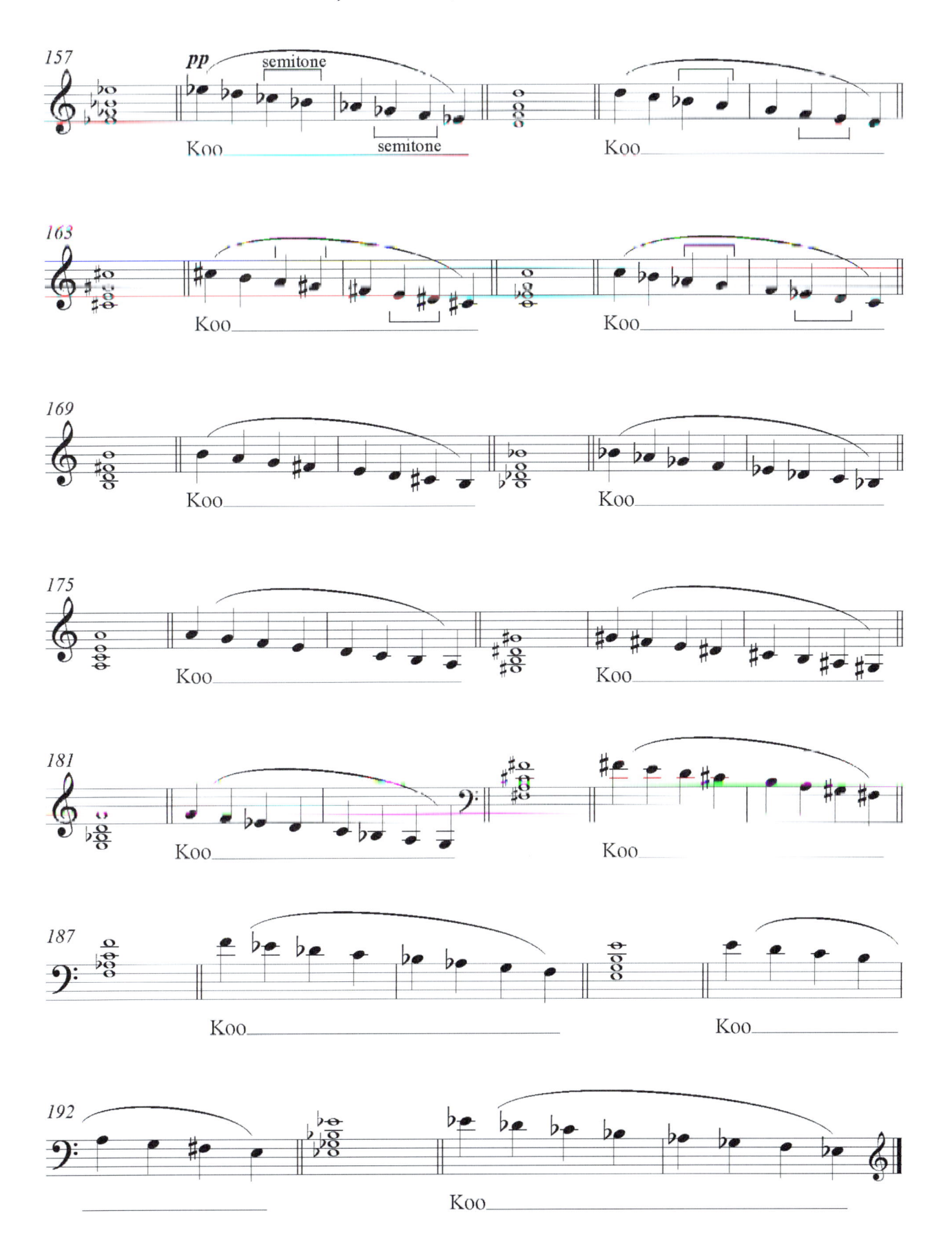

7 The Locrian Mode
Starts and finishes on the seventh note of the major scale.

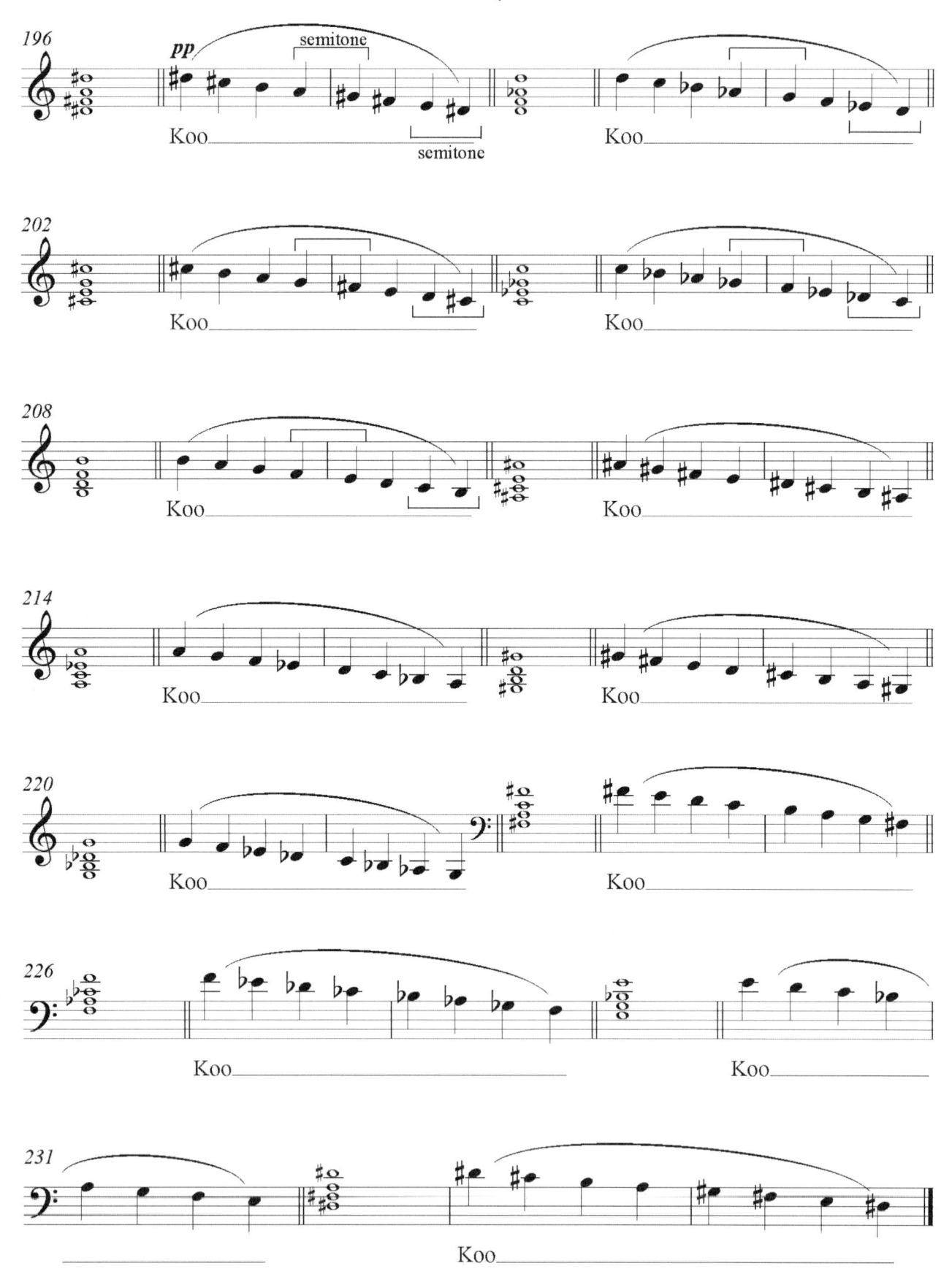

APPENDIX 5

Using The Major Modes To Enhance The Female Mixed Head Voice

1 The Ionian Mode
This is exactly the same as the major scale (see Exercise 21).

2 The Dorian Mode
Starting and finishing on the second note of the major scale.

I haven't written in the key signatures. You can see what they are from the scales.
Write them in for yourself.

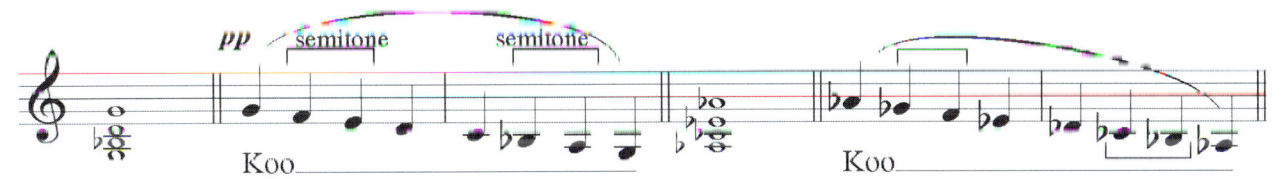

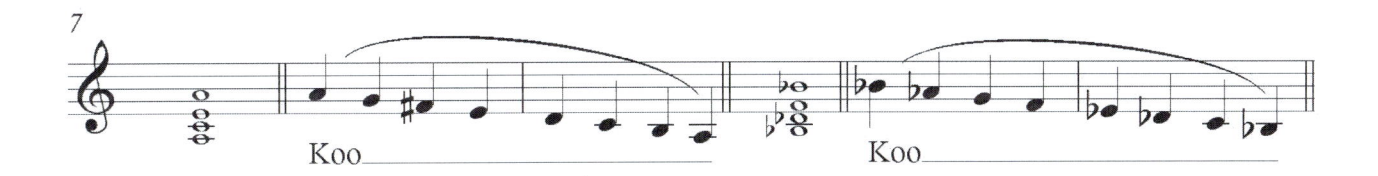

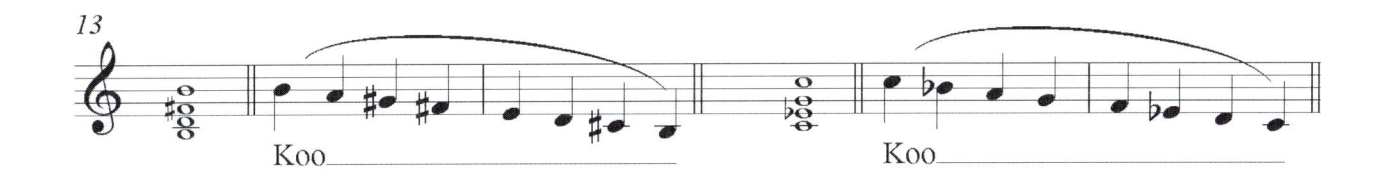

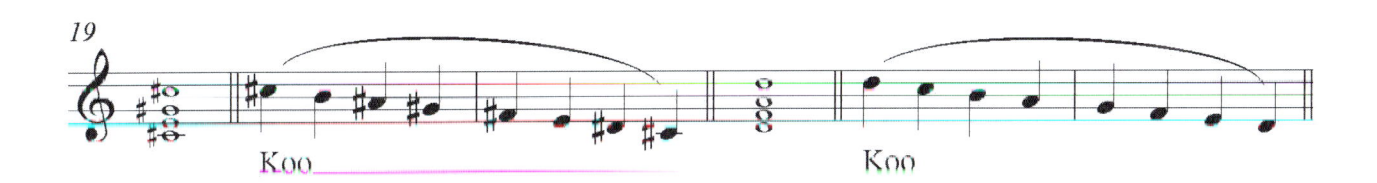

These last two scales are of limited use as exercises.
I've included them to complete the cycle of scales.

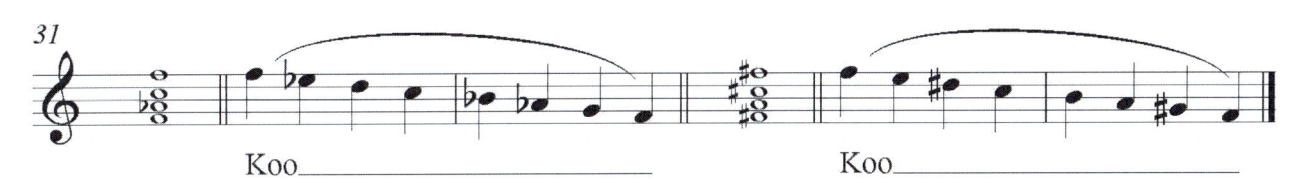

3 The Phrygian Mode
Starts and finishes on the third note of the major scale.

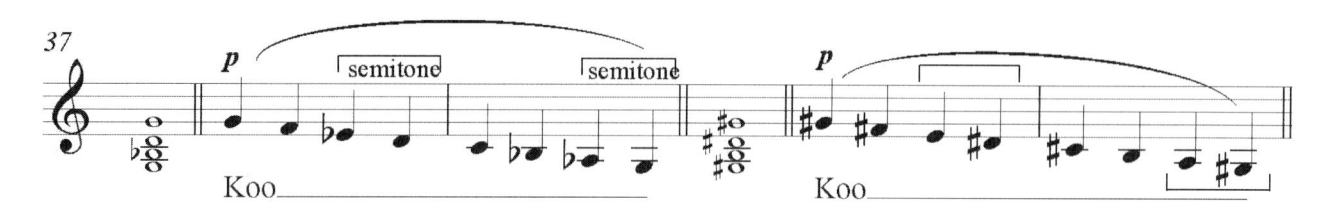

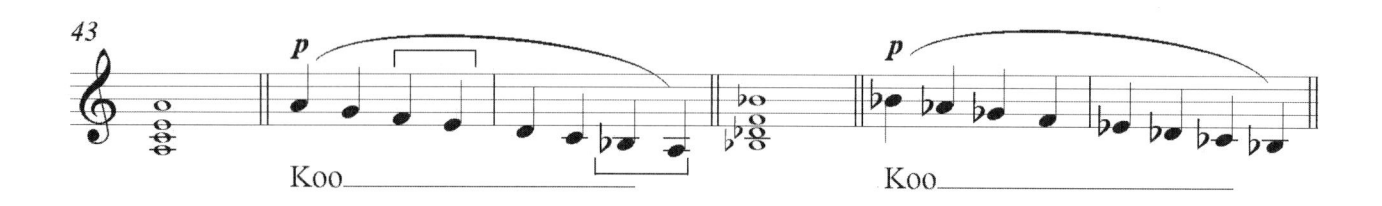

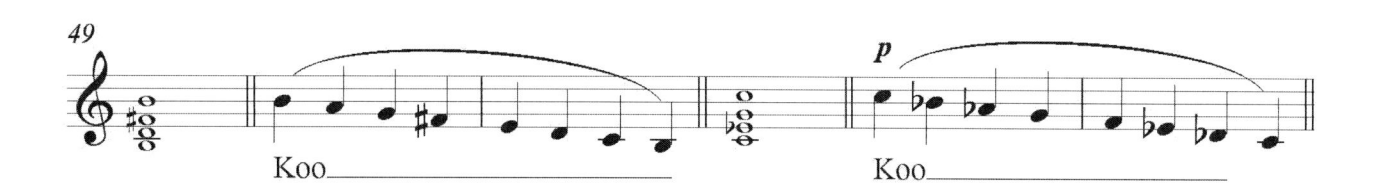

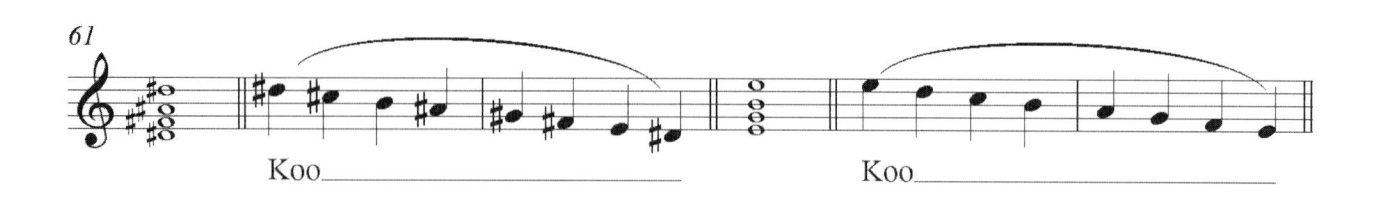

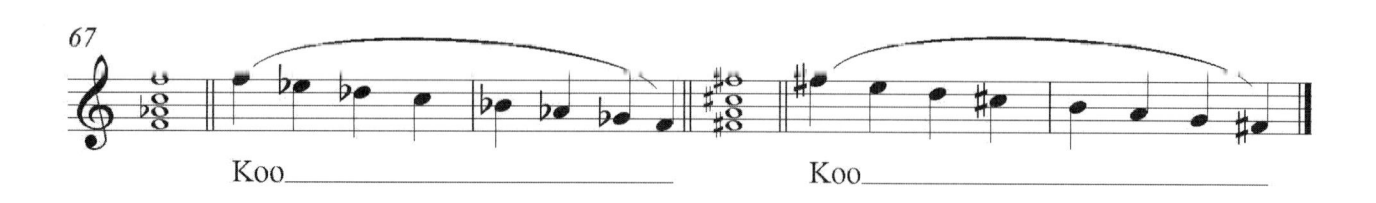

4 The Lydian Mode

Starts and finishes on the fourth note of the major scale.

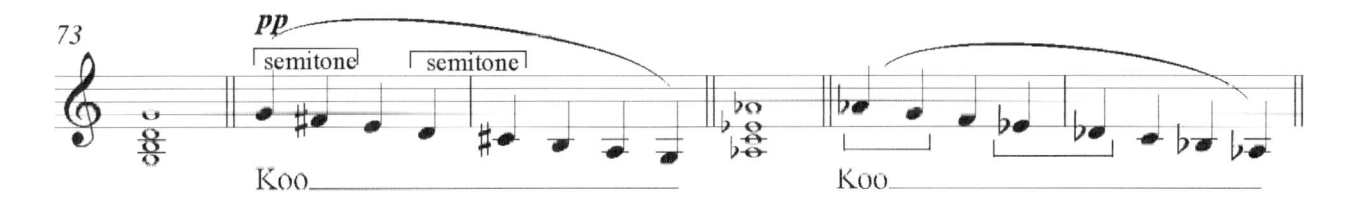

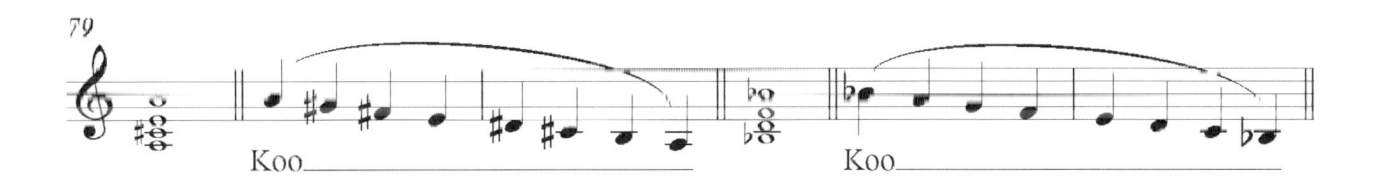

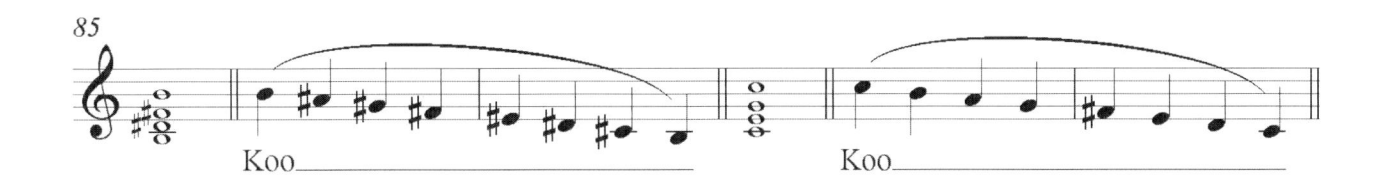

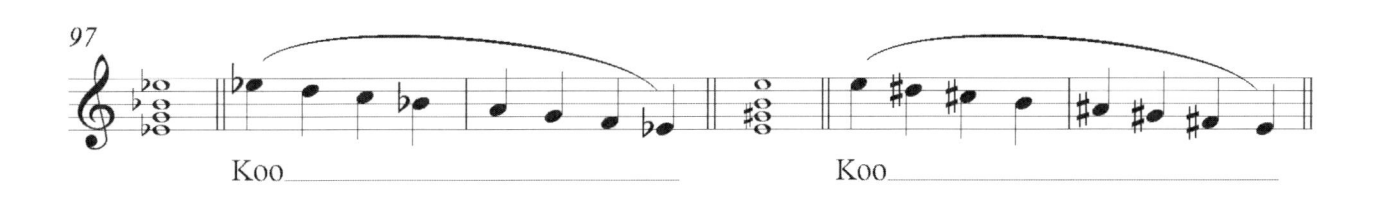

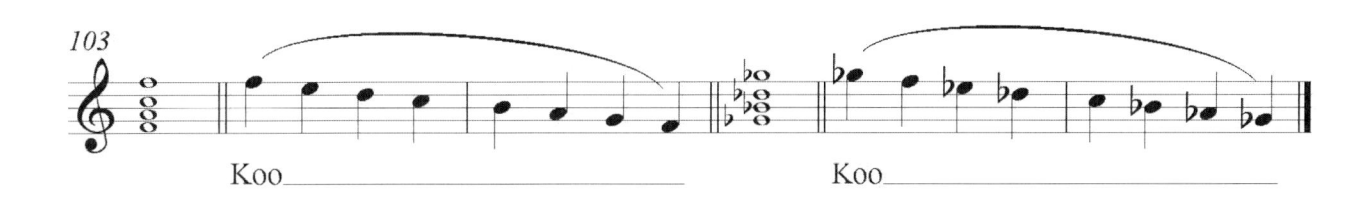

5 The Mixolydian Mode
Starts and finishes on the fifth note of the major scale.

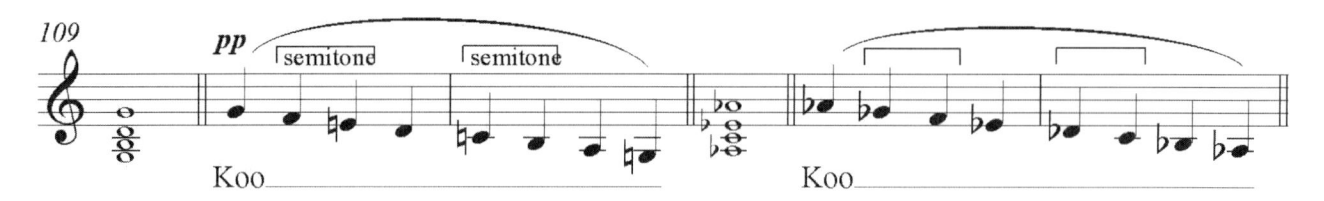

Koo

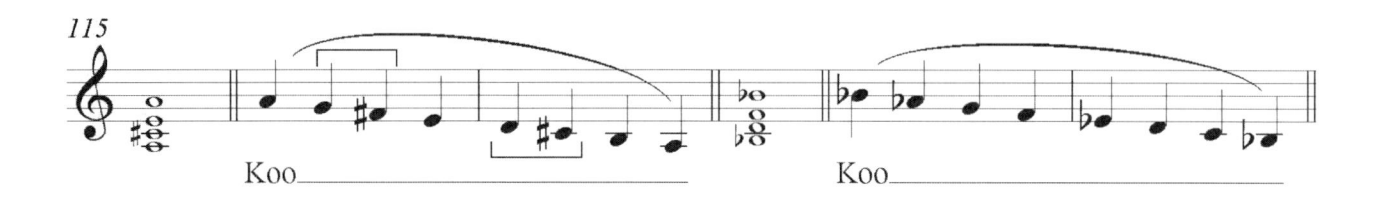

Koo

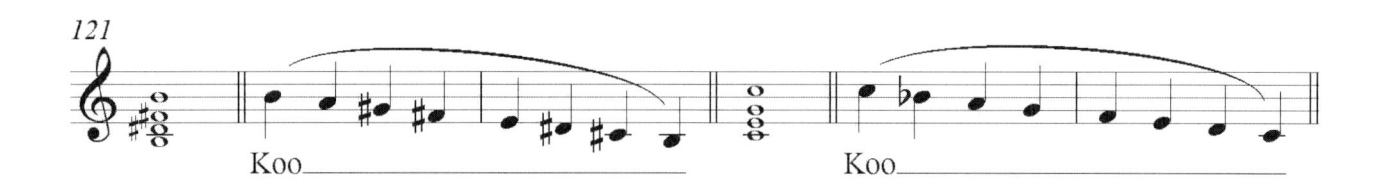

Koo

Koo

Koo

Koo

6 The Aeolian Mode

Starts and finishes on the sixth note of the major scale. This is also known as the natural minor, as if it was more natural than any other scale, or that other minor scales were unnatural!

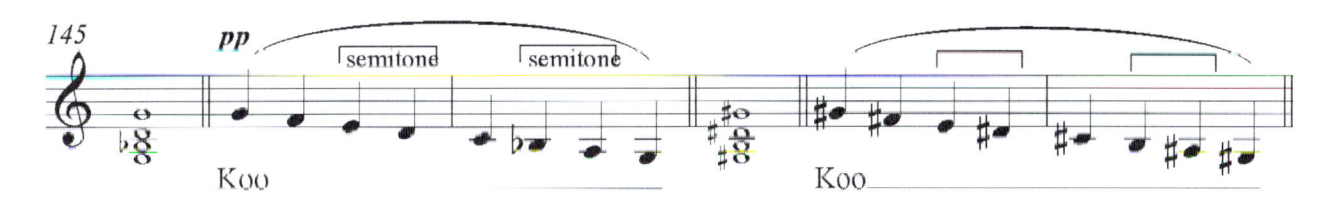

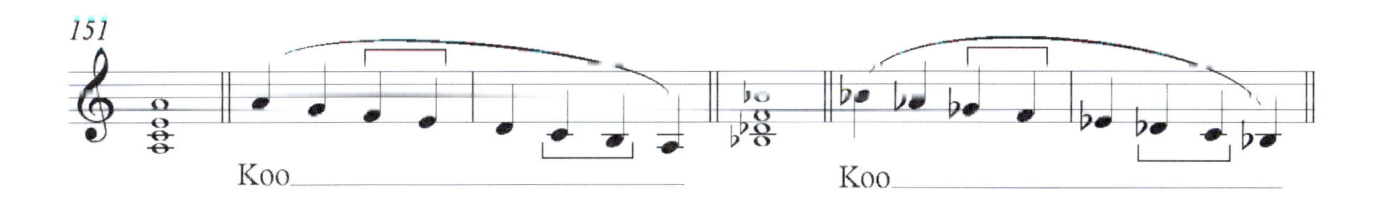

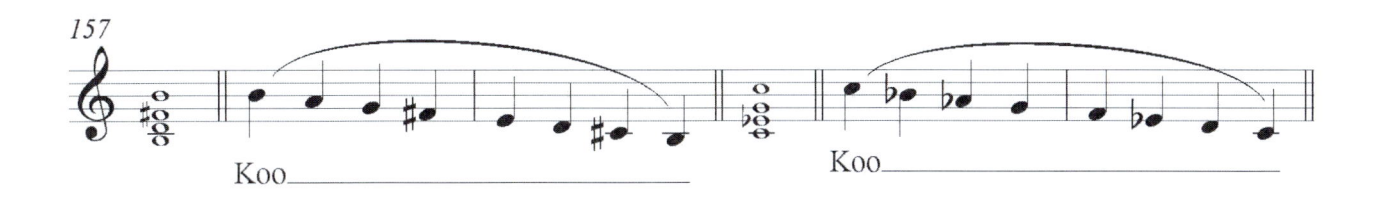

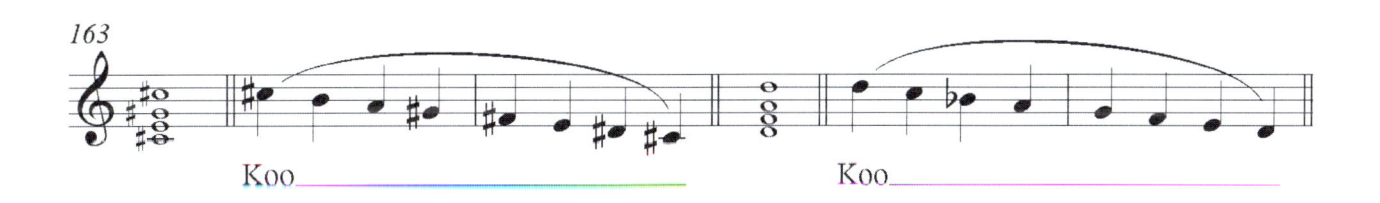

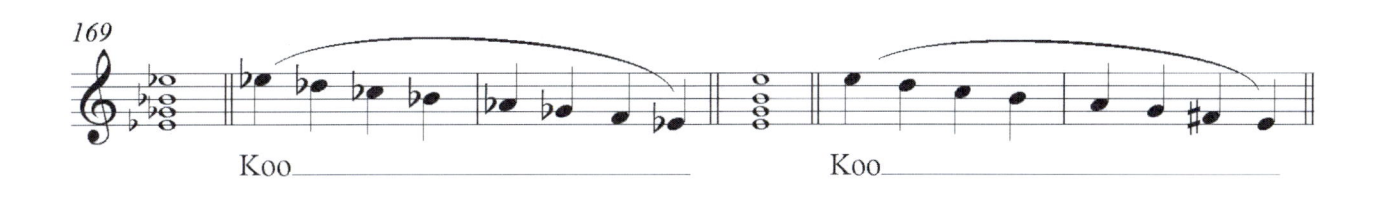

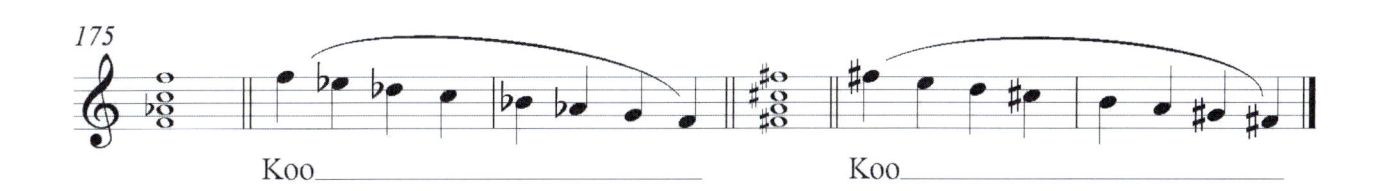

7 The Locrian Mode

Starts and finishes on the seventh note of the major scale.

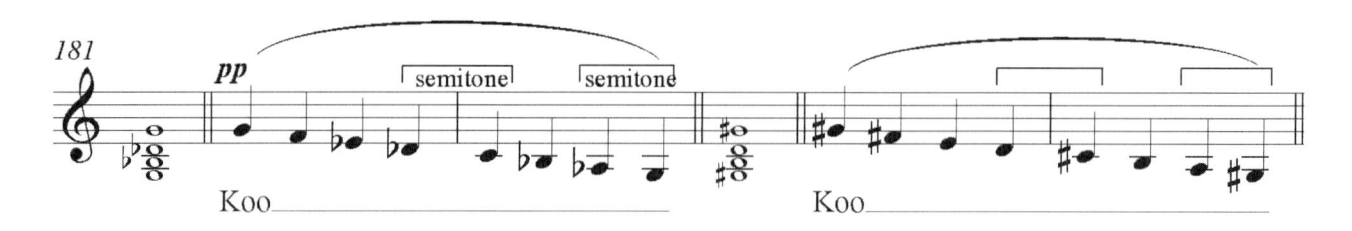

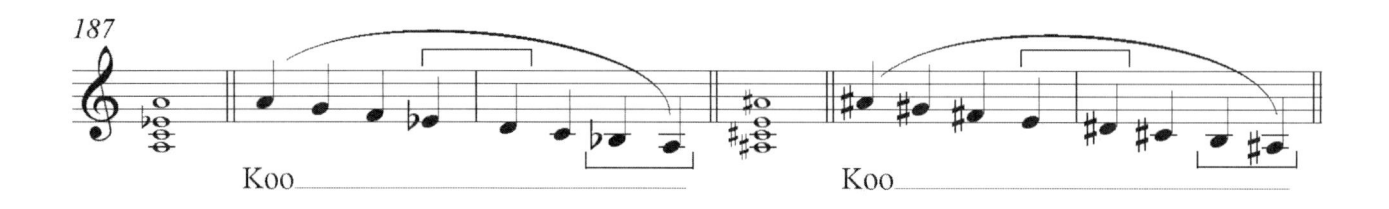

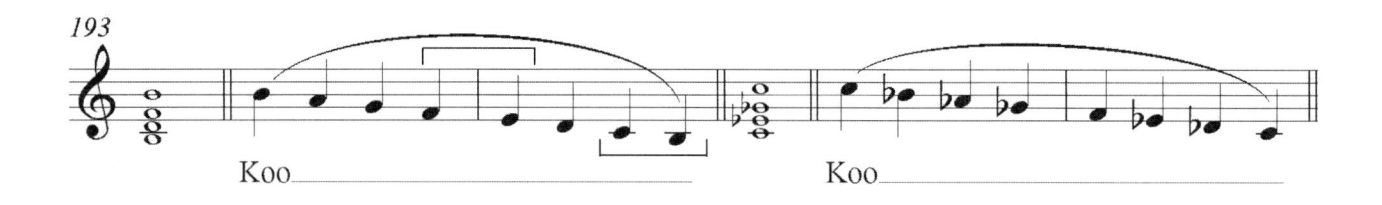

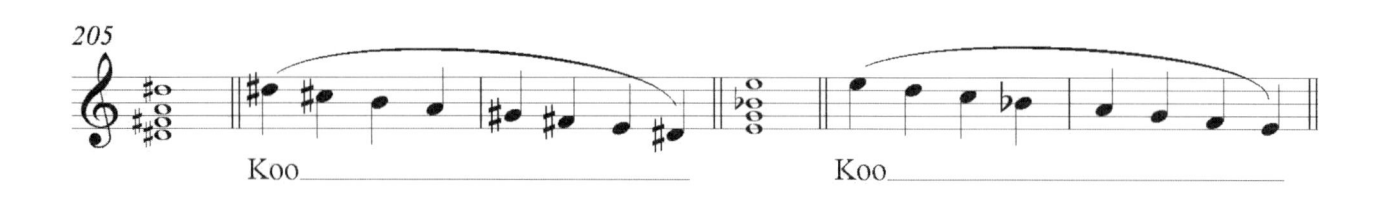

A FINAL NOTE TO TEACHERS

Although some of the exercises in this book ought to be familiar to you, many will be new, and some of them might even shock you. There really is no point in clinging to the theism of 'operatic training for everybody', including rock singers, or to the myth that screaming will ruin the voice, when the evidence is overwhelming that neither is true. This is not to say that you should be reckless with the voices of your students – of course you shouldn't. One of the most important parts of your job is to *listen*. Trust your instinct, but also trust your student's instinct. If he or she wants to explore the screaming voice, don't try to steer them away from it; teach them how to do it. This means that you too must learn to scream, if only to find out where the screaming registers change. A singing teacher's job is to teach the sounds the student wants to make, not to enforce the style the teacher wants to hear. Nearly all my rock singers can sing operatic arias, but very few of my opera singers can manage a serious rock song – they just don't have the range or the acting ability. The trick is to regard singing as pure acting: 'Pretend you're an operatic diva.' 'Now you're Axl Rose.' 'Now sing it as if you're fronting a boy band.'

All singing teachers should be able to demonstrate the sounds they're teaching. You should be able to sing the exercises and songs *with* your students. Don't just pontificate at them. They need a live demonstration of the *scale* of the sound they should attempt, or they'll be too nervous to sing loudly enough to get hold of the sounds they really want.

Singing teachers should be able to read music (both treble and bass clefs) and to have basic keyboard skills; it discredits you if you can't or don't. You don't need to be a brilliant pianist, or even a particularly good one, but you *do* need to be able to play the exercises. The way in which you strike that first E♭ chord for 'May, may may' will make a huge difference to your students' confidence, and also to yours. These skills are, after all,

not very difficult to learn, and if *you* can't be bothered to learn them, you're not likely to motivate your students. They aren't fools, so don't be surprised if they make slow progress.

Research

Research is crucial in every discipline, but singing has suffered appallingly in recent decades from a shortage of serious research. It needs to be done at PhD level, with the discipline that that entails, and this is where the current rules cause problems. The use of human beings as primary source material now comes under the heading of *sociology* in most universities, so now singing can be researched only under one of four independent headings: academic, medical, philosophical or sociological – not musical or artistic.

In the first category, we have musicologists wandering around Europe, ferreting around in archives and reading 500 years' worth of literature on the subject, a great deal of which is in Latin. Fascinating, but already well known.

In the second and most valuable category, we have doctors sending tiny cameras down throats to see what actually happens in the process of singing.

The third category consists of philosophers cogitating on the aesthetic conditions of singing. Philosophers rarely cogitate on the question of *talent* – that's far too difficult.

The fourth category has sociologists considering the role that music plays in modern cultures, which is a watered-down version of what philosophers do. For added mystique, they can turn their inattention to the sexual inadequacies of singers who sing too loudly, too quietly, too high, too low or too anything else that might produce individuality.

As few singing teachers have an appropriate science degree, it has become very difficult to join these disciplines together, so nobody (as far as I know) is researching what singers are actually doing – apart from me!

The upshot of this stranglehold is that most singing teachers, having no other institutional theory, are still operating in the theoretical conditions of 50 years ago – theory which hasn't changed since the days of Mozart and Gluck. Harsh though this judgement may be, I challenge anyone to produce empirical research which has been carried out in the last 50 years on the unprecedented developments in singing during that time, or on the training of modern rock singers.

There are, however, the productions of the rock and heavy-metal singers themselves, which are central to any research. Not only do these singers achieve phenomenal results, but they also talk a great deal about it, and I take their evidence very seriously. There are, however, three shortcomings: firstly, their evidence is anecdotal and unorganised; secondly, they're mostly too young to know about the development of the voice through a lifetime of singing, and so to some extent they are bound to be repeating theories they have heard; thirdly, few of them have the critical faculty required in order to construct any theories on which standard practice can be based. Nonetheless, this constitutes some of the most important evidence available on how the voice works and develops when stretched to its limit.

Do Your Own Research

Keep records of your students and their abilities. Note their ranges at their first lessons with you, and keep track of developments in subsequent lessons. Note where the voice changes, where the natural voice gives out and the full extent of the falsetto, both top and bottom, and that includes screaming. Above all, note their development in stamina and tone quality.

And Finally...

Enjoy the sounds and the styles of modern commercial singing. Don't try to clean them up where it's inappropriate to do so. Teach the sounds your students want to make and they will respond enthusiastically.

GLOSSARY

Absolute Pitch

Also known as *perfect pitch*, This is the ability to pitch or sing any note accurately from your own independent sense of pitch in your head, under any circumstances – that is, without an introductory note, and even if the band is out of tune. If you have perfect pitch, you will still be in tune. From my own experience, I estimate that one singer in 2,000 has perfect pitch. If you don't have *perfect* pitch you can still develop a very good sense of pitch so that you can always start a song you know well on the right note without an introductory note from the band. (See *relative pitch*.)

Adam's Apple

The lump on the front of a man's neck, actually the thyroid cartilage, part of the larynx. Although it's slightly flexible, don't attempt to move it with your fingers, in spite of what some books on singing tell you. Women have a similar structure, albeit smaller so that it doesn't protrude as an Adam's apple.

Breath Control

The ability to sustain long notes and phrases on a single breath. This is achieved by filling the lungs from their base (ie puffing up the stomach) and expanding the diaphragm (the front abdominal muscles) like a balloon. The chest cavity will fill up automatically, but it will help if you stick out your chest and deliberately expand the rib cage as you fill up. Don't move your shoulders; keep them down.

You can do all of this in a split second before you sing each phrase, in one single movement of breathing from the stomach. When your air supply begins to run out, start squeezing the diaphragm and continue until all of your air is completely used up or you finish the phrase. This takes practice.

It's not a bad idea to practice this on short phrases. Deliberately use up all the air on each phrase (by squeezing the diaphragm) – this forces you to take a huge breath very quickly in order to be ready for the next phrase.

There should be no movement in the neck at all during this – no tension, no arteries standing out or taking the strain. Do it all with the diaphragm.

Cadence

This is literally the anglicised form of *cadenza*. It means the close of a musical phrase or the fading out of the voice. In harmony, a cadence usually consists of two chords which, together, make a full stop or comma in the music. There are four standard cadences, listed below; if you can recognise them. Sight-singing becomes very much easier.

1 The perfect cadence – chords V-I (the most important cadence)
2 The imperfect cadence – chords I-V
3 The plagal cadence – chords IV-I
4 The interrupted cadence – chords V-VI

Although *cadence* and *cadenza* began as the same word, they no longer mean the same things. (See *cadenza*.)

Cadenza

An Italian word meaning an extended flourish or bravura piece of singing (usually unaccompanied) designed to show off the performer's capabilities, usually at the end of a piece. It is most commonly used in 18th- and 19th-century music, but it made a reappearance in hard rock and heavy metal when the singer wanted to finish with a bit of outrageousness.

Cappella/A Cappella

Italian for *chapel* or *in a chapel or church style*. It has now come to mean *unaccompanied singing*.

Carotid Arteries

There are two of these on both sides of the neck, one internal and one external. They are the main conduits of blood to the head. It is the external carotid arteries that are visible, looking like pipes when they expand under pressure from poorly prepared singing. This pressure often causes brief headaches and, in extreme cases, fainting. When these arteries stand out, it's generally an indication that the singer hasn't taken in enough breath with the diaphragm, but it can also occur when singing exceptionally high notes. Having these 'pipes' standing out on the side of the neck is never a good sign, but sometimes it is unavoidable. This is probably where the word *garrote* (to strangle) comes from, so take care!

Chest Expansion

This means filling the chest with a huge amount of air so that the rib cage expands and the shoulders are pulled back, making the chest appear to stick out.

Begin by filling the lower part of the chest cavity, thus expanding the diaphragm. From there, fill the chest, sticking it out, and at the same time pull the shoulders right back. The same thing can be achieved with a huge yawn. Make sure that you really are breathing from the diaphragm and not just taking shallow breaths in the upper part of the chest. Expanding the chest gives the voice a lot of power and will often counteract any tightness in the neck and throat. (See *diaphragm*.)

Chromatic

An Italian term meaning, literally, *in colours*, especially bright colours. Musically, it means the inclusion of all 12 notes used in Western music, including those not in the diatonic scale, rising or falling by semitones. The chromatic scale can start on any note.

Constipate The Note

This is an instruction I used to get from my first singing teacher, the late Emelie Hooke, a great operatic diva in her day. Basically, it means that, when you're going flat-out on a big rock number, you're already using everything you've got and there's an even bigger note coming up, you need to push out through your bottom – to be crude, pushing for a fart. PJ Proby was notorious for splitting his trousers on stage, but his technique was right; that's how you get high notes. It is either that or wreck your throat – or miss the note.

Darkening The Note

This is a vague but useful expression beloved of singing teachers and describes the sound of a voice, note or phrase. It has two basic meanings: making a note sound as if it's deeper than it is (ie making a head-voice note sound as if it's in the chest voice); and making a note sound sinister or frightening.

The Diaphragm

The muscle that forms the base of the lungs, often called the 'dome-shaped muscle', despite the fact that it spends a lot of the time more or less flat. For centuries, it was believed that the diaphragm provided support for the voice and that, when you pulled in the stomach for high notes, you were pulling in the diaphragm. We now know that the diaphragm moves very little during singing. When singers talk about the diaphragm, what they really mean is the front abdominal muscles, which are right across the front of the stomach, roughly around the naval. This is the bit of you that really moves when you think you're working the diaphragm. Even so, singers and singing teachers continue to refer to the front abdominal muscles as the diaphragm, and so do I.

You can use the diaphragm for a number of things:

- Controlling the breath (see *breath control*);
- Supporting difficult (usually high) notes;
- Emphasising certain notes or words and generally shaping phrases;
- Power;
- Vibrato;
- Tension in phrasing, emoting and tone control;
- Expanding the chest and rib cage.

Generally, when the pitch rises you pull the diaphragm in; when the pitch falls, you let the diaphragm out.

When the highest note of a phrase is the first note, take a good breath, puffing out the diaphragm and filling the lower part of the stomach before you sing the note. Then, as you sing it, pull the diaphragm in to give you all the support and power you need. As you descend the phrase, let the diaphragm look after itself.

Always take care to expand the chest and rib cage as you breathe with the diaphragm. (See *chest expansion* and *rib cage*.)

In emphasising a note or a word, and in generally shaping a phrase, a useful trick is to choose just one word or syllable that you think makes sense of an entire phrase and squeeze the diaphragm on that word. How suddenly or gently you should squeeze is something you need to work out for yourself – trust your instinct. You'll be surprised by how animated a whole phrase – and sometimes an entire verse or chorus – becomes if you've chosen the right word or syllable.

If you can't get the tension or intensity you want into the sounds, or if they sound flaccid or just plain dull (this can happen in any part of the voice but is most common in the middle register), try tensing the diaphragm slightly for a whole phrase or a series of phrases.

Try thinking of it this way: diaphragm *out* for breathing and *in* for singing. This isn't a hard-and-fast rule, but it's quite a good guide.

You need to experiment with it, making sure that you've taken in a big enough breath in the first place for the diaphragm to work at all. You can also use this trick of tensing the diaphragm when you're uncertain about the type of sound you should be making, or when you don't know what to do with your hands (while you're on stage, I mean), or when you haven't a clue as to why the Hell you're even there! It's an actors' trick that makes you look and sound convincing.

Diatonic Scale

A scale containing all seven notes of any major or minor scale, each eighth note being the same as the first, an octave higher.

Dizziness

More extremely known as a *headrush* this is very common among singers and is usually a good sign. It means that your vocal apparatus is resonating properly and you're not singing from the throat. But what gives you a headrush today won't do so in a months time – you adjust. When it occurs, it's wise to pause in order to let it pass, just in case it's indicative of something more serious. Many hard rock singers don't feel that they've sung properly unless they've had a headrush, so they have to go further and higher in order to get it. This is why so many heavy-metal singers produce such amazing ranges.

The causes of dizziness from singing are a matter of debate. Everyone seems to agree that it results from a demand on the chemical supply that the body isn't ready to provide. Some say that it's a shortage of oxygen while others hold that it's a shortage of nitrogen. The mixed head voice will often make men dizzy while women tend to go dizzy singing long sustained notes in the chest voice – 'Too-wee-yaa', for instance. Dizziness should not be confused with the blinding headaches that are produced by having protruding carotid arteries; these are caused by not breathing properly and lack of support.

Dominant

The fifth note of any diatonic scale and, more importantly, the chord built on it. For example, in the key of C (either major or minor), the dominant is G, while the three notes (ie the *triad*) that make up the dominant chord are G, B and D, in ascending order. This is the chord in its root position, because the G (the *root*) is at the bottom, but it can be used in any position. With B at the bottom, it's in the first inversion, while with D at the bottom, it's in the second inversion.

Dominant Seventh

This is the most important chord in Western music. It gives us the sense of key as no other chord does. (See also *dominant*.) A fourth note is added to the triad at the seventh degree of the chord to make a clash which must resolve to the tonic or submediant (the sixth note of the diatonic scale and the chord built on it).

The dominant seventh is exactly the same in both major and minor keys. If the key is C major, the dominant seventh is G7 and the extra note is F. This resolves to the chord of either C major or A minor. The F must fall to the E, in either case.

If the key is C minor, the F falls to E♭. Apart from this, the same rules apply. Try it out on a keyboard – it will soon make sense.

Falsetto

This is the childish crying or feminine high voice that all human voices can produce from the day we're born to the day we die. It is the healing part of the voice. No matter what the state of your voice, if you can get the falsetto voice working, you'll find that the rest of your voice will also work. You can mix it with the natural voice, to magical effect. You should exercise it every day.

To my knowledge, nobody has ever been able to express in words how the falsetto voice is made. Some say you thicken the vocal cords while others say you widen them. These contradictory statements are, no doubt, partially true, but unhelpful; you can't deliberately thicken or widen your vocal cords or consciously affect them in any way. When you attempt a falsetto sound, you trust your ear – in other words, you act – and your brain does the computing subconsciously.

Falsetto is different for both sexes. A man has a natural head voice and a falsetto head voice, whereas a woman's head voice is the same as her falsetto head voice. Men therefore have an extra voice.

Focus

The focus of the voice is the hard edge on the sound, sometimes called the *metallic edge*, which makes tone control possible. The voice is focused on to the hard palate, but it feels as if it's focused high in the nose, and it's in the nose that you should aim to focus your voice

– it halves the work of singing. An unfocused voice has a woolly sound which is easily drowned out by the rest of the band. To make matters worse, microphones don't pick up unfocused voices very well; you can struggle to yell into a microphone until your throat is raw (and then blame the mic!), but even a poor microphone will transmit a well-focused voice comparatively easily.

A good focus enables you to produce not only very hard and powerful sounds but also quiet, smooth sounds that are difficult to drown out in spite of their quietness.

There are four basic ways to build up and maintain a good focus:

1 Exercise the highest notes you can get (which will be very loud), supporting them with the diaphragm, and constipating the note. This will focus the voice on the hard palate.

2 Men should also work on the mixed voice. Women should work on sustaining the quiet low notes. Do not force any of these notes.

3 Work on co-ordinating and articulating the voice with the diaphragm, fast and slow.

4 Keep the tongue firmly against the bottom teeth.

Forcing The Voice

This is self-explanatory. It means forcing a (usually loud and harsh) sound from the throat without using much technique, such as breathing from the diaphragm, keeping the tongue down, etc.

Don't confuse *forcing* with *struggling* for high notes; struggling is quite all right, but you must take the strain with the power muscles, which are all from the waist down – diaphragm, leg muscles, etc. (See also *constipating the note*.) However, a lot of rock sounds need to be throaty or harsh.

You can sometimes get away with forcing these sounds, as long as you also work at your technique and build up a wide vocal range, but try to avoid forcing.

Glottal Stop

This means closing (or stopping) the glottis in order to make a percussive sound by forcing air through it while it's closed. Essentially, a glottal stop is a cough. It's used in many dialects, notably cockney, in words such as *bottle*, in which the double T is replaced by a glottal stop. It's also used by most English speakers to start words that begin with a vowel, such as *I*, *and*, *all* and so on. Try to weed them out of your singing, for two reasons:

1 Glottal stops are quite hard on the throat.

2 They get between you and the audience. You'll find that, for some reason you can't put your finger on, your wonderful singing isn't having the effect you expected. Neither you nor your audience will understand why; there'll just be an inexplicable sense of mild disappointment.

Glottal stops are a major source of such disappointment in gigs, even though neither you nor the audience even notices them. It's a subconscious habit of many performers in order to hide behind a barrier.

Of course, this isn't a hard-and-fast rule. Occasionally – but not often – a glottal stop is exactly what you want. (See also *glottis*.)

Glottis

The space at the upper end of the windpipe between the vocal folds. By opening, closing, widening and narrowing the glottis, the brain modulates it to produce the sound you're thinking of. Leave it alone – your subconscious mind will look after it, as long as you deal with the glottal stop.

Headrush

See *dizziness*.

Hard Palate

The front half of the roof of the mouth, from the top row of teeth and the bony part of the top gum (the real stiff upper lip – a dreadful cliché!) to halfway back in the mouth, where it meets the soft palate in a V-shaped join. Rock-hard, it forms the floor of the nasal sinus, the large, resonant cavity behind the nose. When focused on the hard palate, your voice will double in size in terms of both power and range.

The best singing teacher I ever knew, John Cameron, set great store by what he called *hard-palate resonance*, and so do I. Whenever you hear a magical voice, you're listening to hard-palate resonance. When you achieve this, it will feel as if you're focusing in the nose.

In order to focus on the hard palate, you need to stretch the soft palate, mostly by singing high notes.

Key

The scale (usually diatonic) around which a song is written. The name of the scale is taken from the keynote.

Keynote

The tonic, or 'home' note. The keynote determines the

key in which a song (or part thereof) is written, the first and last notes in the scale and, usually, the key of the song.

Jaw

The only consciously moveable bone in the human head, hinged to the rest of the skull under each ear. When the jaw drops, the throat opens, but when it's only halfway down, it tends to lock, tightening the throat. This causes problems in the voice when you try to move from one register to another and you find that you can't get up or down to a particular note because your whole throat seems to lock.

Never be afraid to drop your jaw if you find that you need a little more room. Keeping the jaw down (at least on the open sounds, and that means most sounds) is the single most important technique in singing. (See also *the tongue*.)

Larynx

A hollow, muscular organ providing the air passage to the lungs which contains the vocal cords. The larynx is also known as the *voicebox*, which is a self-explanatory term. The problem is that we now know that the voice isn't produced solely by the larynx, so although we know that it's important in singing, we don't fully understand its. It obviously regulates something.

Never touch the larynx with your fingers. Let the brain deal with it.

Legato

The Italian word for *smoothly*. A fine legato (a very smooth, well-focused vocal line) is the most prized ability among professional singers and instrumentalists, from classical to rock. It is really the defining characteristic of the great singer. For women, legato is best achieved by smoothing over the join between the head voice and the chest voice, while for men it requires mastery of the quiet mixed head voice.

Lightening The Voice

Making the voice sound very easy, or making a note or phrase sound higher than it actually is. This is not quite the opposite of darkening the voice.

Major Intervals

An interval is the distance in time, space or pitch between any two things. A major interval (in music terminology) is the number of notes from the first (bottom) note of a major scale and a higher note. Intervals are always calculated from the lower of two notes.

Major Key

A set of notes taken from any major scale. Major keys are complete, and sufficient for entire songs, although many songs modulate into other keys for variety or effect.

Major Scale

The most important of the diatonic scales, distinguished from the others by having the third note (counting from the lowest note) sharpened (ie made a semitone higher). Major scales have eight notes, the first and last being the same pitch separated by an octave, and can start on any of the 12 notes in Western music. The starting and finishing note is called the *tonic* or the *keynote*.

Mezza Voce/Messa Di Voce

Italian phrases meaning *half voice* or *mix of the voice*. American singing teachers use these expressions a lot. In practice, both phrases refer to the quiet mixed head voice. (See *mixed voice*.)

Minor Intervals

This term refers to seconds, thirds, sixths and sevenths that are reduced by one semitone from major intervals. It doesn't work with a fifth, however, which, when dropped by a semitone, becomes a *diminished fifth* or an *augmented fourth*.

Minor Keys

Keys built on the minor scales.

Minor Scales

There is no complete agreement on what a minor scale should be. Two things, however, are accepted:

1   All minor scales are diatonic in nature.

2   All minor scales have a flattened third – that is, the third note (counting from the bottom note, or keynote) is a semitone lower than the third note of a major scale.

There are three minor scales:

1   The *natural minor*, which is what you get if you play a scale starting on A entirely on the white notes of a keyboard. The term *natural* is a misnomer – this scale is neither more nor less natural than any other.

2   The *melodic minor*, which is the one that concerns singers most and has a sharpened seventh note and, therefore, a sharpened sixth in order to avoid an ugly gap.

This is where the big disagreement occurs. Traditionally, this typifies the rising scale of the melodic minor, but on the descent the sixth and seventh are not sharpened. Current fashion has them with the sixth and seventh sharpened in both rising and descending scales.

3   The *harmonic minor* is like the natural minor, but with a sharpened seventh.

Mixed Voice (male)

For the purposes of male rock singers, there are basically two mixed voices: the *quiet mixed head voice*, in which the falsetto voice is mixed with the natural head voice to produce a smooth, magical sound; and the *screaming mixed voice*, which takes the principle to extremes and mixes screaming with the natural head voice.

Mixing the voices is the most difficult of all singing skills. It is also the most important, because it's all about controlling the type of sounds you want. Unlike most singing skills, mixing the voices is not principally about power or range, although both power and range are inevitably improved by it.

After having worked at both mixed voices, you will eventually (after a minimum of four years for some singers) be able to mix the two mixed voices and be able to move smoothly, and in a single breath, from a full scream to a delicately modulated, magical sound without any jolts or 'gear changes'. This is virtuoso stuff.

Mixed Voice (Female)

Although it has generally been thought that the mixed voice is peculiar to men, I've recently found that some women can, after a great deal of work, produce the unmistakable sound of the mixed voice. It's an exhilarating sound developed by quietly blending the head and chest voices in the area of overlap that used to be known as the *feigned voice*. This must be worked slowly, and without pressure. (See Chapter 1, 'The Range'.)

Nodules/Nodes

Few words can make singers panic quite so much as the suggestion that they might get nodules on their vocal cords. A nodule is a small swelling or aggregation of cells, even a small tumour. In other words, nodules are usually warts. If you're prone to warts, you'll get warts.

There is little evidence to suggest that nodules are caused by singing, merely that, if you're a singer, you're more likely to *notice* nodules on the vocal chords than you would if you were, for instance, a bricklayer.

Fortunately, nodules are quite rare. The vast majority of singers never get them, no matter how much they ill-treat their voices. Others, including those who pamper their voices as if they were rare Stradivari, get them no matter how careful they are. It is fashionable to blame them on passive smoking, although so far there is no evidence to support this.

Some singers have had operations to remove nodules, but they usually grow back. If you leave nodules alone, they're likely to disappear in a matter of months. If you suspect that you have them, you *must* seek medical advice.

Modes

This is a wide-ranging term. In terms of ancient music, it means a scale of five or more notes spread over an octave. For our purposes, however, it is best to look at Appendices 4 and 5, which make it clear.

Oesophagus

Medical term for the gullet, a channel between the mouth to the stomach. Part of the alimentary canal.

Pharynx

The membrane-lined cavity behind the mouth and the nose, connecting them with the oesophagus.

Port/Portamento

Italian for *carrying*. In music, it means sliding the voice from one note to the next.

Psycho-/Psychological

Relating to the mind.

Psychological block

A mental inability or inhibition caused by emotional factors. Nearly all singers suffer from this occasionally. It can take many forms – forgetting your words and losing your place on the page just before a difficult note or phrase are common and mild forms. More seriously, a psychological block can cause an entire register to shut down temporarily. This problem usually affects the high registers, particularly falsetto, but sometimes the deep chest voice can be shut off. It's a fear, and you need to outface it. It is rarely serious or long term. Usually the ambition of the singer overtakes the fear. You want that note more than you're frightened of it. Occasionally, it indicates a more deep-rooted cause, and counselling or psychiatric help may be needed, but usually it's no more than an inhibition.

Psychosomatic

The effect of the mind on the body; the effect of the mind and body working together, not always intentionally.

Range

This is the distance between your highest note and your lowest note, not the distance you can make your voice travel. (See Chapter 1, 'The Range'.)

Relative Pitch

This is something that most of us claim to have. Whereas perfect pitch is the ability to identify and sing any specific note under any circumstance, relative pitch is the ability to identify and sing any specific note in relation to any other note. If I played a note on the keyboard and told you it was an A and asked you to sing an F♭ from it, you would be able to do it without hesitation – if you had true relative pitch.

Rest

Musically speaking, a rest is a period of silence that is part of a piece of music, although this doesn't necessarily mean that all instruments or voices are silent at the same time. A rest is any intentional gap of a specific length of time (as opposed to a pause, the length of which might be unspecified) in any of vocal or instrumental lines.

Resonance/Resonating

Magnifying the voice by making it echo in cavities such as the sinuses or the chest and reverberating on part of the bone structure, such as the hard palate. For practical purposes, *resonating* is the opposite of *forcing*.

Rib Cage

The bony cage around the lungs and other organs in the chest, attached to the rest of the skeleton by the vertebrae (backbone). Slightly flexible, the rib cage expands when the lungs fill with air. There is evidence to suggest that the ribs vibrate with the voice, possibly acting as sound posts, although this is unconfirmed. I tend to believe it, because singing in the chest voice is such a pleasant sensation.

Rubric

Rules, instructions, guidance notes, explanations, etc.

Scale

An arrangement of notes in any system of music in ascending or descending order.

Scat

Style of improvised singing using sounds that imitate instruments instead of words. Scat singing is usually either fast and spectacular or slow and discordant, the latter involving playing tricks with the pitch by 'bending' the note or using quarter-tones.

Screaming

The loud extension of the falsetto voice and the loudest sound the human voice can make unaided. This technique is generally practised by children, and often produces a shocking sound. Heavy-metal singers found a way of mixing it with the natural voice by extending the mixed head voice, thus enabling enormous flexibility, harsh one minute and smooth the next. This generally takes about four years to master.

Sight Reading/Sight Singing

This means singing accurately at first sight from written or printed music and is the most lucrative musical skill of all. Recording studios pay very highly for backing singers who can pick up the sheet music and sing their harmony lines correctly first time. If you're a perfect sight-reader with good tone control, you might well earn more money as a session singer than the stars you're backing.

Simile

The Italian word for *the same* or *similarly*, this means that you should continue singing in the same style (ie legato, staccato, loudly, quietly, etc) as in the previous few bars.

Sinuses

Cavities in the head which resonate with the sounds of the voice. The sinuses seem to be where the tone quality is made. When you have a virus, such as a cold, they can become clogged and the voice quality becomes difficult to control. Experienced singers can usually clear out their sinuses in the normal process of singing, or with vocal exercises if the clogging is not too serious. The beautiful tone of the quiet mixed head voice in men, and the quiet head voice in women, is created almost entirely in the sinuses.

Soft Palate

The back half of the roof of the mouth, from the V-shaped join with the hard palate right to the back of the throat. The soft palate controls the tone of the entire voice. Pure muscle, it needs to be stretched in order to work efficiently, like all other muscles. This can be done by singing your highest notes. Conversely, you can improve your ability to reach high notes by arching the soft palate for a difficult high note or phrase, which enables you to focus on the hard palate. If you do not stretch it, it acts like a cushion and your notes will sound woolly. Yawning is a very good way of stretching the soft palate.

Somatic

Relating to the body, as opposed to the mind.

Staccato

Italian word meaning *stopped*. A staccato note is a shortened note followed by a silence, usually represented on the page by a note with a small dot over it. This means that you don't sing the full length of the note; you sing half of it, leaving a silence for the other half of its length. A staccato phrase is a series of short notes separated by silences. Staccato can be very effective for pointing up the words, making them sound clipped.

Teeth

Your teeth are very important for producing a good singing tone. Try to keep the tip of your tongue against the bottom teeth as much as possible during both singing and breathing, particularly if you feel you're in danger of coughing. False teeth should make no difference – sing with them in exactly the same way, as if they were naturally yours.

Tension

In singing, there is good tension and bad tension. Tension in the neck, shoulders or at the base of the tongue is bad, while tension in the sound of the voice is often good – it arrests the ear. Tension in the diaphragm, legs and buttocks is often good – tensing these parts of the body is the principal way of introducing tension into the voice. Experiment with tension in the diaphragm through whole phrases, particularly in ballads, where you might need a better sound on long notes, but keep your shoulders down and relaxed.

Throat

This is a vague term, and I won't weary you with the various names singing teachers use when they mean the throat, or parts of it, and which always cause confusion as to what is actually meant. Where, for instance, does the throat begin and end? As far as this book is concerned, by *throat* I'm referring to the part that is sore when we say we have a sore throat: the inside of the neck. It is the weakest part of the body, containing a series of regulators – larynx, vocal folds,

etc – which are extremely delicate. It is capable of almost no power; it merely regulates and transmits the sound. If you try to force power from the throat for any length of time, not only is it likely to become sore but also your tuning is likely to become uncontrolled; you'll aim for a particular note and a different note will come out instead. This is because the regulators, which control your ability to pitch accurately, have become bruised temporarily.

Nearly all of our defence mechanisms are in the throat – it is the chief way into the body. Under pressure, we tend to 'close the gate', causing soreness or a lump in the throat. The antidote is to drop the jaw and keep the tongue against the bottom teeth.

In order to do nothing with the throat, you must do everything with the diaphragm.

Tongue

The only muscle in the human body that is stronger in a woman than in a man. I'm not being facetious; it's true! Keeping the tongue down to the bottom teeth or gum is crucial – it automatically opens the throat. If the tongue is allowed to wander about aimlessly, your throat will start to work overtime, until it runs out of energy. It's better to keep the tongue down and make the diaphragm do the work.

Tonic

A term referring to the keynote and the chord built on it. (See *keynote*.)

Trachea

The windpipe – ie the passage, reinforced with cartilage rings, which carries the air from the larynx to the bronchial tubes.

Uvula

Pronounced 'yoo-vyoola', this refers to the fleshy extension at the back of the soft palate hanging above the throat. Leave it alone.

Vibrato

Italian word meaning *shaking* or *vibrating*. Singing needs vibrato, particularly on long notes – a totally straight note is not attractive. Some natural vibrato is likely to develop in the tiny muscles in and around the jaw and, in particular, in the lower lip. Neither discourage nor force it; let it develop there of its own volition. If you want to control your vibrato, you should always start it from the diaphragm. Don't fall into the trap of locking the jaw in order to produce a shake; you'll run into all sorts of problems that way, not least that you're likely to look about 80 years old.

Virtuoso

An Italian word meaning someone learned or skilful. For our purposes, it means someone who can show off exceptionally good technique.

Vocal Cords/Folds

These are folds in the lining membrane of the larynx, near the glottis. The edges vibrate in the process of singing, and it is these vibrations that were thought to make the voice, although this theory is now in doubt. They are tiny and flat, and never visible from the outside of the neck. If you think you can see them standing out on your neck, you're probably looking at the carotid arteries.

Warming Up

A warm-up should do two things:

1 Exercise the muscles you need for singing.

2 Stretch the soft palate, which controls the tone and extends the range. The only way to do this is by singing high notes.

There is no easy way of doing either of these.

Within this framework, you can adjust your warm-up for the work you want your voice to do. If you're suffering from a cold or a sore throat, it may be wiser to concentrate on the mixed head voice. You must use your discretion. You are, after all, the only person who knows what your throat feels like.

BIBLIOGRAPHY

BEHNKE, Emil: *The Mechanism Of The Human Voice*
(London, J Curwin & Sons, 1880)

The Hutchinson Concise Dictionary Of Music
(Oxford, Helicon Publishing Ltd, 1998)

MARCHESI, Mathilde: *Marchesi's Vocal Method*
(London, Edwin Ashdown Ltd)

MILLER, Richard: *The Structure Of Singing, System And Art In Vocal Technique*
(New York, Schirmer Books, 1986)

REID, Cornelius L: *Bel Canto – Principles And Practices*
(New York, Joseph Patelson, 1950)

The Free Voice – A Guide to Natural Singing
(New York, Joseph Patelson, 1965)

Voice – Psyche And Soma
(New York, Joseph Patelson, 1975)

NOTES